About Island Press

Island Press is the only nonprofit organization in the United States whose principal purpose is the publication of books on environmental issues and natural resource management. We provide solutions-oriented information to professionals, public officials, business and community leaders, and concerned citizens who are shaping responses to environmental problems.

In 2004, Island Press celebrates its twentieth anniversary as the leading provider of timely and practical books that take a multidisciplinary approach to critical environmental concerns. Our growing list of titles reflects our commitment to bringing the best of an expanding body of literature to the environmental community throughout North America and the world.

Support for Island Press is provided by the Agua Fund, Brainerd Foundation, Geraldine R. Dodge Foundation, Doris Duke Charitable Foundation, Educational Foundation of America, The Ford Foundation, The George Gund Foundation, The William and Flora Hewlett Foundation, Henry Luce Foundation, The John D. and Catherine T. MacArthur Foundation, The Andrew W. Mellon Foundation, The Curtis and Edith Munson Foundation, National Environmental Trust, The New-Land Foundation, Oak Foundation, The Overbrook Foundation, The David and Lucile Packard Foundation, The Pew Charitable Trusts, The Rockefeller Foundation, The Winslow Foundation, and other generous donors.

The opinions expressed in this book are those of the author(s) and do not necessarily reflect the views of these foundations.

Rewilding
North America

Rewilding North America

A Vision for Conservation in the 21st Century

DAVE FOREMAN

Island Press
Washington ✦ Covelo ✦ London

ISLAND PRESS is a trademark of The Center for Resource Economics.

Library of Congress Cataloging-in-Publication data.

Foreman, Dave, 1946-
  Rewilding North America : a vision for conservation in the 21st century / Dave Foreman.
    p. cm.
  Includes bibliographical references and index.
  ISBN 1-55963-060-4 (cloth : alk. paper) — ISBN 1-55963-061-2 (pbk. : alk. paper)
  1. Wilderness areas—North America. 2. Biological diversity conservation—North America. 3. Extinction (Biology)—North America. I. Title.
  QH77.N56F66 2004
  333.95'16'097—dc22

                                                                2004002132

British Cataloguing-in-Publication data available.

Printed on recycled, acid-free paper

Design by Brighid Willson

Manufactured in the United States of America
10 9 8 7 6 5 4 3 2 1

To Michael Soulé and Doug Tompkins
for blazing the trail to 21st century conservation

Contents

List of Maps

Acknowledgments

Since 1972 I have been blessed with mentors and coworkers of the first rank. My ideas and strategies have been sparked and shaped in the smithy of these friendships. I could never begin to tally all the folks who have contributed to my conservation thinking, so I won't try. I will only highlight a few who have made a particular contribution to *Rewilding North America*.

I have dedicated *Rewilding North America* to two conservation visionaries and doers who have shaped the foundation for effective conservation in this new century. Michael Soulé, the "father" of conservation biology, has perhaps done more than any other individual to bring together scientists and citizen conservationists to defend and rewild the diversity of wild nature. He has also brought uncompromising, fearless vision to the science of conservation biology. Michael has influenced me more than anyone else has.

Doug Tompkins is no scientist, but he is a marketing and design genius who throughout the 1990s has used his wealth to fund the most hard-charging conservation groups through his Foundation for Deep Ecology. He has also set a new benchmark of wildlands philanthropy through his awe-inspiring work in buying and preserving the wildest private lands in Chile and Argentina. He and his wife Kris now are protecting private lands in Argentina's Patagonia as newly designated national parks. Doug has been an inspiration to me and a great backer of my work, including during some of my darker times. His unflinching support has allowed me to do things I otherwise wouldn't have been able to do.

Mark Twain wrote that thunder is spectacular and it grabs your attention, but that it is the lightning that really does the work. I want to hold up four of my closest collaborators over the last three decades as bolts of lightning working effectively behind the scenes without a lot of thundering notoriety. Their wise counsel and hard work have not only advanced conservation on many fronts but have also made my thunder far more effective. David Johns, Bob Howard, John Davis, and Nancy Morton have supported me and worked with me even at my worst. I doubt that I would have accomplished very much without their friendship, counsel, and backing.

I have benefited in writing *Rewilding North America* from having leading conservationists review and comment on specific chapters. John Davis copyedited the manuscript (some chapters through several versions) and vastly improved my prose as he long has. His challenging questions made my ideas more solid.

Others who read and commented on one or more chapters are Tom Butler, Bob Howard, David Johns, Paul Martin, Brian Miller, Susan Morgan, Reed Noss, Brian O'Donnell, Dave Parsons, Michael Soulé, and John Terborgh. I owe them much gratitude.

In addition, several of my chapter reviewers and other colleagues read and commented on material in *Rewilding North America* as it appeared in my "Around the Campfire" column in *Wild Earth*, in other articles, or as material in the Sky Islands and New Mexico Highlands Wildlands Networks. They include Matt Clark, Kim Crumbo, Kathy Daly, Barbara Dugelby, Jennifer Esser, Andy Holdsworth, Jack Humphrey, Leanne Klyza-Linck, Rurik List, Paula MacKay, Kurt Menke, Craig Miller, Rod Mondt, Paul Rauber, Todd Schulke, and Kim Vacariu.

I thank Kurt Menke and Todd Cummings for preparing the final maps. I have been awed by their talents while working with them over recent years.

My agent, Joanna Hurley, has toiled for the last several years to get me published and to keep me published. I thank her for how well she has worked for me. It has been wonderful to have real editors like Barbara Dean and Barbara Youngblood at Island Press. Their encouragement and wise suggestions were key for turning a bunch of text-laden pages into a book. And, finally, I'd like to thank my copyeditor, Erin Johnson, for the top-notch job she did with the manuscript.

All of these folks helped to improve the material presented in *Rewilding North America*. Of course, none of them are responsible in any way for my mistakes and opinions. My coauthor, Chama, caused all the mistakes in this book by sitting on my lap while I typed on the keyboard.

DAVE FOREMAN
Foothills of the Sandia Mountains

Introduction

From my earliest days, I have been drawn to the heart of wildness, to wild lands and wild rivers and wild things, to the places and beasts outside the rule of humankind. Long before I learned the ancient English meaning of wilderness—"self-willed land"—I looked up at the Sandia Mountains, rising above the city of Albuquerque, and saw a world where we were not masters of all. Long before I had heard of the Beowulf-time word, *wildeor*—"self-willed beast"—I watched the horny-toads and bluetails scurry through the grama grass and rabbitbrush of the high desert and knew that they ran their errands on their own time in their own way, not on human-time or in human-way.

As I grew older, I began to sense a loss of what was no more, of once-upon-a-time wildernesses and once-upon-a-time wild animals, as I read Ernest Thompson Seton and Mark Twain, as I read about Kit Carson and Buffalo Bill. Unlike many other boys, I did not yearn for the smoking buffalo gun in my hands, but for the buffalo vast as summer cloud shadows across the land.

Older still, I watched the high desert between Albuquerque and the Sandias gradually disappear under a carpet of asphalt and buildings. As a young man, I saw raw roads ripped into the wilderness, forests buzz-cut, rivers dammed, coal torn from the badlands—all where I sought will of the land. And I knew that if my wilderness—no, not mine, but its own—was to endure, I had to fight for it.

Aldo Leopold called the essays in *A Sand County Almanac* "the delights and dilemmas of one who cannot" "live without wild things."[1] *Rewilding North America* is no *Sand County Almanac*, but it is the horror and the hope of another who cannot live without wild things.

Doug Scott, a peerless strategist and campaign leader for the wilderness movement for over thirty years, begins his inspiring and authoritative *A Wilderness-Forever Future: A Short History of the National Wilderness Preservation System* with a vision:

> Here is an American wilderness vision: the vision of "a wilderness-forever future." This is not my phrase, it is Howard Zahniser's. And it is not my vision, but the one I inherited, and that you, too, have inherited, from the wilderness leaders who went before.[2]

Scott quotes Zahniser, "The wilderness that has come to us from the eternity of the past we have the boldness to project into the eternity of the future."[3] The 1964 Wilderness Act, largely written by Zahniser, embodies this vision in Section 2:

> In order to assure that an increasing population, accompanied by expanding settlement and growing mechanization, does not occupy and modify all areas within the United States and its possessions, leaving no lands designated for preservation and protection in their natural condition, it is hereby declared to be the policy of the Congress to secure for the American people of present and future generations the benefits of an enduring resource of wilderness.[4]

As settlement and mechanization yet grind away at wildlands forty years after the passage of the Wilderness Act, the challenge for conservationists in the twenty-first century still is to protect *an enduring resource of wilderness*. But before we can boldly project wilderness from the eternity of the past into the eternity of the future, we must understand what an *enduring* wilderness is. What are its characteristics? What must be done to ensure that wilderness is enduring?

Since the Wilderness Act became law in 1964, our knowledge of what makes wilderness enduring has grown, as has our knowledge of what destroys the eternity of wilderness. And, thus, the task of wilderness areas and other protected areas has evolved. This deepened understanding comes from the ecological research and theory that, after 1978, became known as *conservation biology*.

Of all ecology has learned since 1964, the most important lesson is that Earth is now clearly in a mass extinction event—the Sixth Great Extinction in the last five hundred million years.[5] Although this mass extinction began forty thousand years ago when behaviorally modern humans spread out from Africa,[6] it has reached catastrophic proportions at the beginning of the twenty-first century. Unlike previous mass extinctions, which were caused by physical forces (asteroid strikes and geological events), this Sixth Extinction is caused wholly by the activities of *Homo sapiens*.[7] Biologists widely recognize that direct killing by humans, habitat destruction and fragmentation, disease, pollution, and invasion and competition by alien species are the general causes of current extinctions.[8] Stemming this alarming tide of extinction demands conservation vision and action at local, regional, continental, and global scales.

Both the traditional conservation movement and the recent science of conservation biology have recognized that protected areas are the best way to safeguard species and habitat. In 1980, conservation biology pioneers Michael Soulé and Bruce Wilcox wrote that protected areas were "the most valuable weapon in our conservation arsenal."[9] Protected areas, such as national parks, wilderness areas, and national wildlife refuges, have been cornerstones for conservation strategy in the United States as have comparable areas throughout North America and the world for more than one hundred years.[10] Although the goals of protected areas have included the preservation of an enduring resource of wilderness and of self-regulating ecosystems,[11] we now understand that protected areas systems in North America have not fully safeguarded all species and ecosystems, because of

- Direct killing of native species, especially highly interactive species, inside and outside of protected areas
- Poor ecosystem representation in protected areas, and degraded ecosystems both within and outside protected areas
- Isolation of protected areas and fragmentation of habitat between protected areas
- Loss or degradation of ecological processes, especially fire, hydrology, and predation
- Invasion by disruptive exotic species and diseases
- Pollution
- Global climate change

Drawing on Aldo Leopold's words, I call these causes of extinctions *wounds*.[12]

It is important to understand that national parks, wilderness areas, and wildlife refuges have done much to protect and restore nature. Without existing protected areas systems in North America and the rest of the world, the state of nature would be far bleaker. The problem is that not enough land has been protected, and political and economic forces have thwarted and weakened the establishment of protected areas. And, let's face it, science has only recently understood the depth of ecological problems and even more recently given guidelines for how to solve them.

To make protected areas more effective, conservationists must now (1) work on very large landscapes, probably continental in scope, and (2) undertake ecological restoration based on *rewilding*.[13] Instead of the island-like protected areas currently in place, we need a continental wildlands *network* of core wild areas, wildlife movement linkages, and compatible-use lands to meet the habitat needs of wide-ranging species, maintain natural disturbance regimes, and permit dispersal and reestablishment of wildlife following natural events such as fires. Moreover, this network must be based on the scientific approach of rewilding,[14] which recognizes the essential role of top-down regulation of ecosystems by large carnivores,[15] and the need that large carnivores have for secure core habitats, largely roadless, and for landscape permeability (habitat connectivity) between core areas.[16] Fully protected cores such as wilderness areas are at the heart of this strategy. The Wildlands Project summarizes this approach in its slogan, "Reconnect, Restore, Rewild."

Although such a continental vision is bold and visionary, it follows in the footsteps of other conservation visionaries. In the 1920s and 1930s, eminent ecologist Victor Shelford and the Ecological Society of America called for a careful inventory and planning for a United States system of natural areas protecting all ecosystem types.[17] Wilderness Society founder Benton MacKaye based his vision for the Appalachian Trail on regional planning.[18] In developing the Wilderness Act, Howard Zahniser planned for a national system of wilderness areas cutting across agency boundaries.[19] The peerless system of national parks, national wildlife refuges, national wild and scenic rivers, and wilderness areas in Alaska came from years of careful planning by government professionals, scientists, and citizens to protect entire ecosystems and represent all habitats in Alaska.[20] More recently, conservation groups have undertaken huge, detailed, statewide inventories of potential wilderness areas in western states.[21]

Much conservation work is urgent, responding to immediate threats to wildlands and wildlife, and opportunistic, taking advantage of new political alignments and such to protect certain areas. However, this work needs to be based on an overarching vision and careful long-term planning to be most effective. For example, Reed Noss proposed a conservation area network for the state of Florida in the mid-1980s.[22] Florida state agencies and The Nature Conservancy then carried out detailed planning to refine the network.[23] With this solid, scientifically defensible vision in place, the Florida state legislature was convinced to appropriate $3.2 billion for the purchase of wildlife habitat. Without vision and careful planning, this would not have happened. Similarly, the 2000 release of the Sky Islands Wildlands Network Conservation Plan in southeastern Arizona and southwestern New Mexico by the Wildlands Project, Sky Island Alliance, Naturalia, and other groups has led to conservation groups, outdoor recreationists, landowners, ranchers, and federal, state, and county agencies working together to protect and restore biological diversity across the region.[24] Without the kind of detailed citizen conservation work that has pulled together wilderness area proposals since the 1960s, the current 106-million-acre National Wilderness Preservation System would be far smaller and less ecologically representative.

In 1991, Michael Soulé and I called for a small meeting of farsighted conservation biologists and citizen conservationists. At that meeting, we formed the Wildlands Project to continue visionary conservation planning but with a view encompassing all of North America and grounded in recent ecological research and theory.[25] We believed that producing science-informed wildlands network designs and clear conservation visions would lead to more effective on-the-ground conservation efforts by citizens, scientists, and agencies. And we knew that effective conservation had to be on a larger scale than ever before, that it needed to cross international boundaries just as jaguars and grizzlies do. Many groups throughout the world have been inspired by the Wildlands Project's vision and are proposing similar wildlands networks on their continents.[26]

In *Rewilding North America*, I propose both a vision and a strategy to reconnect, restore, and rewild Four Continental MegaLinkages that will tie North American ecosystems together for wide-ranging species and ecological processes, and to accommodate climate change. These Mega-Linkages are (1) the Pacific MegaLinkage, extending from Baja California to Alaska; (2) the Spine of the Continent MegaLinkage, extending from Central America to Alaska through the Rocky Mountains and other ranges; (3) the Atlantic MegaLinkage, extending from Florida north through the Appalachian Mountains to New Brunswick; and (4) the Arctic-Boreal MegaLinkage, extending from Alaska across Canada to the Canadian Maritime Provinces on the Atlantic coast. They are the basic architecture for a *bold, scientifically credible, practically achievable, and hopeful vision* of an enduring wilderness for North America—a vision that embodies the primary message of *Rewilding North America*.

Ideally, *Rewilding North America* would address the entire North American continent, but in reality it focuses heavily on the geographical area of the United States. For that, I apologize to my friends in Mexico, Central America, and Canada, but the narrower geographic scope allows for a more accurate, comprehensive, and credible treatment of the material. Even so, my hope is that much of what I write can be applied to other countries in North America and the world. In the future, I would hope to address other North American countries in a similarly thorough fashion.

I've written *Rewilding North America: A Bold, Hopeful Vision for Conservation in the Twenty-first Century* for several reasons and for several audiences. First, this is a work of history. I give key historical facts and interpretations of how humans have caused extinctions, how the citizen conservation movement has evolved to be more effective in protecting and restoring the diversity of life, and how conservation biology arose as an applied science working on protected areas and restoration of species. I strongly believe that this history is essential for those who wish to understand our present predicament and those who wish to make things better, because if you don't know how the present came to be, you stand in a nihilistic void and your words and actions lack coherence.

Second, this book is a work of science. I am no scientist, though I'm a fair naturalist, but I have been taught conservation science by the best. I believe that solid science must undergird conservation planning and action if it is to be effective. I try to clearly explain the key theories and research behind continental-scale conservation. I show how they have already been applied and how we can apply them in the future.

Third, *Rewilding North America* is a work of policy—visionary policy, mind you, because we conservationists must be prepared with solid strategies and policy initiatives for when new political or social opportunities arise. These policies and strategies must be part of a bold, hopeful vision, because milquetoast proposals timidly suggested excite no one. It is boldness and hopefulness that grab people's attention and inspire them into action.

I hope to reach at least four audiences: citizen conservationists, conservation biologists, students, and the interested, literate public.

Citizen conservationists—those who belong to and work for conservation organizations—need a deeper understanding of the extinction crisis. They need to recognize that what I propose here is not radical but solidly within the mainstream of conservation history, and that blending in conservation biology is not new, nor does it threaten traditional recreational and aesthetic conservation values or wilderness areas and national parks but instead adds immeasurably to the effectiveness of our efforts and to the meaning of our values.

Conservation biologists—in academia, land and wildlife managing agencies, conservation groups, and other organizations—need to understand the depth and the success of the citizen conservation movement and recognize that traditional protected areas—wilderness areas and national parks—are the cornerstones for wildlands networks.

Students need to understand whose shoulders they stand on, how much work has already been done, where twenty-first century ideas of conservation come from, and how important their future work is for the diversity of life. They must also know that, despite the terrifying extinction crisis in which we find ourselves, there is hope. They can make things better.

And finally, the interested, literate public needs to know more about the true state of nature today and how it has gotten that way. They also need to know that there are positive, workable solutions based on solid science and conservation policy, and that conservationists are not naysayers, doom-and-gloomers, but are powered by a hopeful vision that sees a future in which wilderness can long endure alongside civilization on the continent of North America. And in doing so, we will finally be at home.

Things change. And today things change faster and faster. This is especially so for the good and bad things happening to wild nature and to the policies of conservation. Some of what is discussed in these pages may already be out of date by the time of publication. Please check "For More Information" at the end of the book for Web site addresses that will have up-to-date information.

PART I

BAD NEWS

Soon a millennium will end. With it will pass four
billion years of evolutionary exuberance. Yes, some species
will survive, particularly the smaller, tenacious ones living
in places far too dry and cold for us to farm or graze. Yet we
must face the fact that the Cenozoic, the Age of Mammals,
which has been in retreat since the catastrophic extinctions
of the late Pleistocene is over, and that the "Anthropozoic"
or "Catastrophozoic" has begun.
—Michael Soulé

Let me warn you. There be monsters here.

This first part of *Rewilding North America*—"Bad News," is depressing—"depressing as hell," according to John Davis after he read it. Nonetheless, we must understand the problem before we can craft the solution. Here I set out the evidence for a worldwide mass extinction and explain its causes.

"Bad News" unfolds like this:

Chapter 1, "The Extinction Crisis"—A general overview of the extinction crisis, explanation of biodiversity, early awareness of extinction, and causes of extinction.

Chapter 2, "The Pleistocene-Holocene Event: Forty Thousand Years of Extinction"—The three waves of the current extinction crisis: the First Wave, which began with the spread of modern humans (Stone Age); the Second Wave, which spans the period of European exploration and exploitation; and the Third Wave, occurring now, which is globalization. The chapter explains how each wave caused or is causing extinctions.

Chapter 3, "The First Wave"—How modern humans evolved and spread out from Africa fifty thousand to forty thousand years ago, causing the extinction of most large mammals, birds, and reptiles in Australia, northern Eurasia, North and South America, and remote islands.

Chapter 4, "The Second and Third Waves"—The evidence of past and ongoing extinctions from habitat loss (species-area relationship), specific examples, and human population growth and appropriation of net primary productivity.

Chapter 5, "Ecological Wounds of North America 1: Direct Killing and Habitat Loss"— An overview of seven general wounds humans have caused in North America, and details about wound 1 (direct killing) and wound 2 (habitat destruction).

Chapter 6, "Ecological Wounds of North America 2: Fragmentation, Loss of Ecological Processes, Exotic Species, Pollution, and Climate Change"— Provides in-depth discussion of wound 3 (habitat fragmentation), wound 4 (loss of natural ecological and evolutionary processes), wound 5 (invasion by exotic diseases, plants, and animals), wound 6 (pollution poisoning natural habitats), and wound 7 (global climate change).

I hope that you, the reader, can persevere through these chapters. Should you begin to feel suicidal or murderous while reading Part 1, I suggest you quit and move on to Part 2, "Good News," in which I explain the scientific and historical research that is key to the solution for halting this mass extinction: protecting and restoring an enduring resource of wilderness. In Part 3, "Taking Action," I propose on-the-ground solutions to our ecological crisis. Despite the grim beginning, I think you will find *Rewilding North America* to be positive and hopeful— hopeful as a wilderness-forever future, I believe. As Ed Abbey admonished us: "Joy, shipmates, joy!" And what could be more joyful than halting a mass extinction?

CHAPTER I

The Extinction Crisis

The Crisis

The most important—and gloomy—scientific discovery of the twentieth century was the extinction crisis. During the 1970s, field biologists grew more and more worried by population drops in thousands of species and by the loss of ecosystems of all kinds around the world. Tropical rainforests were falling to saw and torch. Wetlands were being drained for agriculture. Coral reefs were dying from god knows what. Ocean fish stocks were crashing. Elephants, rhinos, gorillas, tigers, polar bears, and other "charismatic megafauna" were being slaughtered. Frogs were vanishing. Even leviathan—the great whales—were being hunted down in their last redoubts of the Antarctic and Arctic seas, and their end was in sight. These staggering losses were in oceans and on the highest peaks; they were in deserts and in rivers, in tropical rainforests and Arctic tundra alike.

A few biologists—including geneticist Michael Soulé (who later founded the Society for Conservation Biology) and Harvard's famed E. O. Wilson—put these worrisome anecdotes and bits of data together. They knew, through paleontological research by others, that in the 570 million years or so of the evolution of modern animal phyla there had been five great extinction events. The last happened 65 million years ago, at the end of the Cretaceous when dinosaurs became extinct. Wilson and company calculated that the current rate of extinction is one thousand to ten thousand times the background rate of extinction in the fossil record.[1] That discovery hit with all the subtlety of an asteroid striking Earth: right now, today, *life faces the sixth great extinction event in earth history*. The cause is just as unsettling and unprecedented: eating,

11

manufacturing, traveling, warring, consuming, and breeding by six billion human beings. For the first time in the history of life on Earth, one
species is killing countless others. For the first time, one species, *Homo
sapiens*—that's us—is waging a war against nature.

The crisis we face is biological meltdown. Wilson warns that the proportion of species driven to extinction "might easily reach 20 percent by
2022 and rise as high as 50 percent or more thereafter."[2] Soulé has said
that soon the only large mammals left will be those we consciously
choose·to protect; that "[the twentieth] century will see the end of significant evolution of large plants and terrestrial vertebrates in the tropics."[3] He writes, "The end of speciation for most large animals rivals the
extinction crisis in significance for the future of living nature. As [Bruce
Wilcox and I] said in 1980, 'Death is one thing, an end to birth is something else.'"[4]

I wish Soulé and Wilson could be brushed away as crackpots hanging off a far edge of science, but not only are they among the most lion-
ized biologists of our time, their dismal views are commonplace in the
scientific community. In 1998, the American Museum of Natural History commissioned the Louis Harris poll to survey the nation's leading
biologists. "Nearly seven out of 10 of the biologists polled said they
believed a 'mass extinction' was underway, and an equal number predicted that up to one-fifth of all living species could disappear within 30
years."[5]

However, few members of the public are aware of the crisis. "Sixty
percent of the laymen polled professed little or no familiarity with the
concept of biological diversity, and barely half ranked species loss as a
'major threat.'"[6] A *Newsweek* Earth Day poll in 2000 found that a mere
5 percent of Americans thought that endangered or vanished species was
the most important environmental problem.[7] Even among members of
nature conservation groups, most seem unaware of the magnitude of
species loss, and few conservation organizations are forthright in putting
the extinction crisis at the top of their agendas and sounding the alarm
about the dead-end road down which humanity is hurtling. The crisis is
made worse by this ignorance.

Considering the biological catastrophe we are in, it is gut-wrenching
to find that only a small percentage of people are aware of the crisis and
our responsibility for it. There may be several reasons for this head
burying. First, scientists and conservationists have not done the best job
of publicizing and explaining the extinction crisis, nor has the media
given it due heed. Second, the money and research time given to the
problems facing nature are so small that we do not even know how many

species there are. That alone makes accurate analysis difficult. Third, anticonservationists have fogged the issue so well that the public and mainstream media have been turned away from the core issues regarding extinction. Fourth, extinction events happen in time and territorial scales that are hard to comprehend. After all, humans have evolved to react to short-term and close-range stimuli. Fifth and closely related, much of the devastation is slow and incremental. Many of us are blind to that which is not sudden. Sixth, the mere thought that we are causing a mass extinction is so soul shattering that most people who hear of it refuse to even consider it. Finally, the values we place on nature make it easy for us to exploit it for our personal economic gain.[8]

The Diversity of Life

Before we can understand the extinction of species, we must know what species are and what their significance is. And before we can understand the extinction crisis, we must know something about biological diversity, or *biodiversity*.

It seems that we humans are adapted to classifying things. Even the act of collecting baseball cards or porcelain figurines comes from this fancy. From our earliest times, we have named, numbered, and classified life forms. Genesis recounts the old Middle Eastern myth where Yahweh brought all the animals before Adam to be named. Not only are we driven to classify things, but we seem to be pretty good at it. We also seem to be consistent at it. Ornithologist Jared Diamond has shown how the classification of bird species by traditional New Guineans is almost exactly that of modern ornithology.[9] Michael Soulé writes that "the taxonomies of aboriginal societies are virtually always the same in structure as those of modern, scientific cultures (both are hierarchical and consist of nested sets of exclusive categories); moreover, aboriginal taxonomies typically recognize the same entities as species as do modern taxonomists."[10]

Modern scientific classification of life is called taxonomy (or systematics) and is based on *binomial nomenclature* developed by Swedish naturalist Carl von Linné (Linnaeus in Latin) about 250 years ago. From the beginning, the goal of taxonomy has been to complete Adam's task and name every creature—a goal we are still far from finishing. In 1990, Soulé wrote that "over 1.4 million species have been described and classified" and that this naming task had been believed to be "about half finished." However, he pointed out, after entomologist Terry Erwin published his research on tropical arthropods in the 1980s, it became clear that there were many more species—perhaps by an order of magnitude or more—than scientists had previously believed.[11] Estimates today from the best biologists range upward to 30 million species, and some think 100 million could be closer to the truth.

Linnaeus gave each organism a double Latin name—popularly known today as a *scientific name*. For example, the wildcat of the Old World is *Felis silvestris*.[12] The scientific name is italicized, and the first name (the *genus*) is capitalized, while the second name (the *species*) is not capitalized. The wildcat is the only cat called *silvestris* (of the forest), but other closely related cats are also part of the *Felis* genus. However, the North American bobcat (colloquially called a wildcat) is in a different genus, *Lynx*, that includes the Canadian lynx, the Eurasian lynx, and the Iberian lynx. All cats, whether they are *Felis*, *Lynx*, or other genera (plural of *genus*) are in the family *Felidae*.

This classification system is based on relationships. In Linnaeus's time (before Charles Darwin and evolutionary theory), these relationships were calculated on gross similarities and anatomy. After Darwin, relationships began to be redefined by evolution, essentially as a family tree. Anatomy (or structural similarity) was still the most significant clue to evolutionary relationships. More recently, classification has become much more accurate as genetic analysis allows researchers to clearly show evolutionary relationships, including how closely related species are to one another and how long ago they split off from a common ancestor. This genetic analysis has not only fine-tuned older classifications, it has also rearranged some relationships. This is not evidence that taxonomists do not know what they are doing, but that they—like other scientists—are constantly improving the description of the world around us.

All life is sorted into five *kingdoms* (although this is not universally accepted). Each kingdom is divided into *phyla* (singular: *phylum*). The wildcat is a member of the phylum Craniata, animals whose brains lie in a *cranium* (skull). Each phylum is divided into *classes*. The wildcat is in the class Mammalia, cranium-possessing animals that have fur, are *homothermic* (warm-blooded, or internally heat-regulated), and with the females bearing mammary glands that produce milk for the young. Within Mammalia, the wildcat is in the order Carnivora, which includes cats, dogs, bears, raccoons, and weasels—flesh eaters. Cats, including the wildcat, make up the family Felidae—-the Cat Family. Among cats, the wildcat and its evolutionary siblings are in the genus *Felis*. As we have already seen, the wildcat is the species *Felis silvestris*. Each of these divisions is called a *taxon* (plural is *taxa*; remember, the science of classifying creatures is *taxonomy*).

Within genera are species. Species are the basic divisions of life. Members of a species can breed among themselves and produce viable and fertile offspring. Within species, however, there are often *subspecies* (or *races*). The subspecies of a species can interbreed, but they usually breed among themselves because of geographical isolation or behavioral differences. Subspecies often look different in coloration, pattern, size, and the like. Within subspecies (or species that are not divided into subspecies) are *populations*. According to Gretchen Daily and Paul Ehrlich, "[P]opulations are geographic entities within species that may be defined either ecologically or genetically."[13] These are the basic breeding groups.

Subspecies and populations are where evolution happens. When genetically isolated for a long period of time, some subspecies and populations evolve into separate species. We must remember that evolution is a process over time. What we see today is a freeze-frame. The process of *speciation* may be at several stages for the variety of creatures we look at—anywhere from initial sorting into subspecies because of more or less isolated populations to clear division into separate species. Things are not at a standstill. Because of evolution, species are always changing (though some change very slowly).

All the populations or subspecies of a species are important because they usually carry a greater diversity of genes than does only one population or subspecies. If conditions change, a population or subspecies unable to adapt to the new conditions will become extinct. However, another subspecies or population within a species may have the characteristics that allow it to adapt to the new conditions thereby allowing it to survive and further evolve while the rest of the species dies out. Daily and Ehrlich write, "If, for example, there is rapid climate change, a widespread species with many populations is more likely to include individuals that are genetically suited to new conditions than a species with just a single local population."[14]

For those who argue that species do not exist, that they are just arbitrary categories scientists have dreamed up, and that therefore we should not be concerned with the extinction of a "species," Niles Eldredge of the American Museum of Natural History responds, "When we compare lists of plants and animals drawn up by local peoples with those of professional biologists, it confirms our notion that species are real entities in the natural world, not just figments of Western-world classificatory imaginations."[15]

Biodiversity is scientific shorthand for biological diversity.[16] Reed Noss and Allen Cooperrider propose this definition: "Biodiversity is the variety of life and its processes. It includes the variety of living organisms, the genetic differences among them, the communities and ecosystems in which they occur, and the ecological and evolutionary processes that keep them functioning, yet ever changing and adapting.[17] They consider four levels of diversity: (1) genetic, (2) population/species, (3) community/ecosystem, and (4) landscape. Within each of these levels are "compositional, structural, and functional components of a nested hierarchy." This is beginning to sound pretty complex. And it is. "Because nature is infinitely complex," according to Noss and Cooperrider, and as is well known to anyone who spends time outside watching, listening, and thinking.

> Composition includes the genetic constitution of populations, the identity and relative abundances of species in a natural community, and the kinds of habitats and communities distributed across the landscape. Structure includes the sequence of pools and riffles in a stream, down logs and snags in a forest, the dispersion and vertical layering of plants, and the horizontal patchiness of vegetation at many spatial scales. Function includes the climatic, geological, hydrological, ecological, and evolutionary processes that generate and maintain biodiversity in ever-changing patterns over time.[18]

Key to the diversity of life is the total number of species. Stuart Pimm and his University of Tennessee colleagues write, "Any absolute estimate of extinction rate requires that we know how many species there are. In fact, we do not." Furthermore, "the problems of estimating their numbers are formidable."[19] As we have seen, some 1.4 million species have been scientifically named and described, but Pimm and his colleagues calculate that the total number of species is between 10 million and 100 million. Tropical insects, deep-sea creatures, bacteria, algae, and fungi are the main groups that could boost the total number of species well above 10 million.[20]

However, we have a close idea of how many species exist for several taxa. Michael Soulé notes that for vertebrate animals, we have certainly identified more than half of all living species, "although ichthyologists are naming some 250 small species of fish each year, most of them small, freshwater species." For "vascular plants, vertebrates except fishes, [and] butterflies," we have probably named and described around 90 percent of the living species.[21]

Five Great Extinctions

To understand the world today, we must first understand yesterday—in the case of extinction, deep yesterdays. Through careful study of geologic layers and the fossils in them, and armed with sophisticated dating tools, geologists and paleontologists have mapped out a remarkably detailed and precise past. We know, for example, that half a billion years ago—or, 570-some million years ago, to pin it down—a phenomenal blossoming in the diversity of life happened. During this Cambrian "explosion," most of the major phyla of animals appeared for the first time, and fungi and plants show in the fossil record soon thereafter.

During the two hundred years in which there has been a serious study of geology, the theories of *uniformitarianism* and *catastrophism* have slugged it out. Uniformitarianism argues that geological change takes place steadily and slowly; catastrophism argues that much dramatic change comes suddenly. Similarly, in evolutionary theory, some argue that most change comes slowly, and others argue that most change comes suddenly, pointing to episodes in the long, unimaginable time of the fossil record that represent catastrophic change when many species become extinct and afterward many new species arise. Of course, both catastrophism and uniformitarianism play a role: widespread extinction and the evolution of many new species associated with rare catastrophes, and "regular" or "background" extinction and evolution in between.

The fossil record reveals five great extinction episodes in the last half a billion years. They are

Ordovician—500 million years ago, 50 percent of animal families became extinct, including many trilobites (a dominant kind of marine organism that looked sort of like a horseshoe crab).

Devonian—345 million years ago, 30 percent of animal families became extinct, including some types of early fishes.

Permian—250 million years ago, 50 percent of animal families, 95 percent of marine species, many amphibians, and many trees became extinct.

Triassic—180 million years ago, 35 percent of animal families became extinct, including many reptiles and marine mollusks.

Cretaceous—65 million years ago, dinosaurs and many mollusks became extinct.[22]

For millions of years after each of these great extinctions, ecological niches became available for other forms of life to blossom into many new species. The demise of the dinosaurs, for example, made it possible for mammals to suddenly diversify into the multitude of forms Earth has known recently. Not that mammals were something new to life. Species of small mammals first evolved out of the advanced group of reptiles called *cynodonts* by the end of the Triassic about 200 million years ago. For 135 million years, early mammals lived in the shadows of the dinosaurs—probably avoiding them by being nocturnal.[23]

Early Awareness of Extinction

Although extinction has been going on for as long as there has been life on the planet, humans have only recently become aware of it. We first began to understand what fossils were only two hundred years ago. Even after educated people accepted that fossils were the remains of long-dead creatures, they were reluctant to believe that such creatures were extinct. At the end of the eighteenth century, biology was wrapped in the idea of the Great Chain of Being, which believed that by removing one link (species) the whole chain could break. Thomas Jefferson, after studying the fossil of a giant ground sloth dug up in western Virginia (he misidentified it as a lion), wrote in 1799, "If this animal has once existed, it is probable on this general view of the movements of nature that he still exists."[24] He asked Meriwether Lewis and William Clark to be on the lookout for living counterparts to the fossil animals being found.[25]

At the time of Jefferson's writing, however, French scientist Georges Cuvier was convincing most natural historians that the fossils being unearthed in Europe were of extinct animals. Religious scientists thereupon changed earlier beliefs to allow for extinction in God's perfect plan. The evidence for extinct mammals grew as more fossils were dug up and described. By 1825, for example, ten extinct North American vertebrates had been described.

After scientists settled on the reality of extinction, the "how" was left to be answered. Suggested mechanisms for extinction depended on whether one was a catastrophist or a uniformitarian. Cuvier proposed localized catastrophes to explain extinctions, while others, led by William Buckland of England, looked to Noah's flood as the universal catastrophe that caused extinct species. Swiss geologist and biologist Louis Agassiz, who emigrated to the United States and became one of the foremost American scientists of his era, argued for mass glaciation as the cause of past extinctions. Buckland went over to Agassiz's glacier theory in 1842.[26]

In the uniformitarian camp, English geologist Charles Lyell was the "early champion of slow, natural changes across the surface of the earth as a cause of Pleistocene extinctions." According to Donald Grayson, Lyell believed that "the extinction of species is a predictable, natural, and ongoing phenomenon, one that can be expected to occur slowly during the course of ages."[27] Although the reality of extinction of species was well accepted before mid-century by both catastrophists and uniformitarians, Lyell and other advocates of gradual, natural extinctions had a hard time explaining what the actual mechanisms of extinction were.

In both North America and Europe, other scientists, including France's Jean-Baptiste de Monet de Lamarck, suggested that humans had caused past extinctions. Lyell rejected human causation because he believed the extinctions came before humans were present. However, by the 1860s, the great French bone digger Jacques Boucher de Perthes changed the minds of Lyell and others. Boucher de Perthes's careful, stratigraphic excavations in the Somme River Valley proved that early humans and the extinct great beasts were contemporaries. After visiting Boucher de Perthes's diggings in 1859, Lyell wrote, "That the human race goes back to the time of the mammoth and rhinoceros (Siberian) and not a few other extinct mammals is perfectly clear. . . ."[28] In 1860, British anatomist Richard Owen acknowledged extinction of the fossil beasts by the "spectral appearance of mankind on a limited tract of land not before inhabited."[29]

Based on the evidence in the ground, educated people by the last half of the nineteenth century recognized that prehistoric extinctions had happened and that it was likely that Stone Age humans had a hand in them. During that same period, some scientists began to turn their eyes to evidence that new extinctions were then taking place and that humans were again responsible. In 1832, nearly three decades before he accepted Boucher de Perthes's views that humans had hunted extinct beasts, Lyell wrote that "the annihilation of a multitude of species has already been effected, and will continue to go on hereafter, in a still more rapid ratio, as the colonies of highly civilized nations spread themselves over unoccupied lands."[30]

It was not long after Lyell's warning that many hunters and naturalists in North America called for an end to the mass slaughter of bison, passenger pigeon, and waterfowl then taking place. Civilizations, in fact, have recorded extinctions since AD 80, when the European lion became extinct.[31] In 1914, famous naturalist William T. Hornaday of the New York Zoo delivered a stirring series of lectures on wildlife conservation to the Yale School of Forestry, which were published as a widely read book, *Wild Life Conservation*. He listed eleven North American species that had become "totally extinct in a wild state between 1840 and 1910": great auk, Labrador duck, Pallas cormorant, passenger pigeon, Eskimo curlew, Carolina parrakeet, Cuban tricolor macaw, Gosse's macaw, yellow-winged green parrot, purple Guadaloupe macaw.[32]

The magnitude of the extinction crisis, however, remained hidden, even to most conservationists and biologists, through much of the twentieth century. Extinction was a problem and conservationists sought to stay it, but the enormity—that the modern extinction event was of the magnitude of the dinosaur extinction event—was unimagined. However, in 1936, leading American conservationist Aldo Leopold, after a trip to inspect German forests, wrote in *Bird-Lore* that "the most pressing job in both Germany and America is to prevent the extermination of rare species."[33]

In 1963, British conservationist Colin Bertram reviewed the status of wildlife in the British journal *Oryx* and expressed his fear, "Even the minority, the preservationists and conservationists, in my opinion, have as yet failed to see in full the awful vividness of the red light before them." He warned that "without sufficient [human] fertility control, we lose inevitably and for ever most of the remaining larger mammals of the world, very many of the birds, the larger reptiles and so many more both great and small."[34]

University of Wisconsin botanist Hugh Iltis spoke at the first Earth Day (1970) at the University of Michigan. He warned that we were "pushing, prematurely, tens of thousands of species of plants and animals toward the abysmal finality of *extinction* by destroying their habitats, by decimating their numbers, by interrupting their life cycles and ruining their supply of food." He said, "Today, 10% to 12% of the mammalian taxa can be considered to be endangered, and birds are faring no better."[35]

The dawning awareness that we were witnessing an extinction event to rival or surpass that of the dinosaurs became widespread in the 1970s with the rapidly accelerating destruction of tropical forests. Michael Soulé credits British botanist and tropical conservationist Norman Myers with being the first to publicly say we were in a mass extinction, in his book *The Sinking Ark*.[36] In 1978, The Wilderness Society excerpted in their magazine a Worldwatch Institute report by Erik Eckholm summarizing the latest thinking on worldwide extinction by lead-ing biologists. Eckholm warned:

> Within sight is the destruction of plant and animal species, and of the genetic heritage of eons they embody, on a scale that dwarfs the combined natural and human-caused extinctions of the previous millions of years. Should this biological massacre take place, evolution will no doubt continue, but in a grossly distorted manner. Such a multitude of species losses would constitute a basic and irreversible alteration in the nature of the biosphere even before we understand its workings—an evolutionary Rubicon whose crossing *Homo sapiens* would do well to avoid.[37]

Twenty-five years ago, then, the conservation movement had every reason to be fully aware of the crisis. By 1980, Soulé and Bruce Wilcox had edited a state-of-knowledge book on the crisis and possible solu-tions—*Conservation Biology*.[38] In its foreword, Tom Lovejoy wrote, "Hundreds of thousands of species will perish, and this reduction of 10 to 20 percent of the earth's biota will occur in about half a human life span. . . . This reduction in the biological diversity of the planet is the most basic issue of our time."[39] Soulé and Wilcox wrote, "There is sim-ply no precedent for what is happening to the biological fabric of this planet and there are no words to express the horror of those who love nature."[40]

The Causes and Processes of Extinction

Many things can push a species into the long, dark night of extinction. However, only a few things can cause mass extinction. For past mass extinctions, cataclysmic events—either terrestrial or extraterrestrial—so altered or harmed the biosphere that many species and whole groups of organisms died out. Scientists have found convincing evidence that the extinction of the dinosaurs 65 million years ago came suddenly (perhaps in a matter of days or weeks) when an asteroid struck Earth in a shallow sea where today's Yucatán Peninsula of Mexico lies. A 180-mile-wide crater was formed at Chicxulub. The shock wave, tsunami, and wide-spread, massive forest fires from associated meteors killed many crea-tures immediately. Then a thick dust cloud in the atmosphere reduced by 20 percent the solar energy reaching Earth for a decade. University of Washington paleontologist Peter Ward writes that "this reduction would have been sufficient to produce a decade of freezing or near-freezing temperatures in a world that had been largely tropical. The prolonged 'impact winter' . . . is thus the most important killing mechanism."[41] Tim Flannery's recently published book, *The Eternal Frontier*, fills in much detail on the ecological effects and long-term consequences of the asteroid impact on North America—the part of Earth especially devastated.[42]

The great Permian extinction may have been caused by massive volcanism (flood basalts across Siberia are evidence) and the release of huge amounts of carbon dioxide from the deep ocean (there was only one ocean and one continent at that time).[43]

The Triassic extinction could have happened from the giant continent Pangaea breaking up and forming the Atlantic Ocean, thereby altering ocean circulation patterns and causing massive climate change.

But what causes "normal" extinctions, the kind that make up the background rate between the few big catastrophes? A species can become "extinct" by evolving into a new species or several new species (speciation driven by natural selection), or a species can become extinct by dying out and not continuing its evolutionary experiment. The latter is real extinction.

Extinction, or evolution into daughter species, is the fate of all species. Careful study of the fossil record of marine invertebrates shows that species usually last for one million to ten million years.[44] What may cause species to become extinct? Michael Soulé lists the possible factors: rarity (low density); rarity (small, infrequent patches); limited dispersal ability; inbreeding; loss of heterozygosity (genetic diversity); founder effects; hybridization; successional loss of habitat; environmental variation; long-term environmental trends (such as climate change); catastrophe; extinction or reduction of mutualist populations; competition; predation; disease; hunting and collecting; habitat disturbance; and habitat destruction.

Soulé points out that some of these factors "do not become operative until one or more of the other factors have reduced the local populations to a very small size."[45] Note that he lumps together natural and human causes. Most of these factors are at play in today's mass extinction.

In *Song of the Dodo*, David Quammen does a masterful job of showing how these various factors could work in concert to bring a species to its night.[46]

Soulé warns, however, that "it is disappointing that we know so little about natural extinction." Why does modern science know so little about this fascinating subject? It is because "no biologist has documented the extinction of a continental species of a plant or animal caused solely by nonhuman agencies."[47]

The grim truth is that *we humans* are the cause of modern extinctions. How do *we* do it?

Extinction expert David Wilcove and his colleagues list five anthropogenic causes of extinction in the United States, in order of current importance: habitat destruction, nonnative (alien) species, pollution, overexploitation, and disease.[48]

Carnivore ecologist Brian Miller of the Denver Zoo tells me that, worldwide, overexploitation is far more important than in the United States today. In Miller's recent book (with Rich Reading), *Endangered Animals*, experts discuss the threats to forty-nine endangered species around the world. For many of them, direct killing by humans remains a major cause.[49] A special section in the June 2002 issue of *Conservation Biology* emphasized the threat that hunting and direct killing pose to many imperiled mammals and birds. "Of the 24% of mammals threatened with extinction, direct loss and overexploitation is considered a major threat to 34%," and 37 percent of threatened birds are so mainly because of overexploitation.[50]

Let me give just a few examples of the ways humans cause extinction in each of these categories.

Habitat Destruction. We reduce, modify, degrade, or transform natural habitat upon which species depend by burning, agricultural clearing, logging, mining, grazing by domestic animals, preventing natural fire, damming rivers, dewatering rivers through irrigation diversion, drying up springs and streams through groundwater pumping, eliminating keystone species like beaver and prairie dogs whose activities create habitat for other species, and urban and suburban development. Furthermore, we fragment habitat—thereby disrupting necessary patterns of movement of many species—through the above activities and by building roads, clearing power-line rights-of-way, and driving vehicles.

Nonnative (Alien) Species. As humans have spread into new lands, we have brought with us disruptive alien species that are generally well adapted to human disturbance and that outcompete native species, in part because their normal enemies, such as predators and diseases, are left behind. Such damaging invaders include plants and animals, both deliberately introduced species such as domestics or ornamentals, and accidentally introduced species such as weeds or pests. These nonnative species include predators (cats, rats, pigs) and competitors (starlings, tamarisk, zebra mussels). Alfred Crosby of the University of Texas offered an early and insightful look at exotic species invasions in *Ecological Imperialism: The Biological Expansion of Europe, 900–1900*. He showed that temperate regions of the world in North America, South America, Australia, and New Zealand had become "Neo-Europes" with the arrival of European colonists and their domestic crops and livestock, and weeds, diseases, and pests.[51]

Pollution. Whether localized or global (acid rain, greenhouse gases), pollution can poison the waters and soils that are habitat for sensitive species, or leach away needed nutrients. Global warming and atmospheric ozone depletion—major threats to life forms worldwide—are caused largely by air pollution.

Overexploitation. Hunting, fishing, trapping, collecting, and government "pest" eradication programs have caused the extinction of many species and seriously endanger others today.

Disease. As humans have spread around the world, we have brought exotic diseases with us. Global trade is spreading many new diseases. An exotic disease caused the loss of the American chestnut in the wild. The black-footed ferret was nearly wiped out by canine distemper, a disease not native to the Americas.

Ernst Mayr, perhaps the biological giant of the twentieth century, writes, "Background extinction and mass extinction are drastically different in most aspects. Biological causes and natural selection are dominant in background extinction, whereas physical factors and chance are dominant in mass extinction. Species are involved in background extinction, and entire higher taxa in mass extinction."[52] As the cause of today's mass extinction, we humans are no longer just a biological phenomenon but are now a physical factor equivalent to an asteroid or continental drift in radically changing biological diversity. We are not exterminating only individual species, but "entire higher taxa."

CHAPTER 2

The Pleistocene-Holocene Event: Forty Thousand Years of Extinction

In 1996, fifteen hundred leading scientists from eighty countries published a comprehensive report on extinction, writing, "During the past 400 years, some 486 animal and 654 plant species are recorded as having gone extinct . . . a rate about 1,000 times greater than the [average] rate of extinction." Moreover, they noted, "No biologist has documented the extinction of a continental species of plant or animal caused by non-human agencies."[1]

Four hundred years ago (AD 1600) was when the European Age of Exploration began to cause extinctions. Spain, Portugal, France, England, Holland, Russia, and other European countries were colonizing continents and islands to the farthest corners of the world. Today's mass extinction event began with European exploration and exploitation—or so the story goes.

But just as it is hard to focus on something right before your nose, so it is hard to clearly see your age, or era, in the context of history—much less in the context of geologic history. Such close proximity to the extinction crisis makes our perspective fuzzy, and we tend to assume that today's extinction crisis began with European colonization. To bring such a fuzzy view into sharper focus, we must step back and project the object of our gaze into a larger scene—into a wider slice of time. In doing so, we ken a more accurate picture of extinction.

The Hawaiian Islands are a poster child for extinctions caused by European contact—between eighteen and thirty species of endemic birds have become extinct in the last two hundred years.[2] But recent research by avian paleontologists Helen James and Storrs Olson of the Smithsonian Institution shows that most bird extinctions in Hawaii did not come after Captain Cook became the first European to visit, in 1778, but after the first Polynesians arrived, in AD 400, well before Cook's arrival. Their research has "unearthed at least 50 previously unknown species of birds which went extinct" before Cook reached the islands, including a close relative of the bald eagle, an accipiter hawk, three species of long-legged owls, four flightless geese, three flightless ibises, and fifteen Hawaiian honeycreepers (a group unique to Hawaii). According to ornithologist Lyanda Haupt, the rigidly hierarchical Polynesian culture that settled Hawaii burned off vast tracts of lowland forest for farming, hunted the large flightless birds for meat, slaughtered the brightly colored songbirds for ceremonial robes (eighty thousand birds were required for one robe), and released pigs and the Polynesian rat, an alien predator.[3] E. O. Wilson writes bluntly, "The Polynesian seafarers . . . broke the crucible of evolution."[4]

If we step out of today and look closely at the historical, biological, and fossil records, we find that the current extinction crisis did not begin only four hundred years ago, and it has not been caused solely by colonial and industrial European empires. Today's extinction crisis—the end of the Pleistocene, in Soulé's words—has been ongoing for forty thousand years, initiated by early Stone Age cultures spreading into previously unoccupied parts of the world. Indeed, only in the last few decades has industrial civilization begun to rival these cultures in the significance of the number of species it has exterminated.

During these forty millennia, human beings have wrought a slaughter in the diversity of life. Duke University's John Terborgh, who, along with Soulé, was selected by *Audubon* magazine as one of the hundred greatest conservationists of the twentieth century, has looked at the loss of big animals in North America and concludes,

> That we should live in a world without megafauna is an extreme aberration. It is a condition that has not existed for the last 250 million years of evolutionary history.
>
> To add perspective to the above, let us reflect on the fact that the entire eastern half of the North American continent south of the North Woods supports only one ungulate, the white-tailed deer . . . eastern North America is unique: all other continental mammal assemblages include a number of ungulates, frequently a half-dozen species or more.[5]

However, even a half-dozen species of large ungulates (hoofed, grazing, or browsing mammals, ranging in size from tiny antelope to elephants) is less than normal. I spent three weeks in southern Africa in 1998. Traveling through an area smaller than the eastern United States, I saw twenty-two species of ungulates out of a total number of forty-two.[6] Eastern North America is truly an empty landscape.

Even western North America has a pitifully small number of large mammals—there are only nine species of large native ungulates in the western United States and northern Mexico.[7] It has only recently been so barren. Thirteen thousand years ago, what is now the western United States and northern Mexico hosted at least thirty-one species of large ungulates, including five species of mammoths and mastodons. While today this area has five species of large carnivores (if we count the very rare and largely absent grizzly bear, gray wolf, and jaguar), thirteen thousand years ago there were ten large carnivores spread across the landscape.[8] By *megafauna* and *large*, paleontologists mean animals weighing 100 pounds (44 kg) or more.

By the middle of the twentieth century, paleontologists had turned away from the views of Darwin, Owen, and the other giants of nineteenth-century biology that humans had caused the Pleistocene extinctions. The new dominant view saw climate change as the culprit. Mid-twentieth-century biologists thought that after the continental glaciers melted and the climate warmed, ecosystems changed and the megafauna lost its food supply. Humans had nothing or little to do with Pleistocene extinctions, or so it was argued. In the 1960s, Paul Martin of the University of Arizona, one of the most brilliant and far-sighted (and hindsighted) individuals I have met, saw the evidence differently. In 1963, he wrote, "Large mammals disappeared not because they lost their food supply, but because they became one."[9] In 1967, he proposed an *overkill* theory: a small group of skilled human hunters spread through North America and South America in an advancing front, leaving extinction in their wake. Martin calculated that this could have happened in perhaps one thousand years. Consistent with overkill, only the large prey mammals sought by humans, along with their predators and scavengers, became extinct.[10] In 1984, he and paleoanthropologist Richard Klein edited an 892-page anthology, *Quaternary Extinctions: A Prehistoric Revolution*, with thirty-eight papers from leading authorities. Martin's paper in the anthology, "Prehistoric Overkill: The Global Model," is a landmark work of science and the best summary of the human role in Pleistocene extinctions.[11] The extinction of twenty-three species of large ungulates and five species of large carnivores in the western United States alone was caused by the arrival of a skilled hunting culture of modern humans from across the Bering Land Bridge.

The Sixth Great Extinction—*our extinction*—should properly be called the Pleistocene-Holocene Extinction or the P-H Event, just as the previous extinction is properly called the Cretaceous-Tertiary Extinction, or the K-T Event. The P-H Event is the consequence of *Homo sapiens* evolving in Africa and spreading out into new lands or, in Richard Owen's words 140 years ago, of the "spectral appearance of mankind on a limited tract of land not before inhabited."[12]

We can see the Sixth Great Extinction occurring in three waves, each caused by new groups of humans armed with new technologies spreading over new lands.[13] The First Wave, the "Spread of Modern Humans," ran from forty thousand to about thirty-five hundred years ago as skilled big game hunters first entered lands where *Homo sapiens* had not previously existed. It continued from three thousand years ago until two hundred years ago, as Stone Age farmers found previously unpeopled islands in the Pacific and Indian oceans. The Second Wave, the "Spread of Europeans," began in 1500 and ended around 1970 as European colonial and then industrial civilization spread over the world. The Third Wave, "Overpopulation and Globalization," began about 1970 as human population exploded and new technologies and business practices tied the world into one exponentially expanding agro-techno-economy.

In the First Wave, extinctions were caused mostly by hunting, and perhaps by fire-setting and introductions of dogs and diseases into areas that had not previously experienced them. The victims were primarily large mammals, birds, and reptiles on continents and islands. In the second phase of the First Wave, Stone Age farmers settled Hawaii, New Zealand, Madagascar, and other islands, and extinctions were caused by agricultural clearing, fire-setting, hunting, and introductions of dogs, rats, pigs, goats, and diseases into areas that had not previously experienced them. The victims were primarily birds and reptiles.

Damaging though Stone Age hunters were, farmers have far deeper and broader impacts on nature. Niles Eldredge of the American Museum of Natural History writes, "When we settled down and became farmers (superficially less of an arrant bloodthirsty occupation), we actually began to pose an environmental threat that none of our forebears had even remotely come close to: We started to destroy habitat instead of species directly."[14] Ian Tattersall, also of the American Museum of Natural History, argues that the impact of hunters and farmers is very different: "But careless hunting to extinction of prey species, based as it may have been on the extraordinary human capacity, does not equate with any conscious attempt to change the environment. . . . What a contrast with settled agriculturists! For the very concept of crop production implies the modification of ecosystems."[15]

The Second Wave was caused by hunting with guns; large-scale fishing; massive habitat destruction by agriculture, forestry, and domestic livestock grazing; river damming and diversion; introduction of exotic predators, browsers, grazers, parasites, and diseases; and later by industrial pollution. Islands lost birds, giant tortoises, and small mammals. On continents, some birds, fish, and large mammals have been driven into extinction, but many more species of birds, freshwater fish, and large mammals have had their numbers drastically reduced to possibly nonviable remnants. In the oceans, sea mammals, shellfish, and many fish have been wastefully exploited so that their populations are mere shadows of what they were four hundred years ago.

The Third Wave has just begun. Its agents of extinction are those of the other waves, but now the human population explosion—from about 10 million people ten thousand years ago to over six billion today—and a globalized agro-techno-economy spread over the whole Earth threaten everything from the last megafauna to plants to insects to coral reef ecosystems.

The five anthropogenic causes of extinction identified by Wilcove— habitat destruction, nonnative (alien) species, pollution, overexploitation, and disease—hold true in each of the three waves, though their order of importance varies. During the First Wave, in rough order of importance the causes were overexploitation, nonnative (alien) species, habitat destruction, and disease. Pollution was a very minor player. During the Second Wave, in rough order of importance the causes were overexploitation, habitat destruction, nonnative (alien) species, disease, and pollution. During the Third Wave, the order of importance is habitat destruction, overexploitation, nonnative (alien) species, pollution, and disease.

In forty thousand years, fully modern humans have spread across the Earth three times, with devastating consequences for the rest of life (table 2.1). In the next chapters we will look at the three waves in more detail.

TABLE 2-1. The Pleistocene-Holocene Extinction Event

Location	Date	Affected Species
THE FIRST WAVE: SPREAD OF MODERN HUMANS 40,000 YEARS TO 200 YEARS BP[16]		
Europe and Northern Asia	40,000 to 13,000 BP	Megafauna, including *Homo neanderthalensis*
Australia and New Guinea	40,000 to 25,000 BP	Large marsupials, reptiles, and birds
North and South America	11,000 to 10,000 BP	Megafauna
Caribbean Islands	7,000 to 3,000 BP	Giant ground sloths, monkeys, tortoises
Mediterranean Islands	5,000 BP	Dwarf megafauna, including elephants
Wrangel Island (Siberian Arctic)	3,500 BP	Mammoths
Pacific Islands	3,000 to 200 BP (AD 1800)	Birds
New Zealand	1500 to 200 BP (AD 1800)	Moas, other flightless birds
Madagascar	1000 to 200 BP (AD 1800)	Large birds, tortoises, lemurs, small hippos
THE SECOND WAVE: SPREAD OF EUROPEANS 500 BP (AD 1500) TO 30 BP (AD 1970)		
Islands		Tortoises, birds, mammals
Continents		Freshwater taxa, and steep population declines of remaining megafauna
Oceans		Steep population declines of marine mammals, large fish, and other species
THE THIRD WAVE: OVERPOPULATION AND GLOBALIZATION AD 1970 TO 2100		
Everywhere		All taxa

CHAPTER 3

The First Wave

Human Evolution

Before looking at human-caused extinctions, we must first glance at what current research tells us about human evolution—because our evolution explains much about the Pleistocene-Holocene Extinction. Until recently, human paleontologists saw a steady progression from early "ape men" to modern human beings. The metaphor for human evolution was a ladder: australopithecines led to *Homo habilis*, who led to *Homo erectus*, who led to Neanderthals, who led to us, with only a single species of *Homo* alive at any one time.[1] This view took many diverse human fossils and categorized them into just a few species. Today, leading experts in the field, using recent fossil finds, more advanced dating and interpretive tools, and genetic analysis, offer a different view. Two of the world's leading students of human evolution recently made an unprecedented personal examination of almost every known human fossil in the world. In *Extinct Humans*, Ian Tattersall of the American Museum of Natural History and Jeffrey Schwartz of the University of Pittsburgh clearly show that, from roughly four to five million years ago until twenty-seven thousand years ago, there were always several species of humans alive at one time.[2] Tattersall provides a good summary of their evidence in *Scientific American*.[3] He recently calculated that "at least seventeen species are represented in the known hominid fossil record."[4]

The evidence also strongly favors an "Out of Africa" scenario,[5] with modern humans evolving recently in Africa and then spreading around the world, displacing other hominid species and causing the extinction of most other large mammals.

Genetic analysis shows that our ancestors split from the ancestors of chimpanzees some five to seven million years ago in Africa. That common ancestor was probably much like a chimpanzee.[6] Some 2.5 million years ago, *Homo habilis* began to make crude stone tools.[7] About 1.8 million years ago, *Homo ergaster* evolved from *Homo habilis* in East Africa and was the first hominid to spread out of Africa, reaching the Caucasus Mountains in what is now the Republic of Georgia by 1.7 million years ago.[8] Still a bipedal ape, *Homo ergaster* likely gave rise to three branches: *Homo erectus* in east and Southeast Asia; a group that culminated in *Homo neanderthalensis* in Europe, western Asia, and the Middle East; and a group that ultimately led to *Homo sapiens* in Africa.[9] Instead of a ladder diagram leading to modern humans, a branching bush is a better model for our family tree.[10]

By one hundred thousand years ago, anatomically modern humans had evolved and were living in Africa. Other species of humans were living elsewhere in the world. Neanderthals lived in the western part of Eurasia. In the Far East lived the Dali people of China and Ngandong people of Java, descendants of *Homo erectus*.[11] It is likely that there was another human species in Africa at this time, too.[12] Therefore, at least three (or maybe four or five) separate species of humans lived in different parts of the world—all using crude stone tools and making some use of fire. Until recently, most human paleontologists viewed Neanderthals as a human subspecies—*Homo sapiens neanderthalensis*.[13] It is now quite clear that Neanderthals were a separate species and that there was no interbreeding between them and *Homo sapiens*. Ian Tattersall writes that "the Neanderthals were not simply a species in isolation, but were in fact the latest survivors of a whole subgroup of species that developed in Europe and western Asia from an ancestor that lived between about a million and half a million years ago, independently of what was going on in other parts of the world."[14] The last common ancestor we share with Neanderthals lived five hundred thousand to six hundred thousand years ago.[15]

Despite the physical evolution of anatomically modern people in Africa sometime before one hundred thousand years ago, our ancestors remained just big animals. Their stone tools were crude, little different from those of a million years earlier. Jared Diamond is a professor of physiology at the UCLA Medical School. He is also a world-class scientist in the fields of ornithology, conservation biology, and linguistics. Furthermore, his book, *The Third Chimpanzee*, is arguably the best book ever written about the human animal. In it, he writes, "There were no bone tools, no ropes to make nets, and no fishhooks." There is no evidence that stone tools were hafted to wooden handles.[16] Because of this lack of sophisticated tools and the lack of innovation in tool making for hundreds of thousands of years, Diamond thinks that these anatomically modern people "were still very *ineffective* big-game hunters"[17] and "just glorified chimpanzees."[18] Stanford University anthropologist Richard Klein, arguably the world's expert on human evolution, writes, "The people who inhabited Africa between 100 and 60 ky ago may have been physically modern or near-modern, but they were behaviorally very similar to Neanderthals and other nonmodern humans."[19]

The real change, which made our ancestors us, came in Africa sometime around 50,000 BP.[20] Diamond and others call this "The Great Leap Forward." Improved, standardized tools and jewelry suddenly appeared in France and Spain about forty thousand years ago. The people moving into Europe with these advanced, innovative tools were the Cro-Magnons, named about the site in France where their bones were first found.[21] Some human paleontologists think that this technological jump came from the anatomical evolution of the voice box, which finally allowed complex language and thus culture.[22] Ian Tattersall and Richard Klein both discuss in detail this emergence of complex language through the evolution of the larynx.[23] More recently, however, Klein writes, "Arguably, the most plausible cause was a genetic mutation that promoted the fully modern brain."[24] Tattersall writes, "*Homo sapiens* is not simply an improved version of its ancestors—it's a new concept, qualitatively distinct from them in highly significant if limited respects."[25] Elsewhere, he writes, "This leap was so great that it is impossible to avoid the conclusion that entirely different sensibilities and capacities were involved."[26] Tattersall and Schwartz argue that, fitting well "with what we know about the evolutionary process . . . the modern human sensibility . . . was acquired as a package, rather than bit by bit over the millennia."[27]

Richard Klein thinks that this Great Leap Forward was such a dividing line that "only fully modern people after 50 ky ago should be called *H. sapiens*, and older African populations would require another name. The most appropriate is probably *Homo helmei*."[28]

This is an important point. We moderns are a very young species. This is proved by the lack of genetic diversity among human beings today. Each of the other four living species of great apes has considerably more genetic diversity than we have. For example, there is greater diversity between two gorillas living in nearby bands in the same forest than between an Eskimo and an Australian Aborigine. "You would find the latter pair (the humans) are more genetically alike than the former (the

gorillas)," writes Christopher Stringer of the Natural History Museum in
London and the primary developer of the Out of Africa model. Although
there are six billion humans, we have less genetic diversity than do gorillas, which number only forty thousand to sixty-five thousand. Chimpanzees (100,000–150,000), bonobos (10,000–25,000), and orangutans
(fewer than 38,500) each have greater diversity than do humans.[29] (This
is why many human evolutionists today think that human races have little meaning. Racial differences are truly superficial and quite recent.)

This lack of genetic diversity may have come about because of a population bottleneck among our ancestors sometime after one hundred
thousand years ago, when their numbers dropped to only ten thousand
adults (this has been determined through complex genetic analysis).
Global cooling from the explosion of Mount Toba on Sumatra seventy-
four thousand years ago may have caused this crash. (Mount St. Helens
was nothing more than a wee hiccup compared to Toba, the greatest volcanic eruption in 450 million years.) With this tiny population, *Homo
sapiens* were far too few to spread out of Africa. Based on genetic analysis of living populations of humans around the world, it seems that our
population rebounded around sixty thousand years ago, consistent with
our spread out of Africa after fifty thousand years ago.[30]

After the Great Leap Forward, humans became very effective big-
game hunters. Big animals had evolved with humans in Africa and the
Levant. They had learned to be wary of hunting chimps and, thus, were
not easy prey even for the culturally advanced *Homo sapiens*. This is why
there have been so few megafauna extinctions in Africa in the last forty
thousand years. Throughout most of the rest of the world, however,
other human species were not very good hunters (Eurasia) or were not
present (the Americas), and big animals had little or no reason to fear us.
During the next forty millennia, we spread. And we killed. Our ancestors drifted into Europe and Asia and replaced the other species of
Homo, although Neanderthals held on in a remote part of southern
Spain until twenty-seven thousand years ago, and the Ngandong people
may have lasted in Java until about that time, too.[31]

John Gittleman and Matthew Gompper in *Science* write, "The most
powerful illustration of how naiveté to danger may lead to elimination
comes from the extinctions of the late Quaternary, during which more
than half of the 167 genera of large land mammals (>44 kg) became
extinct, primarily because of the rapid and catastrophic effects of 'first
contact' with colonizing human hunters."[32]

Richard Leakey of Kenya, one of the most famous scientists and conservationists in the world, writes that "it has become undeniable that the

evolution of *Homo sapiens* was to imprint a ruinous signature on the rest of the natural world, perhaps right from the beginning."[33] Tattersall and Schwartz bluntly state that *"Homo sapiens* interacts with the world around it in an unusual, and unusually destructive, way."[34]

Let us survey that unusually destructive way we have interacted with the world for the last forty thousand years.

The First Wave: Human Expansion 40,000 BP to 200 BP (AD 1800)

After leaving Africa, populations of *Homo sapiens* entered other parts of the world at different times during the last forty thousand years. Invariably, extinction of other species, particularly *megafauna*, coincided.

Europe and Northern Asia: 40,000 BP to 13,000 BP

According to Ian Tattersall, Neanderthals hunted red and fallow deer, but "would rarely have tackled anything much bigger." There is no evidence that they threw spears.[35] Some authorities believe that Neanderthals were mostly scavengers.[36] Mammoths, mastodons, woolly rhinos, and other megafauna had little reason to fear them. The Cro-Magnons who spread into Europe about forty thousand years ago were very good big game hunters, however. As Cro-Magnons spread through Europe, Neanderthals quickly disappeared, hanging on only in areas not taken over by Cro-Magnons. Jared Diamond writes that "Cro-Magnon diseases, murders, and displacements did in the Neanderthals."[37] Our closest relative, then, was one of the first victims of modern humans in the Pleistocene-Holocene Extinction.

During the next twenty thousand years of the Cro-Magnon takeover, twelve genera of large mammals became extinct in Europe, although nine of those genera survived elsewhere. The three permanently lost from Earth were the woolly rhino, giant deer ("Irish elk"), and woolly mammoth. Eleven other genera of large mammals survived into historical time.[38]

Australia and New Guinea: 40,000 BP to 25,000 BP

Sometime before thirty-five thousand years ago *Homo sapiens* were in Southeast Asia; and the Dali people of China and Ngandong people of Java, descendants of *Homo erectus*, were gone or soon would be (Ngandongs may have lasted until twenty-seven thousand years ago).[39]

Another victim of genocide like the Neanderthals? It seems likely. At this time the islands of Java, Sumatra, Borneo, and Bali were still part of the continent of Asia. Australia, Tasmania, and New Guinea were still connected and part of a different continent. Between was a series of islands. Humans arrived in Australia by forty thousand years ago.[40]

In Greater Australia, they found a fauna like no other on Earth. By 30,000 BP, however, most of the large mammals, birds, and reptiles were gone. Thirteen genera and at least thirty-eight species of large marsupials were lost forever. The only megafauna surviving in Australia today are four species of kangaroos in a single genus. Among the extinct giant marsupials were a lion-sized carnivore, three species of rhinolike grazers, half-ton wombats, large koalas, and very big kangaroos. Also lost as hunting and burning humans spread over Greater Australia were a 24-foot-long giant sibling to the Komodo dragon, a massive snake, a huge horned tortoise, and an ostrichlike bird.[41]

North and South America: 11,000 BP to 10,000 BP

By eighteen thousand years ago, *Homo sapiens* of the Dyukhati culture were hunting mammoths and other big game in western Siberia.[42] About 12,000 BP, their likely descendants crossed the Bering Land Bridge linking Asia and Alaska. Around eleven thousand years ago, this Clovis culture of big game hunters was south of the continental ice sheet in what is now the United States.[43] (These people are named after the town in eastern New Mexico where their distinctive stone points were first found.) Within one thousand years of their arrival, thirty-three genera of large mammals were extinct (seven of these still exist outside North America). Seven families and one order of mammals were entirely eliminated from North America.[44]

These big game hunters soon moved into South America, and the extinction of forty-six genera of large mammals swiftly followed. Included in these extinctions were the last survivors of two unique South American orders of ungulates—Litopterna and Notoungulata. Four genera of gomphotheres (cousins of the mammoths with even stranger tusks) were lost.[45]

Caribbean Islands: 7000 BP to 3000 BP

Humans did not reach Cuba and other Caribbean Islands until seven thousand years ago. Giant ground sloths survived in Cuba and Hispaniola until three thousand years ago—about the time of the Trojan War—seven thousand years after they became extinct on the North and South America continents. Other species encountered by the first Antillean Indians included large monkeys, beaver-sized rodents, giant tortoises, and huge, flightless owls. Mammalogist Ross MacPhee, of the American Museum of Natural History, writes that "the chilling conclusion is that roughly 80 percent of all Antillean land mammals living when the Indians came were gone by 1600 or so."[46]

Mediterranean Islands: 5000 BP

From the Balearics to Cyprus, thirteen genera of mammals and several giant land tortoises disappeared long after Pleistocene extinctions in Australia, the Americas, and Eurasia. Among these mammals were dwarf elephants, deer, and hippos. Their extinctions came after humans first arrived.[47]

Wrangel Island (Siberian Arctic): 4000 BP

One hundred miles north of Siberia in the Arctic Ocean lies Wrangel Island. Peter Ward writes, "Mammoths were still living on Wrangel Island when the first pyramids were being built in Egypt."[48] These were dwarf mammoths, only about 6 feet high at the shoulder. They lasted into historic times, then disappeared when *Homo sapiens* first arrived four thousand years ago—at least six thousand years after mammoths were killed off in Eurasia and North America.

Pacific Islands: 3000 BP to 200 BP (AD 1800)

The Hawaiian Islands were not the only islands of the tropical Pacific to suffer mass extinction with the arrival of the Polynesians. Beginning three thousand years ago, these extraordinary seafarers settled island after island throughout the topical Pacific, bringing with them agriculture, dogs, pigs, and rats. Ornithologist David Steadman thinks there was a unique species of flightless rail on each of the eight hundred or so islands. Species of flightless rails remain on only a few remote islands today. Stuart Pimm and his colleagues write, "Adding known and inferred extinctions, it seems that with only Stone Age technology, the Polynesians exterminated >2000 bird species, some ~15% of the world total."[49]

New Zealand: 1000 BP to 200 BP (AD 1800)

Archaeologists Michael Trotter and Beverley McCulloch write: "Thirty-four species of birds that were living [in New Zealand] when Polynesians first arrived about a thousand years ago were extinct by the time of European contact some eight hundred years later. . . . Populations of marine mammals, shellfish, crustaceans, and a terrestrial reptile were seriously depleted. Vast areas of New Zealand forest had been burned as well."[50] The most famous of these extinct birds were moas, "ostrichlike birds comprising a dozen species, and ranging from little ones 'only' three feet in height and forty pounds in weight up to giants of five hundred pounds and ten feet tall," according to Jared Diamond.[51] The moas were incredibly abundant when humans arrived—it is estimated that there are one hundred thousand to five hundred thousand moa skeletons in Maori archaeological sites. Also hunted into extinction were a duck, a goose, and a coot—all huge and flightless. Flying birds, such as a giant raven, a swan, and a pelican were also lost. A thirty-pound eagle, far larger than any living raptor, preyed on moas by attacking their heads.[52] These powerful eagles likely went for the heads of the 6-foot tall Maoris when the humans first arrived.

While human hunting did in the big birds, rats brought by the Maoris led to the extinction of a variety of odd bats, wrens, and huge insects.[53]

Madagascar: 1000 BP to 200 BP (AD 1800)

Along with New Zealand, Madagascar was the last big island to be colonized by humans. Settled by Indonesian traders sailing to East Africa, a culture of farmers and herders developed. Cattle, goats, and pigs were introduced onto an island separated from Africa for millions of years. Present when the Indonesians arrived, but gone (or largely so) when Portuguese sailors stumbled onto Madagascar in AD 1550, were a group of flightless birds even larger than the moas—elephant birds. Among the six to twelve or more species of these birds was one that was 10 feet tall and weighed 1,000 pounds. Two species of giant land tortoises with shells 3 feet long, a dozen species of lemurs (primitive primates), including one almost as big as a gorilla, a "'pygmy' hippopotamus ('only' the size of a cow), an aardvark, and a big mongoose-related carnivore built like a short-legged puma" also lived on Madagascar when humans arrived. Hunting, clearing land for agriculture, burning, and grazing by goats and cattle wiped out this extraordinary megafauna of birds, mammals, and tortoises in the few centuries before Europeans arrived.[54]

It is clear that, well before the heretofore-assumed beginning of the modern extinction crisis in AD 1600, Stone Age Europeans, Australians, Asians, Americans, and Polynesians had exterminated the most magnificent and distinctive mammals, birds, and reptiles of our time. Of large mammals, 14.3 percent of genera became extinct in Africa, 73.3 percent in North America, 79.6 percent in South America, and 86.4 percent in Australia. Our kind, armed with language, culture, fire, and innovative stone and bone weapons stormed through the Earth like an all-consuming typhoon and swept away the majority of large terrestrial mammals that had evolved since our branching off from the other chimps five million years ago.

There are, however, some archaeologists, anthropologists, social scientists, indigenous rights advocates, and others who hotly cast out the demon idea that Stone Age peoples could have caused mass extinction. Their arguments include the following:

• *Where are the bones? If humans quickly killed every mammoth and mastodon in North America, there should be a noticeable layer of their bones in the geological record.*

Stop and think. If every mammoth, mastodon, horse, ground sloth, and other extinct large mammal in North America was killed by Clovis people within one hundred years, would this leap out in the fossil record? Of course not. Because none of these critters would have lived more than one hundred years to begin with. They were dying all the time anyway.[55] What does show in the fossil record is their absence from more recent layers.

• *Climate change at the end of the last glaciation caused mass extinction because of its effect in changing ecosystems.*

Opponents of the overkill hypothesis claim, without evidence, that the North American megafauna was already in serious decline when Clovis people arrived. This hypothesis is based on the assumption that the food supply was dwindling because of wholesale vegetation changes with warming after the Ice Age. The Ice Age ended at the same time around the world. If climate change at the end of the Ice Age was the cause of Pleistocene extinctions around the world, why did not the extinctions occur at the same time—after the end of the Ice Age? Why did some extinctions happen thirty thousand years ago and some only a few hundred years ago? The extinctions in various parts of the world were not coincidental with the end of the Ice Age, but were coincidental with the arrival of humans.

Megafauna extinctions were most extreme in Australia, where climate change was less dramatic than elsewhere. Moreover, extinctions in Australia occurred well before the end of the Ice Age.[56]

Richard Leakey and Roger Lewin ask "how do we explain that the plant species that were important in the diets of, for instance, mammoth and ground sloths remained abundant and widespread after these mammalian species became extinct?"[57]

Not all the large mammals in North America became extinct after the arrival of the Clovis people. Moose, bison, elk, and grizzly bear are still here. However, all of these survivors were late arrivals to North America. They had evolved in Eurasia. The species that had evolved in North America—having no experience with hunting humans—were the ones that became extinct.[58]

University of Nevada anthropologist Gary Haynes has studied the impact of drought on African elephants. He has found that even with heavy die-off during drought, elephant populations bounce back. Using his studies to speculate about mammoths and mastodons, he writes, "The most important lessons to be learned from studies of modern elephant die offs have to do with the proboscidean responses to climate change and with proboscidean resilience allowing recovery from nearly any environmental stress except human overhunting."[59] He concludes, "In the absence of Clovis hunters, mammoths and mastodons (and other megafauna) should have been able to survive the changing conditions of terminal Pleistocene environments."[60]

Jared Diamond reports that in 1966, when he first came to New Zealand, it was widely believed that climate change had caused the extinction of the moas. But recent studies have shown that the "last moas died with their gizzards full of food, and enjoying the best climate that they had seen for tens of thousands of years."[61]

One of the world's leading experts on evolution, Niles Eldredge of the American Museum of Natural History, asks, "Why are all the big hairies dead except *African* big hairies? The answer is that we humans evolved in concert with, and literally as part of, the African ecosystems." Outside of Africa, "We modern humans were clearly like bulls in a china shop, disrupting ecosystems wherever we went, especially systems that had never had any of the earlier hominid species living in them." In such places, "the larger game animals—the big hairies— were totally unwary."[62] Outside of Africa and tropical Asia, every land mammal weighing more than 2,200 pounds became extinct.[63]

One can argue that all this is circumstantial evidence or simply skilled argument. Fine. However, the smoking gun has now been found. University of Michigan paleontologist Dan Fisher has carefully studied the stories told in the growth rings of mammoth and mastodon tusks. Studies on modern elephant tusks show that growth rings are laid down just as they are in tree trunks. Similarly, good years, when elephants are well fed, are shown by wide growth rings. Chemical traces also tell what food the elephant was eating. Moreover, the tusk rings tell how fast female elephants are breeding. Elephants breed slowly, if at all, when food is in desperately short supply. When elephant populations are under heavy hunting pressure, they breed very frequently. Studies of growth rings in mammoth and mastodon tusks eleven thousand years ago in North America reveal the truth at last. They were well fed. They were not dying from starvation. They were breeding frequently. Ward writes, "Lack of food was not their problem. They were not dying off. They were being killed off."[64]

At a 2003 geoscience meeting, another smoking gun or bloody spear was offered by Guy Robinson, David Burney, and Lida Pigott Burney. Through close analysis of spores of a fungus associated with megafauna dung, microscopic charcoal, and boreal tree pollen, they found that "humans arrived on the scene damningly close to the time of the megafauna collapse, whereas climate change was such a late-comer that it could not have played a major role."[65]

- *The Clovis big-game hunters were not the first people in the Americas.*

Both legitimate archaeologists and crackpots have long claimed greater antiquity for humans in the Americas than twelve thousand years ago. A 2000 article in *Scientific American*—remarkable for its superficiality and one-sidedness—leaves the impression that all American archaeologists accept pre-Clovis populations in North and South America. (One illustration in the article portrays these pre-Clovis people paddling a very modern-looking canoe—complete with thwarts.)[66] In truth, however, there is no consensus among archaeologists. All of the pre-Clovis sites have troubling questions: Are the claimed human artifacts really human-made, or are they geofacts—naturally fractured rocks that resemble stone tools? Are the carbon-14 datings accurate or have the sites been contaminated with older organic matter? Are supposed human hearths really campfires or are they simply residues of natural fire?

Jared Diamond, in his best seller, *Guns, Germs, and Steel*, disputes these pre-Clovis dates, concluding that "if there really had been pre-Clovis settlement in the Americas, it would have become obvious at many locations by now, and we would not still be arguing."[67] Famous paleontologist Don Johanson, discoverer of "Lucy," asks, "If humans were abundant in the Americas before the almost ubiquitous makers of Clovis culture, why did they leave so little trace of their existence?"[68]

Just a month before *Scientific American*'s article, *Natural History* published a review by University of Illinois archaeologist Anna Curtenius Roosevelt pointing out the problems with earlier dates.[69]

But, so what? If other humans were present in the Americas before the Clovis people and megafauna extinction, they were very few and were not big-game hunters.[70] For various reasons, including small population size, they might not have survived long, even if they left some archaeological evidence. Brian Miller writes, "Small waves could have arrived periodically, but only the Clovis people did in a dominating fashion."[71] The leading proponent of pre-Clovis occupation of the Americas by humans, anthropologist Thomas Dillehay at the University of Kentucky, writes, "In fact, pre-Clovis sites add credence to the overkill hypothesis."[72]

Similarly, claims of great antiquity are made for human presence in Australia, as long as sixty thousand years ago. However, John Mulvaney and Johan Kamminga, in their *Prehistory of Australia*, do not find convincing evidence for dates older than forty thousand years ago.[73] Moreover, recent research has disproved a highly touted early human presence. A human burial at Lake Mungo in southeastern Australia was dated at sixty-two thousand years ago in 1998, but better analysis reported in 2003 gave a date of only forty-two thousand years ago.[74] Even if *Homo sapiens* arrived tens of thousands of years before the Australian megafauna extinction, it does not contradict human hunting as a cause. Richard G. Klein, in his monumental text on human evolution, *The Human Career*, points out that Australia may have been colonized twice. And, he writes, "the earliest Australians may have been neither recent African immigrants nor fully modern."[75] Other authorities see some human fossils in Australia as deriving from *Homo erectus* in Java.[76]

Moreover, *Homo sapiens* may not have left the Australian coasts and populated the interior until a bit before twenty-five thousand years ago.[77] Klein writes that "the Australian [extinctions] cannot be attributed to terminal Pleistocene climatic change, which they clearly antedate, and a human role may be even more strongly implied [than in the Americas]."[78]

- *Human hunting did not kill the megafauna, but habitat modification by burning, and/or introduction of diseases and exotic competitors caused die-off.*

In 1997, Ross MacPhee and Preston Marx offered the possibility that *hyperdisease* (a very virulent and very lethal disease) brought by the first humans entering an area caused the megafaunal extinctions, not hunting. They admit, however, "At present, the hyperdisease hypothesis is an abstraction awaiting marriage with suitable empirical data."[79] In other words, the hyperdisease cause of mass extinction is an interesting idea, but there is no evidence to support it—as there is for human hunting. Of course, burning and the introduction of disease and exotic competitors do play parts in human-induced extinction—but it is still human-induced.

- *The overkill model of an advancing front is wrong.*

Some recent research has called into question Martin's original hypothesis of an advancing front. However, even if this challenge is true, it does not refute that humans were responsible for overkill. Long-term hunting may suddenly reach a threshold after which extinction swiftly occurs. Ward writes, "There are many examples of this in case histories of fisheries, where large, supposedly extinction-resistant stocks of fish suddenly crash when the fishing rate is enhanced just slightly. Some threshold is surpassed, and the stock suddenly falls to very low numbers."[80] Furthermore, an *extinction debt* may be caused by slow, steady hunting pressure. Ward again: "Killing *over* 2% of the population (each year) does not cause an immediate population crash . . . but it inevitably consigns the hunted population to extinction several centuries down the road."[81]

- *People—particularly Stone Age people—were simply not capable of causing mass extinction.*

Despite Dan Fisher's bloody spear, I am sure that some will continue to deny a major human role in Stone Age extinctions. MacPhee and Marx, for example, write that their hyperdisease hypothesis for the megafauna extinction "permits the conclusion that aboriginal Americans may *never* have produced extinctions solely as a result of unrestricted hunting"[82] (emphasis in original).

I believe the resistance is based not on evidence or logic, but is simply ideological. Various anthropologists and social scientists cannot bring themselves to see Stone Age humans as the cause of mass extinction. Some Native Americans see overkill as a racist attack, just as they do for the solid archaeological evidence of cannibalism in the Americas. Some Australian aborigines, Polynesians, and other indigenous peoples feel the same way. Many of us want to believe in the inherent goodness of human beings, but it makes no more sense today to deny a major human role in Pleistocene extinctions than it does to deny a Hutu role in the slaughter of Tutsis in Rwanda. Of course, there are those who still deny the Holocaust.

Recognizing a human role in the Pleistocene extinctions does not denigrate any living group. We modern humans are all the same species with the same genetic make-up and behavior. My ancestors participated in causing the extinction of Eurasian megafauna, including Neanderthals. More recently, they helped cause the extinction and near-extinction of many North American species. How then can it possibly be racist to present evidence for human-caused extinctions by early arrivals in Australia, the Americas, Hawaii, New Zealand, and Madagascar?

Carl Swisher, Garniss Curtis, and Roger Lewin write in *Java Man*, "Almost certainly, everyone in the world today is a descendant of a population of newly emerged humans who, in their inexorable spread across the world, caused the extinction of species of humans that were like us, but weren't us. We wonder how much time must pass before that, too, becomes a politically correct version of our history, like it or not."[83]

Even more to the point, E. O. Wilson writes:

> The somber archaeology of vanished species has taught us the following lessons:
>
> - The noble savage never existed.
> - Eden occupied was a slaughterhouse.
> - Paradise found is paradise lost.[84]

Richard Klein and Blake Edgar explain: "If late Paleolithic people in Australia, the Americas, and Eurasia reduced species diversity in the way the data suggest, then the dawn of human culture represents not only a profound behavioral or sociocultural transition. It also marks the transformation of humanity from a relatively rare and insignificant member of the large mammal fauna to a geologic force with the power to impoverish nature."[85]

CHAPTER 4

The Second and Third Waves

The Second Wave: European Expansion
AD 1500 to AD 1970

With the rise of agriculture, cities, civilization, and empires in Eurasia came a slow wave of losses of many species. Although these were seldom complete extinctions of species, they were widespread extirpations. As early as 2500 BC, elephants, rhinos, and giraffes were hunted out in Egypt's Nile Valley. Lions and leopards were gone from Greece by 200 BC, and beavers were also exterminated in Greece.[1] Aurochs were killed off in Britain by 2000 BC, and, during the Roman Empire, tigers were hunted out in much of the Middle East, hippos in the lower Nile, and elephants, rhinos, and zebras in North Africa. Whales were gone from the Mediterranean Sea by the end of the Roman Empire.[2] In Great Britain, bears were gone by AD 1000, beavers by AD 1300, and wolves by AD 1743.[3] Walruses were hunted out of the British Isles by 1500.[4]

Five hundred years ago, sea captains sailing for Spain and Portugal had found the Americas and had rounded Africa to reach India. The era of exploration, colonization, and exploitation that followed has caused sweeping extinctions. For example, in the United States and Canada alone, at least seventy-one species and subspecies of vertebrates have become extinct since 1500, along with 217 documented species of plants.[5] Let's look at some of the evidence.

Mammals

In 1997, Ross MacPhee and Clare Flemming of the American Museum of Natural History, Department of Mammalogy, published the results of their careful review of mammal extinctions since AD 1500. They identified ninety species of mammals that have become extinct during the modern era of European expansion, although they think it likely that the number will be "revised upward to 110 or 115 confirmed losses," or "close to 2 percent of all mammal species on Earth." Using the highest estimate for the rate of natural or background extinction of one mammal species every four hundred years, the loss of ninety species in five hundred years is "a minimum 7,100 percent increase over the natural rate."[6]

Since the arrival of the Spaniards, thirty-six species of mammals have become extinct on Caribbean Islands, including the Jamaican monkey and the Caribbean monk seal. Nineteen species, including the thylacine (Tasmanian "wolf"), have become extinct in Australia since 1843. Most extinct mammals from the Second Wave have been rodents, insectivores, and bats, and most have been on islands (except for Australia), but larger mammals killed off include Steller's sea cow, the Falkland Islands fox, and two species of antelope in Africa.[7]

Birds

"In the last 300 years, Mauritius, Rodrigues, and Réunion in the Indian Ocean lost 33 species of birds, including the dodo, 30 species of land snails, and 11 reptiles," according to Stuart Pimm and his colleagues.[8] European colonization and exploitation of Pacific islands has led to many bird extinctions, as well.

North American Freshwater Ecosystems

North American freshwater ecosystems hold one-third of all freshwater mussels in the world, 40 percent of all stoneflies, 30 percent of all mayflies, two-thirds of all crayfish, and one-tenth of all freshwater fish.[9] David Wilcove writes, "For all sorts of freshwater animals—from crayfish to caddisflies—the United States is the center of diversity." "But," he points out, "no other group of organisms has suffered more from development or benefited less from environmental laws than our freshwater fauna."[10] Stuart Pimm and his associates write, "In the last century, North American freshwater environments lost 21 of 297 mussel and clam species (120 are threatened) and 40 of ~950 fish species."[11]

Anthony Ricciardi and Joseph Rasmussen write that the evidence shows that "North American freshwater biodiversity is diminishing as rapidly as that of some of the most stressed terrestrial ecosystems on the planet." While 123 species of North American freshwater mollusks, crayfishes, amphibians, and fishes have become extinct since 1900, the future bodes far grimmer. Their conservative estimates of extinctions (conservative because they do not consider competition from the invading zebra mussel) of mussels by 2100 are 127 species out of the remaining 262. Their estimates of imperiled freshwater North American fauna are crayfish, 110 of 336 species (32.7 percent); gastropods, 108 of 474 species (22.8 percent); amphibians, 63 of 243 species (25.9 percent); and fish, 217 of 1,021 species (21.3 percent).[12]

David Propst, the endangered species biologist for the New Mexico Department of Game and Fish, wrote in 1994:

> When Europeans first arrived, it is estimated that the streams and rivers of New Mexico supported at least 66 species of fish. Today, only 59 persist. Of that number, 28 are currently listed as endangered by the NM Department of Game and Fish. At least two more should be added and the status of another three is of concern. Two should be removed because they are extinct. Thus, nearly half of New Mexico's native fish fauna is officially imperiled. The imperilment of the native fish fauna of New Mexico has occurred almost entirely in the past 50 years and continues today.[13]

In 1998, the New Mexico Game Commission voted to drop the two extinct fish from the endangered species list. They "disappeared because their habitats have been drying up."[14] Do not think for a moment that this is a result of drought; their habitats had been drying up because of diversion of water from streams to irrigation ditches and by groundwater pumping.

Perhaps as dire as the actual extinctions caused by the spread of European civilization has been the slaughter of many mammals, birds, and ocean fish to the point where they are mere whispers of their former numbers. The extinction of many of these depleted species fast approaches in the Third Wave.

The Third Wave: Economic Globalization AD 1970 to AD 2100

During my lifetime, the world's human population has more than doubled; I don't have to live much longer before it triples. Consumption of resources has vastly grown. New technologies allow the exploitation of even limited resources in very remote areas. With the end of the Cold War, a global business culture straddles Earth like the Colossus of Rhodes. For the first time in history, the entire human population of Earth has become part of a single economy (although there is resistance from a variety of groups). Industrial pollution, whether toxic chemicals, radioactive materials, long-lasting poisons, or greenhouse gases, is now carried around the world. With these unprecedented developments and demands, humans have begun a Third Wave of extinction. This time, every form of life, everywhere on the planet, is in danger.

In the first two waves, modern humans drove the most beautiful and powerful creatures on Earth into extinction or serious endangerment. In this Third Wave, postmodern humans are finishing the job in the most widespread species cleansing imaginable. In one hundred years—AD 2100—the Pleistocene-Holocene Event will be largely over. We will have turned Eden into Hell in only forty thousand years.

The Evidence For Mass Extinction Today

Even if we grudgingly acknowledge past human-caused extinctions, what proof is there that a mass extinction continues today? We can point to at least three different types of evidence in answering this question: We can look at (1) the area-species relationship and the evidence of habitat destruction; (2) the decline of specific living species; and (3) our takeover of Earth's terrestrial and marine net primary productivity (NPP) and our overshooting of ecological carrying capacity.

Remember Charles Lyell's recognition that "the annihilation of a multitude of species has already been effected, and will continue to go on hereafter, in a still more rapid ratio, as the colonies of highly civilized nations spread themselves over unoccupied lands."[15] His words ring even truer today.

Species-Area Relationship

Michael Soulé writes, "One of the principles of modern ecology is that the number of species that an area can support is directly proportional to its size. A corollary is that if area is reduced, the number of species shrinks."[16] In 1980, John Terborgh and Blair Winter wrote that research showed that "extinction is strongly area dependent."[17] The species-area relationship has been shown with birds, mammals, reptiles, and other kinds of animals on the Greater Sunda Islands (the Indonesian archipelago), Caribbean islands, and elsewhere. An ecological rule of thumb is that if a habitat is cut by 90 percent, it will lose 50 percent of its species, or, if 50 percent of the area is lost, 10 percent of the species will disappear. However, within isolated nature reserves the consequences are even worse than this. Bruce Wilcox explains:

> Studies suggest that habitat loss contributes in two ways [to species reduction]: first, by excluding a portion of a fauna, particularly the rare or patchily distributed species; second, by increasing the extinction rate of the remaining species as a result of lower population sizes. Habitat insularization also contributes in two ways: first, by extinguishing species "protected" within an area through the removal of required resources outside the area; second, by reducing accessibility for, and sources of, colonists necessary to offset extinction events.[18]

It is the species-area formula, used with the best estimates of habitat destruction and of numbers of species in various at-risk habitats, that gives us the dramatic forecasts of mass extinction by such biologists as E. O. Wilson. In his book, *The Diversity of Life*, Wilson explains the process in a simple but authoritative way. After carefully going through his calculations, Wilson writes:

> If destruction of the rain forest continues at the present rate to the year 2022, half of the remaining rain forest will be gone. The total extinction of species this will cause will lie somewhere between 10 percent . . . and 22 percent. . . . Roughly, then, if deforestation continues for thirty more years at the present rate, one tenth to one quarter of the rain-forest species will disappear. If the rain forests are as rich in diversity as most biologists think, their reduction alone will eliminate 5 to 10 percent or more—probably considerably more—of all the species on earth in thirty years. When other species-rich but declining habitats are added, including heathland, dry tropical forests, lakes, rivers, and coral reefs, the toll mounts steeply.[19]

A recent study published in the prestigious British science journal *Nature* shows an even higher rate of rainforest destruction than Wilson used. Instead of using only satellite images to calculate the area of Amazonian forest lost to deforestation in 1998, ecologists from Woods Hole

Research Center in the United States and the Institute of Environmental Research in Brazil undertook extensive on-the-ground research that tripled the estimate of official government figures. This new research estimates that "217,000 square miles, or 16 percent, of the original rain forest has been spoiled over the years. The official Brazilian estimate is 13 percent."[20]

Stuart Pimm gives authoritative estimates of the loss of tropical humid forests around the world, which I've adapted in table 4.1.

However, "for every area [that is] cleared of [rainforest], sometimes three to four times more forest nearby is severely damaged by selective logging, firewood collection, and especially fires."[21] Pimm also shows that, once logged, these tropical forests do not come back. "Across much of the world's tropics, forests have become an almost worthless weed patch."[22]

Peter Raven, director of the Missouri Botanical Garden and one of the most respected botanists in the world, warned in 1986 that fifty thousand plants, mostly in the tropics, were likely to become extinct during our lifetimes.[23]

TABLE 4.1. Estimates of the loss of tropical humid forests around the world

Region	Original Forest Amount	1990 Forest Amount
Continental Southeast Asia	3 million km2 (741 million acres)	0.25-0.33 million km2 (61-81.5 million acres)
Southeast Asia Islands	2 million km2 (494 million acres)	more than 1 million km2 (more than 247 million acres)
Central Africa	2-3 million km2 (494-741 million acres)	1.32-2.4 million km2 (326-593 million acres)
West Africa	1.25 million km2 (308 million acres)	140,000 km2 (34.6 million acres)
Mesoamerica	1 million km2 (247 million acres)	300,000-400,000 km2 (74-99 million acres)
Amazon-Orinoco	8 million km2 (1.97 billion acres)	6.5 million km2 (1.6 billion acres)
Atlantic Brazil	1 million km2 (247 million acres)	more than 100,000 km2 (more than 24.7 million acres)

Source: Stuart L. Pimm, *The World According to Pimm: A Scientist Audits the Earth* (McGraw-Hill, New York, 2001), 58–59.

Naysayers of high extinction rates have seized on the area-species relationship to claim that Wilson and others are all wet. "What about the eastern United States?" they ask. Settlers cleared nearly all of it. Why have not more birds gone extinct there?

Stuart Pimm has perhaps presented the most detailed evidence for extinction around the world. The article he and three colleagues wrote for *Science* in 1995, "The Future of Biodiversity," may be the most important short paper written so far to explain today's mass extinction event. He says that critics are interpreting the species-area model "naively."[24] Pimm explains that, although settlers cleared 95 percent of the East, they did so over several centuries. As clearing moved west, the forests near the Atlantic that had earlier been cleared began to recover. At least 50 percent of the area was always forested. Nonetheless, the model predicts that 16 percent of the 160 forest bird species (which is twenty-six species) should have gone extinct. Or does it? No: "[A]ll but 28 of these [160] species occur widely across North America. They would have survived elsewhere even if all the forest had been permanently cleared."[25] Sixteen percent of twenty-eight species is four.[26] Let's see . . . passenger pigeon, Carolina parakeet, ivory-billed woodpecker, and Bachman's warbler have gone extinct. Four.

Moreover, as Peter Ward writes, "[T]he extinction of species established within a forest does not necessarily take place at the same time as the forest's destruction. Although many species are immediately eradicated, others, composed of small numbers of individuals, can hang on for extended periods, giving the impression that they have avoided extinction." This is called *extinction debt*: "Decades or centuries after a habitat perturbation, extinction related to the perturbation may still be taking place."[27] For example, both the ivory-billed woodpecker and Bachman's warbler held on in tiny numbers for several decades after their habitat was severely reduced.

In a study of bird declines in the Kakamega Forest in Kenya, researchers found a lag time between forest fragmentation and extinction among birds. They concluded that "in the first 50 years after isolation, tropical forest fragments of this size [roughly 2,500 acres] suffer half of the total number of extinctions that they are likely to experience."[28] They warned that, because 65 percent of the world's 1,111 threatened bird species are in forests, "We can therefore predict that 50% of these—approaching 500 species—will be extinct in approximately 50 years."[29] Another researcher, studying African primates, predicted future extinctions because of habitat loss that has already occurred.[30]

Niles Eldredge writes, "Other approaches to measuring extinction rates yield more alarming results. Many species in museum collections simply can no longer be found in the wild. Many of my colleagues at the American Museum of Natural History have told me of returning to locales where, a few years earlier, they had found new species—in one case, a new species of spider in Chile—only to discover that the species' habitat had disappeared."[31]

Some nine thousand species of birds are alive today, and 108 are known to have become extinct since 1600, according to the prestigious International Council for Bird Preservation (ICBP). Naysayers casually dispute that figure, asking how can it be proved? Jared Diamond writes, "The ICBP decides to list a species as extinct only after that bird has been specifically looked for in areas where it was previously known to occur or might have turned up, and after it has not been found for many years."[32] If anything, the reported number of recently extinct birds is an undercount because of the lack of investigators, particularly in the tropics. Diamond notes that when he investigated the status of birds in the Solomon Islands, "12 of those 164 species hadn't been encountered since 1953."[33] Another indication of the magnitude of the extinction crisis was a ridge in Ecuador where thirty-eight new species of plants were found. Right after discovery, "the ridge was logged and those plants were exterminated."[34]

Stuart Pimm warns about "mischievous and even malevolent critics like Julian Simon" who dispute extinction rates, despite all the solid science. Pimm says we "should focus on the groups we know" with a "statistical sample." Even economists use this approach. "If you talk about a consumer price index, it's based on a few grocery baskets around the country; the economists don't actually measure the price of everything."[35]

Pimm suggests comparing "current rates of extinction among well-studied taxa to the background rate." With birds, we know the rate "is *several hundred times* what it ought to be." Moreover, this high rate of extinction is "true of mammals, butterflies, flowering plants, fishes, it's true of a whole variety of different samples."[36] For example, Mark Lomolino, an expert on extinction at the University of Oklahoma, says, "Between 1930 and 1990 the diversity of European fungi may have dropped by as much as one-half."[37]

Imperiled Species Today

Those who dismiss the extinction crisis like to claim that the aim of the Endangered Species Act in 1973 was to protect big animals and beautiful birds—not disgusting beetles and other vermin. "I thought we were talking about saving bald eagles and white tigers and things like that," said Senate Republican Leader Trent Lott in 1998 on why he voted for the Endangered Species Act in 1973.[38]

This is a profoundly ignorant attitude, since invertebrates play key roles in maintaining ecosystems. E. O. Wilson famously wrote in 1987, "The truth is that we need invertebrates but they don't need us. If human beings were to disappear tomorrow, the world would go on with little change. . . . But if invertebrates were to disappear, I doubt that the human species could last more than a few months." Wilson goes on describing the impact of invertebrate disappearance, concluding, "Within a few decades the world would return to the state of a billion years ago, composed primarily of bacteria, algae, and a few other very simple multicellular plants."[39]

But we don't need to ground our case for mass extinction on invertebrates. Vertebrates provide plenty of evidence that human-caused extinction is tearing apart nature. Let's survey a few beautiful, interesting groups of animals and see how they are doing, or, in other words, take a statistical sample of groups we know, as Pimm suggests.

In 1995, twenty-two of Earth's thirty surviving species of large mammalian carnivores were listed as "endangered by either the United States or the World Conservation Union."[40] There are only some two thousand breeding adult African wild dogs left in the wild, and the Ethiopian wolf is down "to fewer than 500 individuals."[41] According to the World Wildlife Fund, there may be no more than one thousand giant pandas left in the wild. BBC News reports that "India's Minister of Social Justice and Empowerment has warned that by 2007 'there would be no breeding elephants left in India . . . and the species would die out'" because of poaching, capturing, and habitat destruction.[42] Ten percent of the 608 species and subspecies of primates are in grave and immediate danger of extinction. Cambridge University's primatologist David Chivers says, "I've spent 30 years on [primate conservation], and now we don't seem to be getting anywhere. It's ridiculous."[43] The International Crane Foundation in Baraboo, Wisc., reports that eleven of fifteen species of these tall, beautiful birds are endangered.

The leatherback, the world's largest sea turtle, could "be extinct within 10 to 30 years," according to Larry Crowder of the Duke University Marine Lab. Pacific Ocean populations have "plunged 95 percent in the past 22 years." There are probably fewer than five thousand breeding females. The culprit? Drift nets and long-line fishing.[44]

In 1996, George B. Rabb, director of the Chicago Zoological Park and one of the world's leading experts on endangered species, wrote:

"Nearly half of all primates, the order that includes monkeys and apes, are threatened with extinction. Thirty-six percent of shrews and moles are threatened, 33 percent of pigs, antelope and cattle, 26 percent of bats, 26 percent of wild dogs, bears and cats and 17 percent of rodents. Twenty-two percent of the order that includes rhinos, horses and tapirs are critically endangered and, under one criterion, have a 50 percent chance of becoming extinct within three generations."[45]

Following are a few groups of mammals and birds I've picked to show how dire the extinction threat is.

Cats. Of the thirty-seven species of wild cats that still exist in the world, sixteen (41 percent) are listed as endangered by the United States. These include such fabled and beautiful beasts as the cheetah, tiger, and snow leopard. Seven other species have subspecies listed as endangered (all subspecies of the leopard are listed either as endangered or threatened).[46]

In 1979 and 1980, 1.2 million cat pelts are known to have gone into the fur market, although the International Fur Traders Association instituted a voluntary ban on spotted or striped big cats by the early 1970s. There had been ten thousand leopard skins imported into the United States in 1968 alone.[47]

In the last fifty years, the Bali tiger, Caspian tiger, and Javan tiger have gone extinct. Only five of the original eight subspecies of tiger now remain.[48] There are fewer than six thousand tigers left in the wild; over one hundred thousand lived just in India one hundred years ago. Superstitious ideas about the health benefits of tiger bones and other body parts drive a deadly poaching trade wherever tigers are left.

African lion populations have crashed since 1980—from two hundred thousand to twenty-three thousand today. This is almost a 90 percent decline. Numbers of African cheetahs are down to a mere fifteen thousand. Rifles and poisons have become widespread in Africa, and stockherders and farmers are using them to kill off predators.[49]

Whales. Only the growing popularity of whales during the last forty years has saved several species from extinction by hunting. The largest animal ever to live, the blue whale, was reduced from an estimated historical population of two hundred thousand individuals to only six thousand by 1965 (twenty-nine thousand were killed in the southern summer of 1930–1931 alone). Hunting of the right whale brought it to the brink of extinction, with fewer than four thousand remaining; and the bowhead was harpooned down to a population of a mere three thousand.[50] Meanwhile, Japan and Norway ignore world opinion to resume their destructive industrial whaling practices of the past.

Rhinos. The very symbol of strength, the rhinoceros family has been around for over 40 million years through all kinds of ecological change, but it may not survive humankind. Five species in three distantly related subfamilies live in Africa and southern Asia today.[51] Big they may be, but their populations are tiny. The U.S. World Wildlife Fund estimates surviving numbers as follows: black rhino, 2,700; white rhino, 10,337; greater one-horned (Indian) rhino, 2,500-plus; Javan rhino, fewer than 75 ("likely the world's most endangered large mammal species"); Sumatran rhino, 250–300.[52] The steep decline in numbers of black rhino over the past century says it all: one million in 1910; 65,000 in 1970; 15,000 in 1980; 4,800 in 1985.[53] Today, there exist only 2,700 black rhino. Hunting and habitat destruction are wiping out these extraordinary beasts.

Great Apes. Our three closest relatives, the bonobo (pygmy chimpanzee), chimpanzee, and gorilla, are all endangered, and the orangutan is considered vulnerable (it may actually be more endangered than the others). In the last fifty years, bonobos, chimps, and gorillas have declined by half, and orangutans have declined by perhaps half in the last decade. Cheryl Knott, an orangutan researcher from Harvard, warned in 2003, "At the current rate of habitat destruction [in Borneo], orangutans could be extinct in the wild in 10 to 20 years."[54] Richard Cincotta and Robert Engelman report, "Some experts believe that the growing *bushmeat* trade—the uncontrolled harvesting of wildlife, and the butchering and marketing of their meat—could eliminate all viable populations of African apes within the next fifty years."[55]

In Gabon, the center of gorilla and chimpanzee populations along with the Democratic Republic of Congo, the apes "have declined 56% since 1983," mostly from hunting. Now Ebola is also devastating them. *Science* reports, "Researchers are warning that a relentless epidemic of Ebola hemorrhagic fever in central Africa, combined with hunting, could push Africa's apes close to extinction within the next decade."[56] While habitat destruction has led to the rapid decline of our nearest relatives, their final demise may well be caused by our eating them, which is what we may have done to our even closer relatives, the Neanderthals and Ngandongs.

As for monkeys, many species are faring as poorly as their larger cousins. John Oates, who has studied primates in West Africa for more than thirty years, describes the loss of monkeys to hunting and habitat destruction in his eye-opening *Myth and Reality in the Rain Forest.*[57]

Parrots. Parrots are one of the most popular kinds of birds, and that is a good part of the reason so many are in danger of extinction today.

The 1980 meeting of the Parrot Working Group of the International Council for Bird Preservation (ICBP) led to the 1992 publication of the authoritative *New World Parrots in Crisis*. At least twelve parrot species have become extinct since 1600. The most abundant and most northerly parrot was the Carolina parakeet, which ranged throughout the eastern United States. Shooting and habitat destruction shoved it down the funnel of extinction in the 1800s. Of the 330 or so living species of parrots (including parakeets, macaws, cockatoos, lories, and lovebirds), 71 (21.5 percent) are at risk of extinction and 29 (10 percent) are "near-threatened." So one hundred species (30 percent of the total) of these fascinating birds face the end of the line.[58]

N. J. Collar and A. T. Juniper of the ICBP write that, of 140 species of parrots in the Americas, "no fewer than 42 (30%) may be considered at some risk of extinction. . . . Of these 42 species, 17 are at risk from habitat loss only, 7 from trade, 15 from a mixture of the two, and 3 from other factors. Of the 98 non-threatened parrot species, almost all are declining and many require conservation measures to offset the current impacts of habitat conversion and trade."[59]

The discussion above shows that estimates of extinction rates are not flights of fancy, and indeed many other species have experienced the same sharp declines in population. *Time* reports that "the crisis may be even more acute than everybody feared" after the IUCN Red List of Threatened Species from the World Conservation Union was released in September 2000. "Of the 18,276 organisms investigated, 11,046—including 24% of mammals and 12% of birds—are threatened with extinction."[60]

Net Primary Productivity and Carrying Capacity

Besides the species-area relationship and direct evidence of extinction, the amount of Earth's productivity we use is further evidence for mass extinction. In their 1990 book, *The Population Explosion*, Paul and Anne Ehrlich used the formula I = PAT to explain the human impact on Earth. The variable I stands for impact, P for population, A for affluence, and T for technology. Affluence (A) represents "some measure of the average person's consumption of resources" and technology (T) represents an "index of the environmental disruptiveness of the technologies that provide the goods consumed."[61] Multiply these and you get human impact.

But is it really possible to calculate the human impact on Earth? Actually, we can, and we can even put a number on it. We've had that number for over fifteen years. A group at Stanford University, including Paul and Anne Erhlich, published the results of their research in *Bio-Science* that showed human beings were using about 40 percent of Earth's net primary productivity (NPP) in 1986.[62] This basic ecological measure is defined by Paul and Anne Ehrlich as "[a]ll the solar energy annually captured worldwide by photosynthesizers and not used by them to run their own lives."[63]

The Stanford group's calculations were strongly confirmed in 2001 by Stuart Pimm in his book, *The World According to Pimm: A Scientist Audits the Earth*. Pimm gives a detailed accounting of our appropriation of net primary productivity. In laying the groundwork for his calculations, he defines two key terms: "*Biomass* is how much living stuff the planet has. *Production* is how much new stuff grows each year—the products of photosynthesis."[64]

He convincingly goes through the numbers to explain that about 132 billion tons of biomass are produced on Earth each year.[65] Of this, humans directly consume about 4 percent—what we eat, what our livestock eats, and the "wood we consume for heating and building." However, the scientists at Stanford found we used around 40 percent of NPP. What gives? Pimm explains, "To get the food and fiber that we consume directly, we use and destroy much more plant production."[66] He then takes ninety-four pages to carefully recalculate the data. His bottom line is this: "Each year we use 26 billion tons of plant production for crops, 14 billion tons from forests, use and forgo 17 billion tons for grazing, and forgo 3 billion tons for urban areas. That comes to a total of 60 billion tons." Now add to the total 132 billion tons of NPP another 10 billion or so tons that the land could produce if we humans weren't mucking things up, for a rough figure of 141 billion tons. The 60 billion tons is 42 percent of 141 billion tons.[67]

This is only terrestrial NPP, however. What of the oceans, those supposedly inexhaustible supermarkets? Using the same meticulous approach and sixty pages of calculations, he estimates that humans consume "a quarter to a third of the oceans' production."[68]

How about freshwater? Total annual terrestrial rainfall is 110 trillion tons. Of that, 40 trillion tons flow down rivers to the oceans; 12.5 trillion tons of this are accessible to human use.[69] Pimm concludes, "We consume 60 percent of the accessible runoff each year."[70]

This is how much we use now, with a world population of six billion humans. However, we continue to pile baby upon baby. The exponential growth of human population multiplied by rising affluence and more invasive technology is the main driver of the Third Wave of extinction. Let's quickly see how we've grown and will continue to grow. The widely accepted world population estimate for AD 1 is 250 million.[71] Physician and University of Colorado anthropology professor Warren Hern writes that "the human population doubled 4 times from A.D. 0 to 1976, with the doubling times dropping from 1650 years (est. 500 million at 1650 A.D.) to 46 years (from 2 billion in 1930 to 4.29 billion in 1976). People who are 40 years old or more in 1998 are among the first people in history to have lived through a doubling of world population; people who are 75 years old have seen the human population triple."[72] We have added almost one billion people to Earth's human population in the last decade. This increase is what "the *total* global population [was] in the year 1800 . . . and is approximately *triple* the estimated world population at the height of the Roman Empire (ca. 300 million)."[73]

Where will it all end? Many demographers predict that human population will stabilize at 11–12 billion—twice what it is today. This figure could be too low, however. Hern quotes a leading demographer that the forecast of a stabilized human population of 11–12 billion people is based on "the informal insertion of unspecified assumptions." One such assumption is that a projection of higher population numbers seems "implausible."[74] In other words, stabilization at 11–12 billion is guessed because anything higher seems like too much. If we double our population, and affluence and technology continue to increase as world leaders, corporate heads, and economists believe, what becomes of our taking of NPP? Double our population and we will take over 80 percent. This is conservative because it does not incorporate increasing affluence and technology. Is this sustainable? How many species could continue to exist on less than 20 percent of the earth's net primary productivity? Clearly an ecological crash will happen before we reach this point.

Some two hundred years ago, Parson Thomas Malthus wrote in his famous *An Essay on the Principle of Population*, "Population, when unchecked, increases in a geometrical ratio. Subsistence increases only in an arithmetical ratio."

William Catton in *Overshoot* explains the real meaning of Malthus's principle: "Throughout the essay Malthus was referring to human population, and by subsistence he meant food. . . . these conceptions were unduly narrow. But the really basic Malthusian principle is so important that it needs to be restated in the more accurate vocabulary of modern ecology. It states a relationship of inequality between two variables: *The cumulative biotic potential of the human species exceeds the carrying capacity of its habitat.*"

We cannot understand the Third Wave of extinction without this bedrock principle. *Biotic potential* means how many children a couple could theoretically produce, and *cumulative biotic potential* means "the total number of people that could result after a series of generations if every generation fully exercised its reproductive power." *Carrying capacity of its habitat* "is simply the maximum number of living individuals the available resources can indefinitely support." In other words, humans always have the potential to produce more humans than any area, including the entire world, can support.[75]

This is what we are now doing. And the piper's bill is ecological holocaust.

No Speciation

Not only are many species becoming extinct under the human onslaught on Earth, but so much habitat has been destroyed and fragmented that leading biologists fear the further evolution of new species of large terrestrial animals is over. In 1983, Hugh Iltis wrote that, as a consequence of the destruction of tropical forests, "life will lose forever much of its capability for continued evolution."[76]

Michael Soulé writes that "the minimum area for speciation . . . can be solved empirically. All that is necessary is to determine the size of the smallest island on which a particular taxon has speciated autochthonously (in situ)—that is, where there is sufficient room for a species to split into two or more species." The smallest island where this has occurred for large mammals is the huge island of Madagascar—far, far larger than any protected area. Soulé also points out that Madagascar has been isolated for tens of millions of years, giving much time for speciation to happen.[77] He concludes that the twentieth "century will see the end of significant evolution of large plants and terrestrial vertebrates in the tropics."[78]

In other mass extinctions, Niles Eldredge writes, "New species evolve, and ecosystems are reassembled, only after the cause of disruption and extinction is removed or stabilized." However, for today's mass extinction event, "*Homo sapiens* will have to cease acting as the cause of the Sixth Extinction—whether through our own demise, or, preferably, through determined action, before evolutionary/ecological recovery can begin."[79]

It is important for us to overcome the misunderstanding that today's extinction crisis has been going on only since 1600 and is caused only by the spread of Western civilization across the planet. Acknowledging that the Pleistocene Extinction is a single event stretching back forty thousand years to the early spread of hunting humans into new lands, and continuing through today with the spread of vast numbers of humans at various technological levels into wild places, allows us to understand what is really going on, and—maybe—learn enough about ourselves to take action to stop the holocaust.

Ian Tattersall and Jeffrey Schwartz warn with frightening clarity that "our species is an entirely unprecedented entity in the living world. . . . This central fact of human uniqueness is one with which we urgently need to come to terms, because evolution has done nothing to prepare the biota that not only surrounds but also supports us to cope with this highly destructive new element on the landscape."[80] Harvard biological anthropologist Richard Wrangham and coauthor Dale Peterson seem to agree when they write: "The real danger is that our species combines demonic males with a burning intelligence—and therefore a capacity for creation and destruction without precedent. That great human brain is nature's most frightening product."[81]

The central reality of our era is extinction. Nothing is more important. Mass extinction is our legacy as a species so far. No other moral challenge is so great as controlling our destructive power over nature. In the following chapters, we will look for the reasons behind our destructiveness and seek determined actions that can halt the causes of extinction.

CHAPTER 5

Ecological Wounds of North America 1: Direct Killing and Habitat Loss

If we are to effectively plan conservation action that will protect and restore the diversity of life, we need to ponder the causes of today's mass extinction. In the previous chapters I gave an overview of extinction. In this and the next chapter I will more specifically describe the ecological harm humans have done to the continent of North America. From this will flow the goals and action steps I propose in later chapters.

Aldo Leopold was the greatest American conservationist of the twentieth century. His insights more than a half a century ago still cut trails for the rest of us. One of his tree-blazes reads, "One of the penalties of an ecological education is that one lives alone in a world of wounds. . . . An ecologist must either harden his shell and make believe that the consequences of science are none of his business, or he must be the doctor who sees the marks of death in a community that believes itself well and does not want to be told otherwise."[1]

Leopold came to understand land health and ecological wounds from his field work with the U.S. Forest Service in New Mexico and Arizona from 1909 to 1924 and bow-hunting trips to the Sierra Madre in Chihuahua in the mid-1930s. In 1937, he mused, "For it is ironical that Chihuahua, with a history and a terrain so strikingly similar to southern New Mexico and Arizona, should present so lovely a picture of ecological health, whereas our own states, plastered as they are with National Forests, National Parks and all the other trappings of conservation, are so badly damaged that only tourists and others ecologically color-blind, can look upon them without a feeling of sadness and regret."[2]

Far ahead of his time in his skill to wisely read the story of the land, Leopold understood that free Apaches kept settlement out of the northern Sierra Madre Occidental well into the twentieth century. Without livestock grazing and with hearty populations of mountain lions and wolves, mountain ecosystems in Mexico were ecologically healthy, whereas similar mountain ecosystems in the United States were deeply wounded. Unfortunately, since Leopold's time, the mountain fastness of northern Mexico has been as carelessly wasted as the southwestern United States.

In recent years, ecological and historical researchers have greatly improved our understanding of ecological wounds. Even in the best-protected areas, such as national parks and wilderness areas ungrazed by domestic livestock, preexisting wounds may continue to suppurate.[3] For example, without wolves and natural fire, Rocky Mountain National Park in Colorado is not a healthy landscape; without restoration—in the form of wolves and natural fire—its health may continue to worsen. Indeed, the flagship of American conservation—Yellowstone National Park—was declining in health until wolves were reestablished in the mid-1990s.

Efforts to protect the land and create a sustainable human society will come to naught without understanding these wounds and their underlying causes—and then doing our best to heal them. More than sixty years ago, Leopold worried that "our own conservation program for [the southwestern United States] has been in a sense a post-mortem cure."[4] This is true for most of North America. Medicine for the land, or ecological restoration theory and practice, has advanced much in the last sixty years (or so we trust). Perhaps we can raise this Lazarus of a North American landscape to robust good health. It is, at the very least, our duty as citizens to try.

Retired pathologist and board president of the Wildlands Project, Bob Howard, helped me work out a medical-diagnosis approach that differentiates between wounds or illness and their causes. This process evolved during the course of designing two wildlands networks, one for the Sky Islands and the second for the New Mexico Highlands. For example, cigarette smoking is not a human illness, but it can be a cause of several illnesses, including emphysema, lung cancer, mouth and throat cancer, and heart disease. Likewise, grazing by domestic livestock is not a wound to the land, but it can trigger several landscape wounds. Wildlands network conservation visions planned by the Wildlands Project and cooperating groups throughout North America now identify actual land wounds or illnesses (pathologies) and consider the human causes for each (the etiologic agents that perturb natural systems). Just as a medical doctor seeks not only to treat the symptoms and the disease but also to understand the root cause(s) of the illness, so do ecological "doctors" seek both to heal the wounds of the land and to understand their underlying causes.

The end point of human-caused wounds to the land is today's extinction crisis—death, in medical terms. In chapter 1, we saw how David Wilcove and his colleagues list the current causes of extinction in the United States. We need to revisit the causes here:

• Habitat destruction
• Nonnative (alien) species
• Pollution
• Overexploitation
• Disease[5]

The Wildlands Project adapted this list to describe seven primary ecological wounds to the land:

1. Direct killing of species
2. Loss and degradation of ecosystems
3. Fragmentation of wildlife habitat
4. Loss and disruption of natural processes
5. Invasion by exotic species and diseases
6. Poisoning of land, air, water, and wildlife
7. Global climate change

Each wound has more than one cause, and many of the causes contribute to more than one wound. The overall impact of these wounds is greater than their sum, and they are highly synergistic. Although they were first described for the southwestern United States, they apply anywhere on Earth, including to the oceans. Among the leading causes of these wounds in North America are overhunting, overfishing, and trapping (including poaching); predator and "pest" extermination (shooting, poisoning, trapping); removing native animals and plants for collectors; agricultural clearing; livestock overgrazing; livestock fencing; logging and fuelwood collection; mining; energy exploitation; industrial recreation (ski areas, resorts, golf courses, etc.); off-road vehicle recreation; urban, suburban, and "ranchette" (semi-rural subdivisions) sprawl; agricultural and forestry biocides; intentional or accidental releases of nonnative species; road building; fire suppression; dam building; irrigation diversions; groundwater depletion; channelization of streams and rivers; air, water, and land pollution; and human overpopulation (which is the fundamental cause).

During the past five hundred years, these wounding agents, or *proximate causes*, have brought about the seven ecological wounds in North America, and they continue to threaten species with extinction. Therefore, we need to look at both the historical wounding and the continuing threats of future wounding.

Before we look at the wounds we've caused, though, we must understand the lay of the land as it was before the arrival of Europeans. The North America that early European explorers and colonists found was by no means pristine, but much of it was quite wild and natural, despite claims by some ideologically driven scholars and popularizers.[6]

Credible estimates of human population in 1500 for what is now Canada and the United States range from as many as 3.8 million[7] to as few as 2 million.[8] There may well have been 23 million in what is now Mexico and Central America.[9] Where populations were dense and agriculture intense, as from Central America to central Mexico, ecosystems were degraded and many species extirpated. In what is now the United States, agricultural societies in the Southwest, along the Mississippi River, and elsewhere had strong localized impacts on biodiversity.[10] For example, hunting by Native American agricultural societies in the Southwest before the Spanish conquest may have extirpated elk and bison from many areas in New Mexico and Arizona. There is also evidence that agricultural tribes in the Southeast hunted out bison in large areas before European settlement.[11] Agricultural tribes along the Missouri River and other Great Plains rivers may have locally exterminated grizzly bears.[12]

During a seventy-five-year period around AD 1100, people from Chaco Canyon in northwestern New Mexico cut some one hundred thousand ponderosa pine logs from surrounding mountain ranges up to 60 miles away. Other Anasazi, Mogollon, and Hohokam villages in the Southwest also overcut forests for timber and firewood. Thousands of acres were cleared for agricultural fields, and serious soil erosion from logging and farming happened.[13]

However, three million people with a much lower technological level north of the Rio Grande had far less impact than do over 300 million Americans and Canadians today. Despite the loss of the megafauna, the diversity and abundance of life in North America before 1500 (and even more recently) is unimaginable to us at the beginning of twenty-first century.[14] Passenger pigeons numbered in the billions. One 1810 flight in Kentucky was estimated by ornithologist Alexander Wilson to contain over two billion birds.[15] Also extraordinarily abundant, compared to today, were Carolina parakeets (now extinct), shorebirds, and waterfowl. Eskimo curlews were called "prairie pigeons" because they seemed as beyond numbering as the passenger pigeon.

Some 60 million beaver filled streams in North America before 1600.[16] Through dam building, they governed stream runoff and created vast wetlands and riparian forests. Some five billion prairie dogs tilled the soil of North America's grasslands and provided habitat for many other species.[17] Between 30 and 60 million bison, some 40 million pronghorn, and 10 million elk ranged freely. Bison and elk inhabited most of what is now the eastern United States, as well as much of the West. Mountain lions lived from coast to coast and from the southern Yukon to South America. Gray wolves lived from central Mexico north to the Arctic. Grizzly bears stalked the forests, mountains, plains, and tundra west of the Mississippi and Hudson Bay. Walruses hauled out on Cape Cod. Woodland caribou were common in northern New England, Minnesota, the Upper Peninsula of Michigan, and the U.S. northern Rocky Mountains.

The most diverse temperate forest in the world blanketed the land from the Atlantic to the Great Plains. White pines and tulip poplars grew to over 200 feet in height and individual chestnut trees spread their branches over a quarter of an acre.

This was the New World that explorers, colonists, and settlers found. What we did to it is as sobering as a head-on collision with an 18-wheeler. The following historical and ecological discussion of human-caused wounds and continuing threats concentrates on temperate North America, particularly on the United States. It draws heavily on the weighty two-volume *Status and Trends of the Nation's Biological Resources* from the U.S. Geological Survey, which is a detailed reference on the subject. Peter Matthiessen's classic *Wildlife in America* and David Wilcove's more recent *The Condor's Shadow* are also excellent overviews.[18] I've previously outlined the factors that have destroyed and degraded wilderness in North America in my books, *Confessions of an Eco-Warrior* and *The Big Outside*.[19] I'll further highlight key papers and books about specific wounds as they come up. I use direct quotes from the experts more than is customary in the pages that follow to show how grimly they see things. I encourage the reader to refer to the original sources cited for more detail.

What follows is not a comprehensive discussion; that would easily take an entire book. Rather, it is a survey that gives a sense of what we've lost and how, since 1500, we've caused those losses.

Wound 1: Direct Killing of Species

Causes: During the preceding five hundred years or so, native animals—
especially fish, carnivores, large ungulates, keystone rodents, and birds—have
become extinct, regionally extirpated, or greatly reduced in number by commer-
cial fishing and seabirding; whaling; subsistence hunting and game-hogging;[20]
market hunting; trapping; predator and "pest" control; and collecting.

Commercial Fishing

(Note: *fishing* as used here refers to the taking of any marine species,
vertebrate or invertebrate.) Daniel Pauly and his colleagues at the University of British Columbia Fisheries Centre showed in a landmark article in *Nature* that commercial fishing has historically been unsustainable
and that "many exploited fish populations and eventually fish species
will become extinct."[21] This holds true for the continental shelves of
North America, as well as for the rest of the world's oceans.

Well before European settlement in North America, British, French,
Basque, and Spanish fishermen began to gobble up the mind-boggling
wealth of ocean fish and seabirds off New England and the Canadian
Maritimes. Perhaps as early as 1480, British fishing boats were bringing
back prodigious catches of cod from North American waters.[22] The
great auk, a large flightless seabird that nested on islands in the North
Atlantic in vast numbers, was heavily exploited for food and oil by the
earliest explorers and those who came after until the last two were killed
in 1844.[23] The huge Steller's spectacled cormorant (or Pallas cormorant)
off the coast of Alaska was hunted into extinction in little more than one
hundred years after its discovery in 1741.[24]

Numbering in the tens of millions in 1500, sea turtles along the
Atlantic Coast and Caribbean Sea were hunted close to extinction by
1800. Bermuda passed protective legislation in 1620 because of the
slaughter. In recent years, the shrimping industry has become a major
threat to sea turtles. The southeastern U.S. shrimp fleet was drowning
forty-four thousand sea turtles a year before turtle excluder devices were
required.[25] Despite protections afforded by the Endangered Species Act,
many sea turtles still die in shrimp nets.[26]

According to Jeremy Jackson of the Scripps Institution of Oceanography and his eighteen colleagues writing in *Science*: "There are dozens
of places in the Caribbean named after large sea turtles whose adult populations now number in the tens of thousands rather than the tens of
millions of a few centuries ago. Whales, manatees, dugongs, sea cows,
monk seals, crocodiles, codfish, jewfish, swordfish, sharks, and rays are

other large marine vertebrates that are now functionally or entirely extinct in most coastal ecosystems."[27] This devastation is primarily caused by overfishing and applies as much to the continental shelves of North America as to anywhere in the world.

The magnificent cod fishery off New England and the Canadian Maritimes collapsed in the late 1980s and early 1990s from industrial overfishing.[28] "Haddock, yellowtail flounder, and Atlantic cod stocks on Georges Bank have collapsed," according to *Status and Trends*.[29] Among pelagic Atlantic fish off North America, swordfish, bluefin tuna, and marlin have been the most thoroughly overfished.[30]

The most desirable fish in North American waters are largely top carnivores, as they are in all the oceans. Gerald Smith at the University of Michigan writes that "the biomass of top predatory fishes has diminished by more than two-thirds in the past five decades."[31] According to fisheries biologists at Dalhousie University in Nova Scotia, overfishing has caused a more than 50 percent crash in northwest Atlantic shark species (except for the mako) "in the past 8 to 15 years."[32]

Not only are target fish species being vacuumed from North American oceans, but even more nontarget species—*bycatch*—are caught and killed. Bottom trawling, for example, sometimes takes in bycatch "more than 17 times the target catch."[33] Most of the bycatch dies before it is swept overboard.

White abalone were so overfished along the California coast during the late 1960s and early 1970s, that their populations crashed from somewhere between two to four million to possibly only 2,500.[34] This is a decline of 99.9+ percent. Delaware Bay, on the Atlantic coast, is an essential stopover and feeding site for migrating red knots, which feed on the eggs of the once-plentiful horseshoe crab. Unbridled taking of horseshoe crabs has caused them to dwindle by half. Since 1998, red knots have fallen from 33,741 to a mere 5,376. Some studies predict extinction by 2010.[35]

Atlantic salmon became extinct in the Lake Ontario watershed in the 1800s from overfishing and habitat destruction, as did arctic grayling in northern Michigan streams by the early 1900s.[36]

Overfishing has occurred in most Alaskan lakes and rivers reachable by road; lake trout, burbot, arctic grayling, rainbow trout, chinook salmon, northern pike, and whitefish are among the looted species.[37]

According to *Status and Trends*, "Alaska's anadromous and freshwater resident fishes are managed primarily for human use. Little or no consideration is given to their value and use by other vertebrates or to their value to the natural community as a whole."[38]

Whaling

Stuart Pimm writes, "By 1800, whalers had nearly exterminated the northern Atlantic populations of right and bowhead whales. . . . Whalers *did* exterminate the Atlantic population of the gray whale."[39] Atlantic right whales may have been butchered down to fewer than fifty individuals by 1900. There are now about three hundred, but they are still being killed by ship collisions and entanglement in fishing nets.[40]

After World War II, whalers zeroed in on fin and sperm whales in the North Pacific. Over half a million whales were torn from the sea and whale biomass dropped from "about 30 to 3 million metric tons."[41]

Today, many whales and other marine mammals are killed and injured by ship collisions, bycatch, and entanglement in fishing lines and nets.[42]

New genetic research on whale populations in the North Atlantic shows that original numbers of humpback, fin, and minke whales were vastly greater than is generally believed. There may well have been 240,000 humpbacks, 360,000 fin, and 265,000 minke whales in the North Atlantic. Today's populations are estimated to be 9,300–12,100 humpbacks, 56,000 fins, and 148,000 minkes—a stunning drop, largely from hunting.[43]

A giant manatee, Steller's sea cow, grazed on the kelp forests of the Bering Sea. Discovered by Russians on the 1741 exploration cruise of Vitus Bering, it was hunted to extinction a quarter century later.[44] However, it had largely been exterminated by aboriginal people throughout most of its range long before Bering arrived. Bering found them only around Aleutian islands not occupied by Aleuts.[45]

From 500 BC on, the Aleuts had overhunted sea otters.[46] After 1741, the Russians and others cleaned out what were left for their luxuriant fur; in the 1800s otters crashed throughout their range to fewer than two thousand—1 percent or less of their earlier population.[47] Preeminent otter researcher Jim Estes reports that in 1740 there were one hundred thousand to two hundred thousand sea otters in the Aleutians, but only one hundred to two hundred in 1911.[48]

The Atlantic walrus subspecies, which ranged south to Massachusetts, was quickly set upon by the first colonists and pretty much hunted out south of Labrador during the 1600s.[49] It now survives only far to the north.

In the early 1800s, British, Americans, and Russians nearly hunted out Guadalupe fur seals and elephants seals along the California coast.[50] The monstrous northern elephant seal was slaughtered to fewer than one hundred by 1900.[51] The northern fur seal, once numbering five million on the Pribilof Islands in the Bering Sea, was hunted down to one hundred and thirty thousand by 1911.[52] During the 1870s, half the walruses in Alaska were killed.[53] Canada, still frozen in a frontier mind-set of wildlife exploitation, again plans to allow hundreds of thousands of harp and gray seals to be butchered in the St. Lawrence Gulf region over the next few years.

Subsistence Hunting and Game-Hogging

The Pilgrims and Puritans remarked on the abundance of deer and waterfowl in Massachusetts. So quickly were they overhunted, however, that a closed season on deer was instituted in 1696, and in 1710 Massachusetts prohibited boats for waterfowl hunting.[54] This carefree hunting was a sign of things to come. Because of overhunting, white-tailed deer dropped to fewer than five hundred thousand in the United States in 1900 (but they are now unnaturally abundant, numbering between 18 and 25 million, largely due to eradication of top predators).[55]

Woodland bison were hunted out of North Carolina by 1765 and from the entire Southeast by 1825.[56] They were exterminated by hunters east of Appalachians by 1801, and elk soon suffered a similar fate.[57]

Hunters killed the last caribou in Michigan by 1900.[58] In the U.S. northern Rocky Mountains, woodland caribou were a common resident, but hunting and logging caused populations to drop to only one hundred in northern Idaho in the 1950s. The U.S. population is highly imperiled now, numbering a mere thirty or so in 1998.[59]

According to *Status and Trends*, bighorn sheep are down to "2% to 8% of their [population] sizes at the time of European settlement," because of overhunting and disease transmitted from domestic woollies.[60]

Spring and winter subsistence hunting by native people of brant, Canada, emperor, and greater white-fronted geese in the Yukon-Kuskokwim delta in western Alaska caused major population drops from the mid-1960s to mid-1980s.[61]

Market Hunting

Market hunting (commonly known as commercial hunting) began early in the North American English colonies. For example, the port of Savannah, Georgia, shipped out six hundred thousand deer hides to England between 1755 and 1773.[62]

Market hunting of native birds in North America caused some of the most spectacular extinctions in modern times and the near extinction of other species. The passenger pigeon, the most abundant bird on Earth, ranged from Florida to Ontario and west to the Great Plains. It was slaughtered as though there was no end during the 1800s. Wagons and trains hauled millions of birds from single hunts back to big cities for sale. Hunters wiped out the last big nesting of passenger pigeons in 1878 and the last known wild pigeon was shot in 1900.[63]

Market hunters also slaughtered ducks and geese with wild abandon, causing many species to crash and one—the Labrador duck—to become extinct by 1875.[64] Market hunters went after curlews, sandpipers, and other shore birds just as they did the passenger pigeon. Eskimo curlews, numbering in the many millions, were slaughtered by the wagonload as they made seasonal migrations up the Great Plains and down the Atlantic Coast. Their numbers were reduced to almost nothing by 1900. The last known Eskimo curlew was seen in 1963. Some other once-abundant shorebirds, including the golden plover, almost met extinction, as well.[65] Hunted not for food, but for their plumes used in fashionable ladies' towering hats in the late nineteenth century, populations of egrets, terns, and herons plummeted.[66] In 1886, five million birds were killed each year to decorate hats.[67] Even songbirds were much hunted for food in those benighted days.[68]

After the Civil War, market hunters spread out across the Great Plains to slaughter the tens of millions of bison ranging there. Newly built railroads hauled the meat, hides, and bones (for fertilizer) back East. The southern herd of bison was exterminated before 1880 and the northern herd by 1883.[69] Market hunters fed the mining camps springing up all over the West after 1850, as well as railroad construction crews and cavalry forts. After 1870 and the introduction of the repeating rifle and railroads, market hunters could ship tons of meat east to city markets.[70] Half a million tule elk in California were nearly extinct by 1870,[71] and Merriam's elk in the Southwest was hunted into extinction by 1906.[72] Bighorn sheep, deer, other elk subspecies, pronghorn, turkeys, and, in the Southwest, thick-billed parrots were cleaned out to feed miners. In 1914, leading conservationist William T. Hornaday of the Bronx Zoo calculated that only about 2 percent of the total population of game birds and mammals from fifty years earlier still existed.[73]

Trapping

As early as 1621, a thriving fur trade in beaver, otter, mink, marten, and bobcat was supporting the Jamestown colony in Virginia.[74] In the 1700s, fur was a major export from both English and French America. Indeed, it was economically more important than fish and timber for the colonies.[75] In the year 1620 alone, French and Dutch fur traders took thirty thousand beaver in the Northeast. In 1690, the take was three hundred thousand.[76] That pretty much wiped them out in New England. By 1840, mountain men had essentially trapped beaver out of what is now the western United States.[77] Today's tiny populations of Pacific fisher and California wolverine are so low mostly due to trapping a century ago,[78] and some populations declined even in Alaska,[79] where six million "furbearers" were exported during 1925–1945.[80] Heavy trapping of mink, river otter, wolverine, fisher, and other "furbearers" cleaned them out in much of the United States and decreased their numbers north in the boreal forest. It is unknown what impact this decline of carnivores has had on ecological integrity.

Predator and "Pest" Control

In 1630, the first bounty was offered for wolves in Massachusetts Bay Colony. Virginia quickly followed suit.[81] One of the first tasks of settlers in a new area on the frontier was getting rid of the hated predators. A telling example comes from central Pennsylvania in 1760 when two hundred men surrounded a 700-square-mile area and marched through it, killing everything they could. The tally: 41 cougars, 114 bobcats, 109 wolves, 112 foxes, 18 black bears, 3 fishers, 1 otter, 12 wolverines, 2 elk, 198 deer, 111 bison, 3 beavers, and over 500 other animals.[82] As late as 1897, New York paid six wolf bounties,[83] and in 1890 it paid 107 cougar bounties.[84]

The Carolina parakeet, which ranged from Florida to New York and west to Colorado, was exterminated in the wild by the late 1800s because it ate wheat and orchard fruit.[85] Not so long ago, hunters were encouraged to kill hawks and owls—even bald eagles—on sight in order to protect "good" birds. Some states even paid bounties on raptors.[86]

From the 1880s on, many ranchers called for the slaughter of wild ungulates, seeing them as competitors with cattle and sheep for forage.

With their natural prey gone in the West, wolves, grizzlies, and mountain lions turned to cattle and sheep.[87] In the United States, the Department of Agriculture's Predatory Animal and Rodent Control (PARC) agency used traps, guns, and poison to exterminate predators, including gray wolves, red wolves, mountain lions, grizzly bears, black bears, bobcats, lynx, wolverines, and coyotes.[88] The National Park Service took a leading role in predator extermination; in fact, wolves were killed out of Yellowstone and other parks by 1930.[89] From 1904 to 1925, the Park Service officially killed 121 mountain lions and 132 wolves in Yellowstone (although it is probable that more were killed).[90] By the mid-1930s, grizzlies were extirpated (except from a few sites in the northern Rockies) and wolves were functionally extirpated from the West.[91] Mountain lion populations were greatly reduced.

There have been massive wolf kills even in the supposedly pristine far north of Canada. In the 1950s and 1960s, the Canadian Wildlife Service ran a wolf extermination campaign in one of the world's great wildernesses, the Thelon Game Sanctuary in the Northwest Territories. Thousands of wolves were killed by contracted trappers using poison bait to reduce wolf predation on caribou.[92] Government programs to kill or sterilize wolves continue across Canada. The state of Alaska still wages a nineteenth-century war on wolves in the twenty-first century.

Jaguars and ocelots maintained breeding populations in the southwestern United States from the Lower Rio Grande Valley in Texas to Arizona. They, too, were exterminated as livestock-killing vermin by PARC agents and ranchers. Sixty jaguars were reportedly killed in New Mexico and Arizona during the twentieth century, including at least four females. Two ocelots are documented as having been trapped or shot in Arizona during that time, too. Jaguars and ocelots continue to be regularly killed in northern Sonora, despite their protected status in Mexico.[93]

Amazingly, this slaughter of predators continues today. The U.S. Department of Agriculture's "Wildlife Services" Program (formerly known as Animal Damage Control or ADC, and before that as Predatory Animal and Rodent Control or PARC) "spends more than $10 million in federal funds to kill nearly one hundred thousand predators nationwide each year."[94] Where wolves, supposedly protected under the federal Endangered Species Act, have recolonized or have been reintroduced in the northern Rockies and the Southwest, government agents regularly kill them if they dare harass or prey on domestic cattle or sheep being grazed on federal lands.

In blatant violation of the protected status of grizzly bears in the U.S. northern Rockies, sheep ranchers and unethical outfitters continue to illegally kill them as depredators or nuisances. "During the last 20 years, about 88% of all grizzly bears studied in the northern Rocky Mountains were killed by humans," according to *Status and Trends*.[95]

Prairie dogs were exterminated to ecologically insignificant levels as a result of a taxpayer-sponsored, government poisoning program that continues today. Many ranchers dislike prairie dogs because of the mistaken belief that they damage the range. Brian Miller and his coauthors write, "Between 1915 and 1960, the total area covered by prairie dog colonies was reduced from somewhere between 40 million and 100 million hectares [100 million and 250 million acres] to about 600,000 hectares [1,500,000 acres]."[96] The once-common black-footed ferret was lost from most of its habitat because of the sweeping kill-off of prairie dogs and became the most endangered mammal in North America.[97] Prairie dogs, despite being proposed for protection under the Endangered Species Act, continue to be poisoned.

Native fish in the Colorado River, including Colorado pike minnow (formerly the Colorado River squawfish), humpback chub, and razorback sucker, were poisoned as pests to make way for sport fisheries of nonindigenous trout.[98]

In Alaska, *Status and Trends* reports that "misguided predator-control efforts to protect salmon species" led to killing "more than 6 million Dolly Varden [trout] between 1921 and 1946 and more than 100,000 bald eagles between 1917 and 1952."[99]

Collecting

Populations of many species of snakes, lizards, and turtles have been hacked down by professional collectors supplying the pet trade. Parrots, macaws, and other tropical birds are similarly imperiled in Mexico and Central America. Rare cactus species and other plants are fast disappearing in the wild because of professional nature looters selling to collectors in Japan and Germany. Commercial reptile collecting is still legal in Nevada. *Status and Trends* states, "In 1993, 19 commercial pet collectors reported a harvest of 21,794 reptiles in Nevada at an estimated total value of $250,000."[100] Species at high risk from legal and illegal collecting include chuckwallas, desert iguanas, Gila monsters, and Panamint rattlesnakes.[101] In the Sonoran Desert, collectors have reduced populations of rosy boa, chuckwalla, and desert tortoise.[102]

Wound 2: Loss and Degradation of Ecosystems

Causes: For almost four hundred years in North America, ecosystems have been degraded and even destroyed by agricultural clearing, logging, grazing by domestic livestock, burning, elimination of keystone species, mining, wetlands draining, urbanization, suburbanization, exurban sprawl, bottom trawling, dams, water diversions, groundwater pumping, channelization, and oil and gas development.

Status and Trends warns, "Both worldwide and in the United States, land cover today is altered principally by direct human use: agriculture, raising of livestock, forest harvesting, and construction."[103] Two publications coauthored by Reed Noss are the best reviews of the loss and degradation of U.S. ecosystems: the 1995 *Endangered Ecosystems of the United States* for the National Biological Service and the 1995 *Endangered Ecosystems* for Defenders of Wildlife.[104] An ecosystem or a portion of an ecosystem is lost if it is entirely converted to another use (agricultural field or pavement, for example). It is degraded if its "structure, function, or composition" is changed.[105] Noss and Robert Peters write, "The more an ecosystem is degraded, the more species decline or become extinct."[106] For example, the southeastern coastal plain's longleaf pine/wiregrass ecosystem, with a 98 percent loss, has twenty-seven species listed under the Endangered Species Act and ninety-nine species proposed for listing.[107]

Agriculture

New England was the first area to be heavily deforested, primarily by agricultural clearing, although commercial lumbering played a role.[108] Vermont, for example, went from being 95 percent forested "in 1620, to 25 to 35 percent around 1850 to 1870. . . . "[109] The scrubby second- or third-growth forested area in 1850, moreover, had little ecological resemblance to the towering ancient forest of 1620.

Tallgrass prairie, which once swept over tens of millions of acres from Texas to Manitoba, has been largely replaced by farms. Iowa once had 30 million acres of tallgrass prairie; now it has a mere 30,000 acres— a 99.9 percent loss. Manitoba has only 750 acres out of a former 1.5 million. Kansas is the best of the lot with only a 82.6 percent loss.[110] There has been a 99 percent loss east of the Mississippi.[111] The conversion of Iowa's prairies, wetlands, and forests to agriculture caused the extirpation of seventy species of animals and plants from the state.[112]

During the 1800s, agricultural clearing along the Rio Grande and its tributaries in New Mexico removed or damaged the most productive and extensive riparian forests (*bosques*). Water diversion for irrigation, groundwater pumping for agriculture and (later) urban use, and the downcutting of arroyos (because of watershed destruction from livestock grazing and logging) have lowered the water table, resulting in dried-up *ciénegas* (wet meadows), dewatered rivers, and dying bosques.[113] This destruction of vitally important habitat and weakening of ecological resilience has greatly aided the spread of exotic species and the loss of sensitive native species.

California's Central Valley was originally a scene of eye-popping wildlife abundance—grizzlies, pronghorn, tule elk, and clouds of waterfowl amidst and above vast fields of wildflowers. "Millions of hectares of native grasslands, marshes, and seasonal wetlands in the Central Valley and delta . . . have been converted to agriculture," according to *Status and Trends*.[114]

The agricultural settlement of Oregon's Willamette Valley led to the loss of 99.5 percent of the oak savannas and native grassland.[115] One of the richest grasslands of North America—the Palouse Prairie in southeastern Washington and adjacent states—is at less than 1 percent of its former extent, due to wheat farming.[116]

The most tropical of continental U.S. ecosystems—the Tamaulipan brushland—has suffered grievously from agricultural clearing. This dense subtropical woodland of the Lower Rio Grande Valley in Texas, which harbors the last U.S. populations of ocelot and jaguarundi, as well as a couple dozen tropical bird species, was more than 95 percent cleared in the twentieth century. More than 90 percent of the valley's lush riparian forest was cleared.[117]

Unsustainable farming practices throughout temperate North America have caused severe losses of topsoil—it can take one hundred to ten thousand years, depending on aridity, to produce an inch of topsoil. The average annual loss of topsoil in the U.S. is about "three times greater than that being formed."[118] A detailed discussion of erosion is beyond the scope of this chapter. Classic studies on soil erosion and how it has led to the collapse of civilizations include *Deserts on the March* and *Topsoil and Civilization*. *Dust Bowl* is a history of the U.S. Dust Bowl and a study of the attitudes that led to it.[119]

Logging

While much attention is properly directed at the unsustainable logging of tropical forests today, the destruction, conversion, and degradation of North American forests for the last three hundred years and continuing today rivals it in irresponsibility. In the lower forty-eight states, only 2 to 5 percent of old-growth forests remained by 1990; only 1 percent of old-growth eastern deciduous forest is left.[120]

Despite talk for over a century about sustainable, scientific forestry, most logging, yesterday and today, on private lands or public lands, has been shortsighted scalping of forests, with little heed paid to ecological integrity or wild species. The national forests originally had very few timber sales, but after World War II, commercial saw timber operations dramatically increased throughout the national forest system.[121] The Forest Service wanted to eliminate old-growth forests and replace them with what they believed were "more efficient young forests."

Twenty-four sawmills were working in Maine by 1682.[122] Over 100 million acres of the great eastern forest in the United States had been logged by 1850, but between 1850 and 1859 another 40 million acres were stripped of trees.[123] The rate of deforestation in the Midwest (specifically in Illinois) from 1820 to 1870 is comparable to current rates in tropical forests.[124]

In the decade after the Civil War, logging companies moved into the North Woods of the Upper Great Lakes States and quickly liquidated most of the old-growth white pine, leaving "a gloomy wilderness of pine stumps," according to one concerned sawmill owner.[125]

Arguably the most magnificent trees in the world, California's coast redwoods have been more than 85 percent logged.[126] The westside forests of the Pacific Coast from northern California to southeastern Alaska are the classic ancient conifer forests, with several species of trees easily exceeding 200 feet in height. Once thought limitless, these forests have been heavily logged for over a century. Ninety-six percent of Oregon's and 75 percent of Washington's coastal rain forests have been logged, and 37 percent of what remains is in stands smaller than "162 hectares [300 acres] surrounded by clear cuts, young plantations, and nonforest habitats."[127]

Logging has degraded 95 percent of surveyed streams in Oregon. Along with other disturbances, logging in headwaters can "alter downstream flow regimes, increase sediment loads, and reduce recruitment of woody debris and nutrients to fish-bearing streams," according to *Status and Trends*.[128] Logging of headwaters habitat, along with dams and overfishing, has devastated salmon and anadromous trout stocks in the Pacific Northwest.[129]

Clearcut logging dries out forest floors, thereby harming amphibians.[130] American marten populations sharply declined in the Pacific Northwest because logging destroyed their old-growth forest habitat.[131] In the ancient temperate rain forest of southeastern Alaska, clearcutting is harming wolves, bears, deer, marten, mink, river otter, mountain goat, northern flying squirrel, and bats.[132]

The scientists contributing to *Status and Trends* write:

As a result of more than a century of logging and fire control, the forests of the Pacific Northwest presently consist of a highly fragmented mosaic of clear-cuts, thinned stands, and young (and often single species) plantations interspersed with uncut natural stands. . . . The road density often equals or exceeds the density of natural stream channels. . . .

Since 1940 nearly 76% of the Olympic Peninsula's ancient forests have been logged. In 1940, 87% of the ancient forest was in patches greater than 4,000 hectares [10,000 acres], whereas by 1988, the forest was so fragmented that 60% of the ancient forest occurred in patches of fewer than 40 hectares [100 acres].[133]

The eastside forests in Oregon were primarily ponderosa pine; 92 to 98 percent of the old growth has been logged.[134]

The extensive bosques along Arizona and New Mexico rivers were heavily cut for fuelwood and timber during the 1800s.[135] This logging of cottonwood, willow, mesquite, and other tree species harmed critical wildlife habitat and accelerated channel erosion. Southwestern watersheds were damaged by the widespread clearcutting of piñon-juniper and oak woodlands for mine timbers and fuelwood, as well as by livestock grazing.[136] Sawmills were set up to supply Army forts in the Southwest early in the Mexican War in 1846. The Forest Service reports, "Every accessible ponderosa pine forest in New Mexico and Arizona was heavily logged in the 1930s and 1940s."[137] Some two dozen ponderosa pine forest birds have declined due to logging.[138]

For all Arizona and New Mexico National Forests, the Southwest Forest Alliance reports, "About 90 percent of the old-growth has been liquidated, including 98 percent of the old-growth ponderosa pine."[139] Wallace Covington, forestry professor at Northern Arizona University, writes, "The cumulative effects of old-growth logging, non-native species introductions, overgrazing, predator control, and fire exclusion has been ecosystem simplification so great that Southwestern forest ecosystems are at risk of catastrophic losses of biological diversity."[140]

Michael Bogan and his fellow researchers summarize the health of Southwest forests as follows:

Fire suppression, commercial forestry practices, and overgrazing have pervasively altered the structure and species composition of most southwestern forests. Old-growth forests have been greatly reduced by high-grading and even-aged management practices that targeted the most valuable old trees, especially ponderosa pine. In addition, until 20 years ago, snags (dead trees) were systematically removed as fire and forest health hazards, while extensive road networks aided those who poached fuelwood (poachers often focused on snags). Hence, most managed forests now lack desired numbers of large-diameter snags, which serve important ecological roles such as cavity-nesting sites for many breeding birds and probably for many bats as well. Today's forests are characterized by unnaturally dense stands of young trees, a variety of forest health concerns, increasing potential for widespread insect population outbreaks and unnatural crown fires.[141]

Large snags are also important hibernation dens for black bear; removal of snags is tough on bears.

Between 48 and 60 percent of Canada's old-growth forests have been logged, 90 percent of the rain forest in southern Mexico is gone, and 60 percent of Guatemala has been deforested.[142] The Sky Islands Wildlands Network Conservation Plan describes the situation in northern Mexico:

Seventy-three percent of the natural forest ecosystems of Chihuahua and Sonora have been severely altered. From the original 23 million acres occupied by old-growth pine-oak forests in Mexico, only 0.6% (41,000 acres) remains. This in turn has led to the decline of species dependent on the old-growth forest, like the extinct imperial woodpecker, and the endangered thick-billed parrot and Mexican spotted owl. Nearly all the Sierra Madre Occidental has been logged at some point, and because of this, the present vegetation may be different than the original cover. For example, small oak forests surround large (over 100 feet high) conifer trees, reminders of the forest that once was.[143]

Livestock Grazing

The grazing of domestic cattle and sheep has been the leading cause of watershed and stream destruction,[144] and of degradation of grassland and desert shrubland ecosystems in the West. The late grasslands ecologist Joy Belsky and her colleagues gave an excellent summary of live-stock impacts on western streams in the *Journal of Soil and Water Conservation* in 1999. They wrote, "Grazing by livestock has damaged 80% of the streams and riparian ecosystems in arid regions of the western United States. . . . Livestock grazing affects watershed hydrology, stream channel morphology, soils, vegetation, wildlife, fish and other riparian-dependent species, and water quality at both local and land-scape scales."[145]

The degradation of ecosystems and loss of species began swiftly, as cattle, sheep, and goats entered regions of the West. Cattle were brought to northern and central New Mexico by the Spanish in 1598; overgrazing was noted as early as 1630. Heavy grazing continued during the Spanish period, even on alpine tundra in the Sangre de Cristo Mountains. Navajos were grazing sheep by the early 1700s. Not counting the Navajo herds, one to three million sheep grazed New Mexico during the 1820s.[146]

By 1850, heavy livestock grazing allowed exotic annual grasses to replace native perennial grasses in California's Central Valley. This native prairie is now essentially gone.[147]

After the Civil War, numbers of sheep and cattle exploded to the north and west of Texas. Nancy and Denzel Ferguson write:

> In 1850 the number of sheep in western states other than California was only about 514,000 but the numbers soared to nearly 20 million by 1890.
>
> In 1870, the total number of cattle in the Arizona Territory was only 5,000. . . . by 1891 the population of cattle in the territory had grown to an estimated 1.5 million. . . . In 1870, the cattle population in 17 western states was estimated to be 4–5 million head; by 1890, that had grown to 26.5 million.[148]

Massive overgrazing and erosion followed the livestock. Rancher H. C. Hooker described the San Pedro River in southern Arizona before the cattle explosion in 1870 as "having an abundance of timber with large beds of sacaton and grama grasses. The river bed was shallow and grassy with its banks with luxuriant growth of vegetation." Thirty years later, he wrote that "the river had cut 10 to 40 feet below its banks with its trees and underbrush gone, with the mesas grazed by thousands of horses and cattle."[149]

Craig Allen of the U.S. Geological Survey and his colleagues follow up on Hooker's report of the consequences of livestock grazing: "One of the most remarkable changes in southwestern landscapes involved late nineteenth and early twentieth century channel entrenchment. Between 1865 and 1915, arroyos developed in alluvial valleys of the southwestern United States across a wide variety of hydrological, ecological, and cultural settings."[150] This arroyo, or gully, cutting lowered the water table, thereby killing riparian trees and other plants because their roots could no longer reach groundwater.[151]

Status and Trends summarizes the impact of livestock grazing on Southwest ecosystems:

> The extremely high historical stocking rates and concomitant overgrazing and livestock preferences for certain more palatable plants (for example, grasses) led to significant alterations in the species composition of vegetation across the Southwest. ... Cool-season grasses and other preferred forage species declined ... while unpalatable and weedy species, such as broom snakeweed, and shrubs, such as creosotebush and mesquite, increased. ... Livestock also altered vegetation composition by serving as an agent for the spread of weedy and nonindigenous plant species such as Lehmann lovegrass. ... Concentrated livestock use of riparian zones has had particularly significant negative ecological effects. ... Overgrazing is also widely considered a major trigger of soil erosion, flooding, and arroyo cutting in the Southwest.[152]

Long-term livestock grazing has diminished and changed herbaceous vegetation in piñon-juniper woodlands "leading to widespread desertification of understory conditions."[153]

Due to overgrazing, blizzards, and drought, cattle numbers crashed in the late 1800s in the West. Since that cattle crash, herds have built back up (cattle numbers on western rangelands grew from 25.5 million in 1940 to 54.4 million in 1990).[154] Across the arid West, in spite of the improvement from near-desertified conditions at the turn of the century, millions of acres of grazing lands remain in only poor or fair condition (moreover, in these ratings the federal Bureau of Land Management is looking only at forage, not biological diversity). Riparian areas are considered by many authorities to be in their worst condition ever.[155] Aldo Leopold wrote, "I sometimes wonder whether semi-arid mountains can be grazed at all without ultimate deterioration."[156] The land has sadly answered his question.

Overgrazing in the Southwest led to extinction in the United States of the masked bobwhite in Arizona one hundred years ago; Montezuma quail, and Botteri's, Baird's, and rufous-winged sparrow populations crashed.[157] Belsky and her colleagues report that "a recent U.S. Forest Service report found livestock grazing to be the fourth major cause of species endangerment in the United States and the second major cause of endangerment of plant species."[158]

Livestock grazing on the Colorado Plateau has been a leading cause of conversion of bunchgrass ecosystems to shrublands, and similarly in the Chihuahuan Desert of New Mexico and Texas, and in the Sonoran Desert of southern Arizona—possibly an indication of "irreversible decline" for these ecosystems. Researchers have shown "that even limited grazing in marginal ecosystems dominated by saguaro has caused long-term, possibly irreversible, declines of that cactus species."[159] Some desert grasslands were transformed into creosotebush desert by the overgrazing/drought/soil erosion "triple-whammy."

"The effect of livestock on riparian habitats in the Great Basin is often so severe that those habitats no longer represent natural vegetation," reports *Status and Trends*. Making up only tiny parts of the Great Basin, riparian areas are "critical centers of biodiversity," especially for birds and butterflies, and as migration corridors.[160] Degradation and loss of riparian habitats are considered "the most important causes of the decline of land bird populations in western North America." Furthermore, livestock grazing harms most shrub-steppe nesting birds.[161] Overgrazing has also led to heavy losses of the important browse species, winterfat.[162]

A good summary of how livestock grazing has led to the endangerment of wildlife, including plants, was published in 1994 by the National Wildlife Federation, a moderate conservation group: *Grazing to Extinction*. Two other excellent and sweeping discussions of the damage caused by livestock grazing are *The Western Range Revisited*, by University of Wyoming Law School professor and range ecologist, Debra Donahue, and the truly monumental coffee-table book, *Welfare Ranching: The Subsidized Destruction of the American West*, from the Foundation for Deep Ecology.[163] A key paper by Jerry Freilich and fellow researchers asks, "How different are rangelands now from the way they were before ranching?" Their sober, fair analysis looks at six often-overlooked impacts of grazing on native biodiversity: "problem animal" removal; truncation of the food web by removing carcasses, and the like; fencing, roads, and fragmentation; exotic weeds and poisons to control them; alteration of fire regimes; and impacts to water supplies and riparian areas.[164]

Keystone Losses

I'll discuss keystone and foundation species in more detail in later chapters. For now, know that they are ecologically highly interactive species whose removal from an ecosystem leads to a loss of habitat for other species and a breakdown of ecological integrity. Beavers, prairie dogs, and large carnivores are examples of these strongly interacting species.

After beavers were trapped out in various parts of North America, the elimination of beaver-dam-created wetlands and high water tables led to loss of riparian forests and habitat for many species.[165]

Widespread extermination of prairie dogs led to poor nutrient turnover in grassland soils and degradation of grasslands, along with woody plant encroachment—and the near extinction of the black-footed ferret.[166]

Kelp forests in the Pacific Ocean from the Aleutians to California largely collapsed from sea urchin grazing when their keystone predator, the sea otter, was hunted out. Gulf of Maine kelp forests also crashed from sea urchin grazing after predatory Atlantic cod were fished out.[167] The ecological extinction of green turtles is a major cause of the "recent die-off of turtlegrass beds in Florida Bay."[168]

Extermination of big cats, wolves, and other large carnivores has led to a breakdown of various ecosystems because of the loss of their top-down regulation of prey species. I'll discuss this issue in chapter 7.

There has been a fifty-two-fold decline in Chesapeake Bay oysters from habitat destruction by mechanical dredging. Because oysters were able to filter all the water in the bay in only three days, their decline has led to much of the collapse of the ecosystem.[169] In general, "overfishing [of filter feeders such as oysters] may often be a necessary precondition for eutrophication, outbreaks of disease, or species introductions to occur," write Jeremy Jackson and his colleagues in *Science*.[170]

Nonmotorized Recreation

In general, the more intense and motorized recreation is, the more it harms nature. Even the most benign kinds of recreation, such as backpacking and canoeing, can cause damage and disturb wildlife, however. For example, research has shown that cliffs popular for rock climbing have more exotic plants and a marked decline of native plants. In many areas, cliffs hold most of the remaining old-growth forests. For example, the Niagara Escarpment near Toronto, Ontario, supports nine-hundred-year-old eastern white cedars. Bryophytes are largely exterminated on climbing routes.[171] Wolverines are known to abandon their maternal dens and kits because of cross-country skiers passing nearby.

Urbanization

Housing developments both destroy and fragment habitat. Therefore, urbanization is covered here and also under the fragmentation wound. Urban sprawl is a primary factor "for declines in more than half of the species listed as threatened or endangered." Species in California, Texas, and Florida are particularly hard-hit.[172]

Suburban sprawl in the East is leading to the clearing and fragmentation of second-growth forest there. David Wilcove reports that this is causing the decline and even disappearance of Neotropical songbirds around Washington, D.C.[173]

Development on barrier islands has led to loss of nesting habitat for sea turtles. Moreover, lights from developments confuse just-hatched turtles when they try to find the ocean.[174]

Although overblown by apologists for the livestock industry, exurban sprawl in the West is an important cause of habitat loss. Such damage is especially severe in mountain valleys near ski areas and other resort areas. Suburban sprawl in the West paves over habitat and pushes wildlife out of key habitats, including vital winter range. Private lands near Yellowstone National Park are a case in point.[175]

Between 66 and 90 percent of the coastal sage scrub in Southern California has been lost since settlement, largely because of urbanization.[176] Based on careful research in San Diego, Michael Soulé writes, "Most canyons [with remnant native vegetation] lose at least half of their [chaparral-requiring] birds within 20 to 40 years after isolation."[177]

Bottom Trawling

Bottom trawling is the most grotesque and destructive form of fishing. Huge nets—some over 300 feet wide—with heavy chains and rollers are dragged across the seafloor, scooping up everything in their path and bulldozing away "structurally complex habitats."[178] Thousands of square miles of the North American continental shelf are regularly trawled. Researchers from the University of British Columbia Fisheries Centre say of bottom trawling that "if an analogy is required, it should be that of clear cutting forests in the course of hunting deer."[179]

Wetlands Draining

According to *Status and Trends*, "53% of the wetlands of the contiguous 48 states have been lost. The former wetlands slowed the flow of water, and their loss greatly increases the chances and severity of flooding."[180]

The prairie potholes region of the northern Great Plains in Canada and the United States is responsible for around "half of the continental waterfowl production," according to *Status and Trends*. Losses of these wetlands in the U.S. range from 99 percent in Iowa to 35 percent in South Dakota; major declines in breeding waterfowl have followed.[181]

California has lost over 95 percent of its original 2 million hectares (5 million acres) of wetlands, which had supported immense winter flocks of ducks and geese.[182] Extensive riparian forests grew around wetlands and waterways. Only 11 percent is left. Riparian-dependent birds such as Bell's vireo and yellow-billed cuckoo are now imperiled.[183] Once astonishingly productive, California's estuarian marshes have been drained, filled, and built on, thereby endangering native birds, mammals, and plants.[184]

Water Control

The various ways we try to remake rivers and streams into plumbing destroy, degrade, and fragment habitat. We'll look at the habitat destruction here, and fragmentation in chapter 6. There are some seventy-five thousand dams and an uncountable number of other developments plugging and diverting rivers in the United States today.[185] In 1982, there were 2,654 large dams (those that store more than 212 million cubic feet of water), 50,000 smaller dams (those that store 2.1 million to 212 million cubic feet), and over 2 million small dams and farm ponds.[186]

By 1988, only 9 percent of all river miles in the United States were considered undeveloped.[187] Most of this was found in very short stretches. How many stretches of free-flowing river of 125 miles or more are left in the lower forty-eight states? Forty-two.[188]

According to *Status and Trends*, "Before European settlement, the estimated amount of riparian land in the 100-year floodplains of the lower 48 states was 49 million hectares [125 million acres]. By the 1980s it was reduced by 81%, to 9.3 million hectares [23.25 million acres]."[189]

This mass of river plumbing causes extinctions. "Of the 27 species and 13 subspecies of freshwater fishes that have become extinct in North America during the last century, habitat degradation contributed to at least 73% of these extinctions," reports *Status and Trends*.[190] Damage to

Alabama's Coosa River has led to the probable extinction of 62 species of freshwater snails.[191]

Dams have especially harmed anadromous fish, including sturgeon species, American shad, river herring species, striped bass, and Atlantic salmon. "Atlantic salmon abundance has declined precipitously," according to *Status and Trends*.[192] The other side of the continent fares only a little better: "Of 214 stocks of Pacific salmon, 74% have a high or moderate risk of extinction, primarily due to habitat loss from dams, logging, roads, and grazing."[193]

Navigational structures, bank stabilization, and channelization of the Missouri River caused commercial fish catches to drop "by 80% between 1947 and 1963."[194]

According to *Status and Trends*, fourteen major dams on the Columbia River "inhibit or block migrating fishes, and, by flooding spawning grounds, cause changes in competition between species, changes in predator-prey relations, and a decline in the variety and numbers of native fish species. In 1911 the commercial fish harvest on the river was 24,400 metric tons, but by the early 1970s it had declined to 6,800 metric tons."[195]

Dams have immediate and delayed effects. First, migration of fish is stopped, the downstream is dewatered, and the water becomes colder and clearer, and the upstream becomes a reservoir. Native fish have trouble surviving and exotic game fish take over. Second, the downstream channel degrades and widens, flood flows are lost, sediment is lost, and there is less over-the-bank flooding, leading to loss of sandbars and riparian forests, and invasion by exotic plants.[196]

Despite its aridity, the Great Basin has many wetlands and lakes in basins. However, water diversion and other uses have dried up 52 percent of the wetlands in Nevada. Heavy metals are accumulating to dangerous levels in several lakes because of the decreased water inflow. Waterbirds and fish are suffering.[197] Eight percent of the fish in the Great Basin–Mojave Desert are extinct and 62 percent are imperiled. Dams, diversions, and channelization (along with watershed damage by livestock grazing) are the leading causes. Four of the larger native fish in the Colorado River are endangered because of the grandiose plumbing designs imposed on that river by humans. Pupfish species endemic to isolated springs are extinct, endangered, or imperiled because of groundwater pumping and other water use leading to the drying up of their habitats. Cutthroat trout strains and other fish have similarly suffered.[198] According to *Status and Trends*, bonytail chub are "functionally extinct" in the Colorado River because of dams; "no young individuals have been found in recent years." Their crash from abundance to near extinction has been compared to that of the passenger pigeon.[199] Western fishes are in bigger trouble than those elsewhere in the United States. *Status and Trends* warns that "we could witness the disappearance of most of the region's endemic fish fauna" if recovery efforts are not successful.[200]

Michael Bogan and his colleagues report, "In New Mexico and Arizona, 11 of 40 (27.5%) land bird species known to have declined in numbers over the last 100 years may have done so because of degradation and destruction of riparian habitats."[201] They conclude, "Most declines and extirpations of aquatic organisms in the Southwest can be traced to the construction of dams, either for water storage or flood control, and to other developments on or near waterways, such as diversion structures and drainage of wetlands."[202]

Water diversions and dams have played havoc with native freshwater fish in California where 57 percent "are either extinct or on the road to extinction if present trends continue." Dams have also caused the crash of chinook salmon runs in Central Valley rivers, where two to three million were common in the nineteenth century. Steelhead have also steeply declined. In the Sierra Nevada, "22 of the 40 native fishes are threatened, declining rapidly, or otherwise in need of special protection." But fish are worst off in California in urban Southern California, where all native fish are either listed as endangered, or should be.[203]

The southeastern United States has the greatest freshwater fish diversity of any temperate area in the world, with 535 species. Habitat destruction from dams and other water projects imperils 19 percent of these species.[204] Peter White, of the University of North Carolina at Chapel Hill, and his colleagues, observe that the Southeast has "90% of the freshwater mussel fauna of all of North America north of Mexico"— 270 species and subspecies. Because of habitat loss from dams and channelization, along with pollution, exotic species, and other human impacts, 48 percent "are endangered, threatened, or possibly extinct."[205]

CHAPTER 6

Ecological Wounds of North America 2: Fragmentation, Loss of Ecological Processes, Exotic Species, Pollution, and Climate Change

As discussed in chapter 5, I categorize the ecological harm humans have caused into seven wounds. Chapter 5 provided an introduction and discussion of two of the wounds: direct killing of species and habitat loss. In this chapter, I continue with a discussion of the other five wounds.

Wound 3: Fragmentation of Wildlife Habitat

Causes: Fish and other wildlife habitat have been fragmented by all of the factors causing ecosystem loss and degradation, and by road and highway building, off-road vehicle (ORV) use, pipelines, power lines, and ranchettes.

Michael Soulé and John Terborgh remind us that "connectivity is not just another goal of conservation: it is the natural state of things."[1]

Most of the causes of ecosystem loss and degradation discussed in the previous chapter also fragment habitat. In this section, I'll emphasize the specific causes of fragmentation.

Habitat for wide-ranging species such as wolf, mountain lion, lynx, pronghorn, and bighorn sheep has been fragmented by roads, fences, agriculture, and urban, suburban, and ranchette development. Even smaller roads and developments fragment habitat for reptiles, amphibians, small mammals, and birds.

Roads

As I wrote in 1992, "Napoleon's army may have marched on its stomach, but the army of wilderness destruction travels by road and motorized vehicle."[2] In the modern era, species extinction most frequently travels by road, as well. There is a vast body of research documenting the various ways roads harm natural ecosystems, but in this small space, I can only touch on them. A sweeping summary of the ecological effects of roads on both terrestrial and aquatic ecosystems was given by Steve Trombulak and Chris Frissell in *Conservation Biology*.[3] (The Wildlands Center for Preventing Roads provides an extensive bibliography of research papers documenting the effects of roads on its Web site: www.wildlandscpr.org/databases/index.html.)

The acreage in the lower forty-eight states affected by roads is staggering. In the same issue of *Conservation Biology* in which Trombulak and Frissell's paper appeared, Richard Forman of Harvard made a state-of-knowledge estimate. As of 1985, he calculated there were 3.85 million miles of roads, not counting private roads or four-wheel-drive routes. His study concludes that "22% of the contiguous United States is estimated to be ecologically altered by the road network."[4] The U.S. Forest Service is the largest road-managing agency in the world, with an official 386,000 miles on the 192 million acres in the national forest system.[5] The road density of national forests averages 1.6 miles of road for every square mile of land. However, this figure does not include some 60,000 miles of unofficial roads and vehicle routes on national forests as estimated by the Forest Service. Such roads push the total road mileage to 440,000. The Bureau of Land Management does not maintain an accurate inventory of roads, but there are certainly several hundred thousand miles of roads on its lands.

Trombulak and Frissell suggest "seven general effects" roads have on natural ecosystems: "mortality from road construction, mortality from collision with vehicles, modification of animal behavior, alteration of the physical environment, alteration of the chemical environment, spread of exotics, and increased use of areas by humans."[6] Their article summarizes the variety of impacts under each of these categories. David Parsons, former leader of the Mexican wolf restoration project for the U.S. Fish and Wildlife Service, prepared a detailed study of focal species for the New Mexico Highlands Wildlands Network. He detailed the negative impacts of roads on wolves, mountain lions, black bears, bighorn sheep, and elk.[7] I'm going to lump the impacts of roads on biological diversity into three broad categories: (1) physical impact, (2) fragmentation of habitat, and (3) access.

Regarding physical impact, Trombulak and Frissell write that road construction has "destroyed at least 4,784,351 ha [11,817,346 acres] of land and water bodies that formerly supported plants, animals, and other organisms." In other words, what once lived there was killed. These impacts can extend out many feet from the roadway.[8] Moreover, they show that "soil density, temperature, soil water content, light, dust, surface-water flow, pattern of runoff, and sedimentation" are altered by roads.[9] Roads also spread "heavy metals, salt, organic molecules, ozone, and nutrients."[10]

Fragmentation is a huge problem. Interstate highways are formidable barriers to many kinds of wildlife. Even two-laned paved roads cause many deaths of animals trying to cross. An example of how much habitat fragmentation from roads has increased in national forests comes from New Mexico's Jemez Mountains, where road length increased from 447 miles in 1935 to 5,240 miles in 1981 and the "[e]stimated total area of road surfaces grew from 0.13% of the map area in 1935 (247 ha [610 acres]) to 1.67% in 1981 (3,132 ha [7,736 acres])."[11] This, unfortunately, is typical for national forests.

Millions of creatures die every year from collisions with vehicles. Moose, deer, elk, raptors, other birds, snakes, toads, and a host of invertebrates are prominent victims. According to Trombulak and Frissell, "Amphibians may be especially vulnerable to roadkill because their life histories often involve migration between wetland and upland habitats."[12] Dispersing predators, such as the Florida panther, are frequently killed. In 2002, for example, 120 black bears were victims of roadkill in Florida.[13]

Roadkill isn't the only impact. There are many studies showing significant changes in animal behavior because of roads. Large mammals, in particular, "shift their home ranges away from areas with high road densities."[14] Movement patterns are altered by roads, as well.

Although paved roads are barriers to wildlife movement and sources of roadkill, dirt roads can be deadly because of the access they provide to poachers and other land abusers. Dirt roads fragment the landscape for wolves, mountain lions, bears, and other species vulnerable to opportunistic poaching. For example, at least five released Mexican wolves were shot alongside roads in Arizona's Apache National Forest in 1998, and several have been killed by automobile collisions. In 2003, thirteen lobos were found dead near roads in and around the Gila and Apache National Forests.

Roads associated with oil and gas exploration and gravel mining in Alaska are fragmenting habitat favored by musk oxen and moose. There are fears that opening the Dalton Highway to private vehicles all the way to Prudhoe Bay will lead to more hunting and trapping in northern Alaska.[15]

Off-Road Vehicles

Since their development and subsequent popularity boom in the 1970s, off-road vehicles (ORVs) have become the bane of responsible land management—both public and private. Some four-wheel-drive (4WD) users are responsible and use their vehicles to gain access to remote areas on bad roads. I have a 4WD, for example, as do most of my friends. However, too many ORVers—whether in four-wheel-drive vehicles, dune buggies, dirt bikes, all-terrain vehicles (ATVs), snowmo- biles, personal watercraft, or powerboats—drive to tear up the ground, harass wildlife, and act like maniacs. Many of these folks are unaware of the damage they cause, while others revel in it.

It's not as though land managers and policy makers are unaware of research documenting the damage caused by ORVs. In the 1970s, Texas A&M supported a study and research summary on such impacts.[16] In 1978, David Sheridan prepared a detailed report to the President's Council on Environmental Quality about the growing problem.[17] Lead- ing American statesmen called for their control thirty years ago: "I hope there is some way we could outlaw all off-road vehicles, including snow- mobiles, motorcycles, etc., which are doing more damage to our forests and deserts than anything man has ever created. I don't think the Forest Service should encourage the use of these vehicles by even suggesting areas they can travel in. . . . I have often felt that these vehicles have been Japan's way of getting even with us."[18] The author of this letter to the Southwest Regional Forester was none other than Senator Barry Goldwater of Arizona.

Had federal agencies taken Goldwater's advice, we would not have the ORV problem today. Conservationists have worked for years, but perhaps not hard enough in the last thirty, to control vehicles off road on public and private lands. The wilderness area protection movement was launched in the early 1920s to halt the spread of automobiles throughout the national forest backcountry.[19]

As with roads, I'm going to clump together the impacts of off-road vehicles on biological diversity into three broad categories: (1) physical impact, (2) fragmentation of habitat, and (3) access.

Howard Wilshire of the U.S. Geological Survey (USGS) and others did considerable research in the 1970s showing the terrific and probably irreversible damage ORVs caused in Southern California through gully erosion on hills, massive wind erosion of chewed-up soils, damage to plants, and dumping of oil and other pollutants. Tank activity on military lands and off-road vehicles in the Mojave Desert cause long-lasting harm to soils, vegetation, and wildlife. Recovery may take one thousand years.[20]

Because they travel on a layer of snow instead of on the ground, snowmobiles have long been claimed to have no impact. However, the passage of snowmobiles compacts the snow in which many small mammals and even birds find refuge, some with elaborate tunnel systems that can be crushed. Snow compaction also damages plants and soils.[21] Moreover, snow compaction allows coyotes to enter winter lynx habitat and compete with them for prey or even kill lynx. The loud noise caused by snowmobiles (and ATVs) disturbs wildlife at a time of year when it is most vulnerable and sensitive. The air pollution that snowmobiles put out is legendary. Park rangers in Yellowstone now wear gas masks because of the blue haze.

Off-road vehicles are a major disrupter of beach-nesting birds.[22] Western snowy plovers or their nests are frequently run over by ORVs driving on beaches in California.[23] Off-road vehicles have heavily damaged beach life in California: at one area, "almost all life forms have disappeared under the onslaught of off-road vehicles."[24]

Off-road vehicle use and fragmentation from roads, sprawl, and agriculture harm the threatened desert tortoise.[25] Even dirt tracks can fragment the landscape for slow-moving reptiles and amphibians, especially when some off-road vehicle enthusiasts run over these animals for thrills. (I once found an approximately fifty-year-old desert tortoise in the desert near my home in Tucson. Its shell was crushed and its internal organs spilled out. Knobby tire tracks showed that an ATVer had deliberately swerved to kill the tortoise for a sick thrill.) Use of dune buggies and other vehicles on Great Basin sand dunes is threatening various endemic insects.[26] Jet Skis or, as the industry calls them, "personal watercraft," and powerboats disrupt roosting waterbirds and cause them to flush.[27] Powerboats and Jet Skis kill dozens of manatees in Florida waters every year and could well cause the extinction of this slow-moving seacow. Water and air pollution from thrillcraft of all sorts is a huge yet scarcely regulated problem.

Some 4WD operators stay on roads, as they should, and are responsible campers when they get to their destination. Unfortunately, an outlaw element uses the machines to gain access for poaching, archaeological site looting, and to disqualify roadless areas from future wilderness area designation. The combination of guns with ATVs or snowmobiles for hunting is an ethical abomination, but, even worse, it puts "if-it-moves-shoot-it" he-men with guns and powerful, nimble vehicles into the most sensitive habitat refugia for wolves, mountain lions, lynx, and other sensitive species. For example, "63% of known human-caused grizzly deaths occurred within 1 kilometer of roads."[28] Others don't need guns to harass wildlife. There are many cases of snowmobilers and ORVers running down wildlife for the thrill of it. Seventeen-year-old Corey Dygert, for example, drove 50 miles per hour on a beach in Washington trying to hit sandpipers, sanderlings, dunlins, and dowitchers. He tallied 450 dead birds.[29]

Dams and Diversions

Major dams on rivers, smaller dams on headwater streams, irrigation diversion dams, and dewatered and degraded stretches of once-perennial streams have fragmented riverine habitat for native fish, amphibians, and aquatic invertebrates.[30] Fragmentation of the Middle Rio Grande and its sidestreams in New Mexico, for example, is largely responsible for the sharp declines and losses of native fish by drying up their dispersal routes.[31] Destruction and degradation of riparian forests have fragmented habitat and migratory routes for riparian-dependent birds and other species.

Dams on the Columbia-Snake river system "create barriers to salmon and white sturgeon movements and alter river flow rates and patterns to the detriment of many fish populations."[32] Salmon once ran nearly 600 miles up the Columbia-Snake segment to central Idaho and twice as far on the Columbia River itself. Historical estimates are between 10 million and 16 million salmon total per year in the Columbia-Snake system. Over 50 percent of the Snake River drainage has now lost salmon runs.[33]

Agriculture

Agricultural fields not only destroy wildlands by replacing them with domesticated or industrial landscapes, but also fragment migration and dispersal of wildlife trying to move between habitat patches. Farms can be deadly places to cross.

Artificial treelines in grassland areas fragment habitat for grassland birds.[34] Fragmentation of riparian areas in California by industrialized agriculture allows the brown-head cowbird to expand its range and parasitize nests of riparian-breeding songbirds. *Status and Trends* states, "Cowbird parasitism is the main reason that the least Bell's vireo and the willow flycatcher are endangered in California."[35]

Livestock fencing blocks the movement of pronghorn—who don't jump fences—to seasonal ranges and water sources. For over a century, barbed wire and net-wire livestock fencing has crisscrossed pronghorn habitat. Such fencing was a big part of the pronghorn's rapid decline and its agonizingly slow recovery.

Logging

Clearcuts, and even selective logging, can create deadly barriers for interior forest species. Spotted owl, marten, and others are loath to travel across clearcuts because it exposes them to their predators. In chapter 7, I discuss how forest fragmentation by logging harms songbirds.

Sprawl

The extraordinary sprawl of suburbs into wildlife habitat, and the ranchette boom in wildlands, is probably the fastest-growing form of ecosystem fragmentation, though the cancerous spread of off-road vehicles is close behind. For example, much rural sprawl ("condoization") in and around resorts in mountain areas takes place in narrow valleys, which are primary travel linkages for many species of wildlife, including moose, elk, bighorn sheep, wolves, bears, and mountain lions. These developments often fragment migratory paths between summer and winter ranges.

Ski areas, which can be viewed as linear clearcuts with a packed human presence, fragment habitat for both forest interior species, such as marten, fisher, and many songbirds, and wide-ranging species, such as bears.

Forest fragmentation from East Coast sprawl leads to songbird decline for three reasons, according to David Wilcove: loss of forest interior nesting habitat, good habitat provided for nest predators (raccoons, opossums) in suburbs, and loss of large carnivores.[36]

Resort development along beaches and barrier islands on the Atlantic and Gulf coasts has fragmented and destroyed habitat for nesting shorebirds.[37]

Wound 4: Loss and Disruption of Natural Processes

Causes: Vital ecological and evolutionary processes—especially fire, hydrological cycles, and predation—have been disrupted and even eliminated by logging, grazing, fire control, beaver trapping, dams and other flood control measures, and killing of keystone species—especially large carnivores.

Daniel Simberloff and his coauthors in chapter 4 of *Continental Conservation* identify fire, hydrology, and predation as the ecologically most essential natural processes to restore.[38] All have been severely disrupted throughout North America south of the boreal forest.

Fire

Many ecosystems in North America coevolved with frequent fire. Noss and Peters write, "Many of our most endangered ecosystems—grasslands, savannas, barrens, open forests such as longleaf pine and ponderosa pine—have declined largely as a result of fire suppression."[39]

In the Southeast, according to *Status and Trends*:

> Fire was and is important to many southeastern ecosystems, including many Coastal Plain and south Florida ecosystems, pine-dominated forests of the Coastal Plain and Appalachian Highlands, oak and oak-hickory forests, oak savannas, glades, barrens, and prairies. Because most natural communities in the Southeast are dependent on fire, more than 50% of the rarest plants in the region also possess this dependence. Fire may also explain the occurrence of canebrakes, dense stands of the Southeast's only native bamboo, which were frequently described by travelers but which have vanished from the landscape except for small remnant patches.[40]

Because of control of natural fire in the Southeast, "there is a general trend toward an expansion of mesic species and a contraction of dry-adapted and fire-dependent species."[41]

Collapse of the once-extensive longleaf pine forests through fire suppression[42] (and other human impacts) has led to serious losses of red-cockaded woodpecker, Bachman's sparrow, fox squirrel, and gopher tortoise. Population of the tortoise is only 20 percent what it was one hundred years ago. Sixty-five species of vertebrates and over three hundred species of invertebrates live in or otherwise use gopher tortoise burrows. No other animal in the region makes this essential microhabitat.[43]

Stopping natural fire in Great Plains grasslands has led to reduced stopover habitat for many migrating birds. Without fire, prairie potholes are taken over by cattails and exotic purple loosestrife, degrading key habitat for native species.[44]

Until a century ago, most Southwestern forests burned in keeping with the two-to-seven-year wet-dry cycles tied to the El Niño-Southern Oscillation.[45] Misunderstanding the ecological role of natural fire caused the Forest Service and other land managers to fight all fires from 1906 on. The Forest Service deliberately used overgrazing by cattle and sheep to get rid of the grass that carried the natural, cool, ground fires between trees.[46] Increasing numbers of scientists recognized fire's important role by the 1960s, but such ideas were heresy to many foresters and ranchers.

Status and Trends concludes, "Fire suppression over the past century pervasively affected many southwestern ecosystems."[47] Wildfire control plus overgrazing by cattle and sheep has helped woody plants to outcompete grasses. Snakeweed, creosote bush, prickly pear, cholla, acacia, mesquite, and piñon-juniper woodland have successfully invaded and replaced many grasslands. Grassland decline has altered the relative numbers of native ungulates that graze or browse. By halting frequent, cool, ground fires in forests, the Forest Service has caused the fuel load to build up, thereby creating conditions for unnatural and catastrophic crown fires.[48]

Fire suppression has increased the time between fires, thereby allowing more time for seedlings to grow into trees large enough to withstand occasional light surface fires. This, too, has led to the forest takeover of grasslands and unnatural tree density within forests and woodlands.[49]

Although Native Americans may have set some fires in the Southwest, Craig Allen and his fellow researchers conclude that "fire frequencies were probably controlled primarily by climate and fuel dynamics, rather than by ignition source."[50] Geographer Tom Vale has effectively made that point for most of North America.[51] Allen and his colleagues further report that

> The importance of intense livestock grazing as a cause of the disruption of natural fire regimes is confirmed by the compar-

ison of different case studies. A few sites in northern New Mexico and Arizona that were grazed by sheep and goats owned by Spanish colonists and Navajos (Dine) show fire frequencies declining in the early nineteenth century, or earlier, and corresponding to the documented timing of pastoral activities in these areas. In contrast, remote sites with no evidence of early, intensive grazing sustained some surface fires into the middle of the twentieth century, when aerial firefighting resources began to be most effective in suppressing fires. Finally, a remote mountain in northern Sonora, Mexico, where neither intensive livestock grazing nor effective fire suppression has occurred, shows episodic surface fires burning throughout the twentieth century.[52]

Aspen stands declined 46 percent in area in New Mexico and Arizona between 1962 and 1986, largely due to fire suppression.[53]

Fire suppression and logging have led to the ponderosa pine eastside forests of Oregon changing over to unhealthy stands of mixed conifer plagued by insect epidemics, unnaturally intense fires, and overcrowding.[54]

Hydrology

The trapping-out of beavers from most western streams by 1840 started the unraveling of watersheds and riparian areas. Beaver dams had created extensive wetlands, controlled floods, stored water for slow release throughout the year, and provided high-quality habitat for many species.[55] Some streams were staircases of beaver ponds for many miles. Without beaver dams, wetlands shrunk and seasonal floods ran unchecked.[56]

Human-made dams and water diversions, in contrast to beaver dams, disrupt natural hydrological processes. For example, halting natural flooding patterns on the rivers that flow east from the Rockies across the Great Plains has led to the growth of forested corridors along river valleys, which had once been wide, rocky, and unforested because of the floods. These unnaturally forested corridors are now leading to hybridization between eastern and western birds as the eastern species follow the riparian forests west. Moreover, white-tailed deer are using the riparian forests to travel west, where they displace mule deer.[57]

Libby Dam on the Kootenai River in Montana has unnaturally

altered stream flows and has led to the population crash of the largest freshwater fish in North America, the white sturgeon.[58]

By eliminating spring flooding, human-made dams threaten the reproduction of riparian cottonwood forests throughout the West.[59] Riparian woodlands were naturally maintained by flooding from snowmelt in the spring and thunderstorms in the summer. Damage to watersheds, loss of the functional role of beavers, artificial dams, water diversions, groundwater pumping, channelization, and flood control structures have done away with this natural disturbance regime (as discussed in "Wound 2: Loss and Degradation of Ecosystems" in chapter 5). *Continental Conservation* discusses the many benefits of naturally fluctuating water levels (both flooding and low flows). Halting natural flooding has also allowed exotic tamarisk to outcompete native cottonwoods and willows in the Southwest.[60]

The loss of flooding disturbance to cottonwood forests has lessened diversity in age classes. Greg Farley and his fellow researchers conclude that the diversity of Neotropical migrant songbirds is "maximized by simultaneous availability of [riparian forest] vegetation of different ages."[61] They further report that "without human intervention to control the spread of nonnative species and enhance recruitment of native species, a near-complete replacement of the native plant community in the Rio Grande Valley could take place within the [twenty-first] century."[62]

Conversion of much of southern Florida to sugarcane has grossly upset the water flow to the Everglades. Wading birds that numbered a quarter of a million only sixty years ago have crashed to fewer than thirty thousand in large part because of the changed hydrology.[63] Everglades National Park was originally set aside because of its huge wading bird populations. Populations are now only "10%–20% of original densities." White ibises no longer nest in the park.[64]

Predation

Recent ecological research has shown the important role played by predation in top-down regulation of ecosystems.[65] Extirpation of the wolf and extirpation or population decline of the mountain lion throughout the United States due to predator extermination programs have disrupted ecological integrity through the behavioral and population release of prey animals. For example, excessive elk browsing harms the regeneration of aspen.[66] After wolves reestablished a functional pres-

ence in Yellowstone, overbrowsing of aspens and willows declined due
to the control by wolf packs on elk behavior. Loss of predators was discussed in "Wound 1: Direct Killing of Species," in chapter 5, and the
necessary role of top-down regulation will be discussed in more detail
in chapter 7.

Wound 5: Invasion by Exotic Species and Diseases

*Causes: Aggressive and disruptive exotic species—plants, animals, and disease
organisms and vectors—have (1) invaded, (2) escaped from cultivation, or (3)
been deliberately introduced, threatening ecosystems and the survival of many
native species.*

Conservation biologists now recognize exotic species as a leading cause
of extinction, second only to habitat destruction.[67] Biologists James
Williams and Gary Meffe (Meffe is editor of the journal *Conservation
Biology*) warn that "this continued homogenization of the world's flora
and fauna, which represents at least millions of years of separate evolutionary histories, is an ecological holocaust of major proportions."[68]

Throughout temperate North America, nonnative plants and animals imperil many native species. Some of these destructive invaders
were deliberate introductions; some escaped from cultivation; others
hitchhiked in. Most do well in disturbed habitats.

Status and Trends reports, "Today, biologists estimate there are more
than 6,500 species of established, self-sustaining populations of nonindigenous animals, plants, and microbes in the United States." These
include plants (3,723), terrestrial vertebrates (193), insects and arachnids
(over 2,000), fish (279), nonmarine mollusks (91), and plant pathogens
(239).[69]

The key factor for successful establishment of exotic species is
human disturbance of natural habitats. Moreover, successful exotics
have escaped the predators and ecological competitors they faced in
their native habitats.[70] Of 392 recent vertebrate extinctions in the world,
exotic species were the main cause in 109 cases.[71] In the United States,
some 315 native species are listed under the federal Endangered Species
Act as endangered or threatened because of exotic species to some
degree.[72] Exotic species can cause the extinction or imperilment of
native species by predation, competition, or changing "basic ecosystem
structure or dynamics."[73] Roads are significant routes for exotic plant
invasions.[74]

Plants

Purple loosestrife invaded from Europe in the early 1800s and has taken over many wetlands in the U.S. Northeast, eliminating native plants and causing losses among birds, mammals, and turtles.[75] It is now invading wetlands in the U.S. northern Rockies.[76]

African lovegrass has caused ten native Arizona species to decline.[77] The exotic grass red brome is spreading through the Mojave Desert.[78] The melaleuca tree from Australia has overrun the Everglades in southern Florida and "has modified soil characteristics and topography . . . displacing native vegetation and changing habitat structure for native wildlife," according to *Status and Trends*.[79] Australian pine, Brazilian pepper, hydrilla, and water hyacinth have also taken over large areas of southern Florida.[80]

Some 13 to 30 percent of species in the prairie are now exotics, including Russian-olive trees, which harm the integrity of riparian ecosystems by sucking up water and replacing native trees.[81]

Exotic spotted knapweed has taken over at least 3.4 million acres in Montana, Idaho, Oregon, and Washington.[82] Overgrazing in the sagebrush-grasslands of the Great Basin has led to wholesale invasion by the exotics cheatgrass and halogeton.[83] Because cheatgrass is highly flammable, fires increase and burn out the natives, thus helping cheat spread farther. There is then a wholesale change to a new ecological system.[84] *Status and Trends* reports, "Cheatgrass is dominant on about 6.8 million hectares [16.8 million acres] of sagebrush-steppe in the Intermountain West and could eventually invade an additional 25 million hectares [62 million acres]."[85] Cheatgrass provides little if any food to native wildlife.

Heavy sheep grazing in the late 1800s so wasted high mountain meadows in New Mexico that "moist meadows in the Jemez Mountains . . . are often dominated now by nonindigenous plants such as Kentucky bluegrass, white clover, and dandelion."[86] Tamarisk (salt cedar), a native of the Middle East, was planted ornamentally in the late 1800s in the Southwest. It was able to outcompete native cottonwoods and willows because dams and flood-control levees prevented the natural cycles of flooding and drying to which the native trees are adapted.[87] Tamarisk is a poor habitat and food source for native species, except for providing critical interim nesting habitat for the endangered southwestern willow flycatcher in a few places where native vegetation has been entirely lost. Tamarisk dries up springs and streams upon which native species depend, as it sucks up large amounts of water through its roots and then transpires this moisture into the air. Tamarisk has also taken over rivers in the Great Basin.[88]

Beaches and dunes along the California coast have become dominated by exotic plants such as European beachgrass and iceplant, with native species losing out.[89] As noted earlier, California's native grasses have been almost entirely replaced by invaders.

Plant Diseases and Pests

Exotic plant diseases and pests have grossly reshaped temperate North American forests. Many of our most majestic trees—including chestnut, elm, beech, red spruce, Fraser fir, hemlock, whitebark pine, valley oak, Port Orford cedar—have been largely wiped out or are threatened with severe decline. One hundred years ago, the American chestnut made up as much as 40 percent of overstory trees in eastern forests. Chestnut blight then invaded from Asia and soon drove the American chestnut to "ecological extinction." Consequently, seven moth species dependent on the chestnut also became extinct.[90]

The chestnut is not an isolated case, unfortunately. According to the United States Forest Service, native trees are assaulted by over three hundred exotic pests. Another alien fungus, Dutch elm disease, has, since 1930, killed American elms in much of their range.[91] In the last thirty or so years, exotic fungi have nearly exterminated butternuts and American dogwoods.[92] Woolly adelgids from Asia and Europe are wiping out hemlocks along the Appalachians and the red spruce-Fraser fir ecosystem in the high country of the southern Appalachians.[93] In Great Smoky Mountains National Park, Fraser fir losses "caused a 35% decrease in the density of breeding bird populations, [and] the loss of two forest interior bird species."[94] American beeches are under threat because of the beech scale insect from Europe that "allows a fungus to invade and kill beech trees."[95] Buckeyes and maples, major components of the eastern deciduous forest, could be widely killed by an Asian beetle.[96] An exotic root-rot fungus imperils the endemic conifer Port Orford cedar in the Klamath-Siskiyou country on the Oregon-California border. It is largely spread by vehicle tires.[97]

Whitebark pine, which grows at high elevations in the West, is being outcompeted by other native trees because of fire suppression. However, an even greater threat is the white pine blister rust, introduced from Europe in 1910 or so, and now killing whitebark pines throughout their range, particularly in moister sites.[98] Grizzly bears in the U.S. northern Rockies are dependent on whitebark pine seeds. Grizzly experts Dave

Mattson and Troy Merrill fear a population reduction of bears because of this loss of one of their major food sources.[99] The blister rust is also attacking other five-needled pines, such as limber pine in the Rockies, which is suffering heavy mortality and may become functionally extinct, and southwestern white pine in New Mexico.[100]

The most frightening of all plant diseases in North America now is sudden oak death. *Phytophthora ramorum*, a European water mold, probably brought in on nursery rhododendrons, is killing off ever-green oaks in California from Oregon to Big Sur. It has now been detected in twenty-six other tree species, including coastal redwood and Douglas-fir. It may be even more deadly to eastern species of oaks. One Forest Service researcher in West Virginia, Kurt Gottschalk, says, "This is the scariest thing to ever happen in my lifetime," and worries that it could be more devastating than the chestnut blight.[101] However, late in 2003, a phosphite spray or injection showed promise in fighting the infection.[102]

Animal Diseases

Devastating epidemics among native species are usually from "intentionally introduced species" or domestic animals.[103] Domestic sheep transmitted diseases to both desert and Rocky Mountain bighorn sheep, causing their near-extinction. Chronic wasting disease, a deadly neurological disease caused by prions, has spread from game farms into many wild populations of elk and deer in North America. How destructive it might become is unknown at this time, but it could be devastating to native deer.

Prairie dogs are particularly vulnerable to sylvatic plague, which can wipe out entire colonies.[104] Plague, which was inadvertently brought here from Eurasia, has been spreading east, north, and south from San Francisco, where it first arrived. Canine distemper and plague are continuing threats to the recovery of black-footed ferrets.[105]

Duck plague has passed from domestic ducks to migratory waterfowl and may cause major dieoffs.[106] Since 1999, West Nile virus has killed hundreds of thousands of birds. Corvids (crows and jays) have been particularly susceptible to the mosquito-transmitted virus, although 157 species have antibodies. There is considerable worry about the effect the killer virus could have on endangered birds, such as the California condor. Captive condors are being immunized with an experimental vaccine.[107]

Amphibians are also victims of exotic diseases. For example, *Status and Trends* reports, "In the past two decades, western toads disappeared from 83% of their historical range in Colorado and from 94% of Wyoming sites." A bacterial infection is at least partly to blame.[108]

Whirling disease, a parasite from Europe, has spread from hatchery trout to wild native trout. Its potential for killing off trout throughout the West is greatly feared.

Invertebrates

Two exotic mollusks, the zebra mussel and Asian clam, have spread in incredible densities through U.S. freshwater ecosystems and contribute to the endangerment of native mussels (73 percent of three hundred native species are imperiled).[109] For example, Lake Saint Clair, upstream of Detroit, maintained its highly diverse freshwater mussel populations (thirty-nine species) even after pollution caused those living downstream to crash. Invasion of the zebra mussel, however, led to the virtual or total extirpation of native mussels in Lake Saint Clair by 1992.[110]

North America has 75–80 percent of the crayfish species in the world and over 30 percent of them are threatened or endangered. One of the leading causes is the introduction of the rusty crayfish outside of its native range where "it has extirpated native crayfish and disrupted aquatic ecosystems."[111] San Francisco Bay has been largely taken over by nonnative invertebrates and fish, including shipworms, striped bass, American shad, Japanese littleneck clam, and green crab.[112] Farmed exotic shrimp have escaped their pens and invaded South Carolina waters.[113]

Fire ants arrived in Mobile, Alabama, about sixty years ago.[114] Since then they have spread widely, wreaking havoc on native species, such as ground-nesting birds, and painfully (sometimes lethally) biting humans. Perhaps the most feared exotic insect is the Africanized honey bee, which arrived in the Southwest in 1990. An exotic snail that is the vector for the human disease schistosomiasis is now resident in Texas and Florida.[115]

Vertebrates

Exotic fish species had contributed to listing forty-nine of one hundred native fish on the Endangered Species List as of 1994, and had contributed to the extinction of twenty-four out of thirty extinct native fish. Williams and Meffe fear that the deadly effects of nonnative fish will drastically increase in the coming twenty-five years because 458 exotic fish had been introduced between 1950 and 1995, whereas only 117 had been from 1831 to 1950.[116] *Status and Trends* reports, "At least 25 non-indigenous fishes have become established in the Great Lakes since the region was settled, and nearly half of them have had substantial ecological and economic effects." Sea lamprey and alewife are two of the most destructive.[117]

Farmed Atlantic salmon regularly escape from their pens and inter-breed with wild stocks, leading to the natives' genetic degradation.[118]

Termed "catastrophic" by *Status and Trends*, the illegal introduction of nonnative lake trout into Yellowstone Lake could be a "staggering" blow to grizzly bears, because lake trout eat native cutthroats. Cutthroat trout spawn in streams and provide a crucial food source for bears just after hibernation. Lake trout do not.[119]

The mosquitofish, native to the eastern United States, has devastated native fish and aquatic invertebrates in the Southwest and else-where where they have been introduced to control mosquitoes (actually they are no better than native fish for controlling mosquitoes). The once most abundant fish in southern Arizona, the Gila topminnow, has become endangered because of mosquitofish; and pupfishes and springfishes in Arizona, California, and Nevada have similarly been imperiled.[120]

More than 90 percent of fish species in the Colorado River system are exotics put there for sportfishing.[121] At least seventy-five exotic species of fish are present in New Mexico, ninety-six in Texas, seventy-one in Arizona, and fifty-five in Utah.[122] Introduced trout in the Rockies have contributed to the decline of native cutthroats: of 13 subspecies, "2 are extinct and 10 have suffered catastrophic declines."[123]

In a landmark article in *Natural Areas Journal*, Michael Murray discusses the ecological impacts of stocking naturally fishless high mountain lakes in the American West with trout. Aquatic invertebrates extirpated from such lakes after stocking include beetles, midges, dragonflies, water striders, mayflies, water fleas, copepods, and side-swimmers. In New Mexico, he writes, "Introducing new fish species has resulted in deterioration of genetic integrity of native races such as Gila trout (*Oncorhynchus gilaea*) within the Gila Wilderness, Rio Grande cut-throat trout (*O. clarki virginalis*) in the Pecos Wilderness." Moreover, some dams were built in the Pecos Wilderness to raise the water level of natural lakes for the sole reason of supporting exotic trout.[124] (This damming of natural high country lakes is common in other wilderness areas, too.) In the North Cascades, introduced trout have gobbled up salamander larvae, which were the main predator in these lakes before trout.[125] Transplantation of trout into naturally fishless Sierra Nevada lakes has likewise led to loss of native amphibians.[126] The mountain yellow-legged frog is gone from more than 90 percent of its Sierra Nevada habitat because of predation by transplanted trout. In the Coast Range, Cascades, and northern Rockies, as well, introduced trout are gobbling up native frogs and salamanders.[127]

Bullfrogs, native to the East, but not the West, eat native frogs where they've been introduced. Decline of various leopard frog species in the Southwest is partly or largely due to bullfrog predation.[128] Native amphibians in California are in big trouble. Habitat destruction is part of the problem, but nonnative bullfrogs, fish, and crayfish have extirpated "much of the local native amphibian fauna through predation on vulnerable eggs, larvae, and juvenile life stages."[129] Bullfrogs are the leading cause of spotted frog declines in the Pacific Northwest.[130]

Feral pigs (including Eurasian wild boar released for sport) are ecologically disruptive in areas of California[131] and the southeastern United States.[132] Releases of arctic foxes on uninhabited Aleutian islands were deadly to ground-nesting birds—"waterfowl, shorebirds, ptarmigan, and burrow-nesting seabirds," as was the accidental invasion by Norway rats from ships in World War II.[133] Barrier islands along the Atlantic and Gulf coasts have been greatly harmed by exotic species, including dogs, cats, rats, nutria, sheep, cattle, horses, pigs, and goats.[134]

Wound 6: Poisoning of Land, Air, Water, and Wildlife

Causes: Farms, feedlots, mines, factories, smelters, power plants, agricultural and public-health biocides, automobiles, oil pipelines and tankers, and urban areas have spread heavy metals, toxic wastes, and chemicals in the air, land, and water, harming species and ecosystems.

Agriculture

Irrigation causes the buildup of toxic minerals such as selenium in wetlands. For over one hundred years these toxic concentrations in the arid West have killed tens of thousands of migrating waterfowl and shorebirds. Irrigated agriculture also leads to elevated selenium concentrations in the Colorado River system where it is a culprit in the imperilment of native suckers, chubs, and squawfish.[135]

Status and Trends reports that "pesticides, primarily from agriculture, were estimated to have caused the deaths of 6–14 million of the 141 million fish that died annually in fish kills from 1977 to 1987, and 672 million birds are directly exposed to high concentrations of pesticides each year in the United States; 67 million of these birds die.[136]

Atrazine, a widely used agricultural herbicide (60 million pounds are used annually in United States), is a major endocrine disrupter in amphibians. Studies are showing that it may be partly responsible for the decline of leopard frogs.[137]

Forestry

Concentrations of DDT and other biocides remain in North American ecosystems from their heavy use in forestry and agriculture in the 1950s and 1960s. Between 1955 and 1963, for example, 1.139 million pounds of DDT were sprayed on 1.18 million acres of northern New Mexico's Santa Fe and Carson National Forests.[138] Similarly heavy use occurred on other national forests. Bald eagles, ospreys, brown pelicans, and other bird species suffered serious declines because of eggshell thinning caused by DDT. Spraying forests with DDT for spruce budworms led to losses of fish and benthic invertebrates in streams.[139]

Mining and Oil Extraction

Hardrock mining releases a witch's brew of toxic metals and byproducts into ecosystems throughout North America. According to *Status and Trends*, "No information on the cumulative effects of metals mining and refining on biota exists, but 557,650 abandoned mines in the United States are estimated to have contaminated 728 square kilometers [180,000 acres] of lakes and reservoirs and 19,000 kilometers [11,800 miles] of streams and rivers."[140]

Mercury from the amalgamation process for extracting gold and silver has contaminated many streams and terrestrial areas in the West, especially on both slopes of the Sierra Nevada.[141] The use of sodium cyanide for mineral extraction has led to "massive and well-documented fish kills" and to major waterfowl dieoffs in leach ponds.[142] Nineteenth-century placer and hydraulic mining devastated many streams in the mountain West. These toxics still impact high country streams throughout the West.

Air pollution (especially from smelters) probably caused the extirpation of the Tarahumara frog from Arizona.[143]

Acid mine drainage from coal mining has hammered the biological diversity of streams on the Cumberland Plateau of Kentucky and Tennessee. Of the once highly diverse mussel fauna there, 22 (or 23 percent of the total number of species) are now extinct or endangered. Fish and other invertebrates have been similarly harmed.[144]

Oil spills cause notoriously large losses of seabirds, mammals, and fish. The wreck of the *Exxon Valdez* killed as many as 5,500 sea otters and 250,000 seabirds.[145] The Alaskan Arctic is being heavily exploited for oil, with consequent air, land, and water pollution.

Industry

Coal-fired power-plant emissions of sulfur dioxide lead to acid precipitation downwind. This particularly harms areas without limestone (which buffers acidity) in the Appalachians, Adirondacks, Canadian Shield, Sierra Nevada, Rocky Mountains, Cascades, Ozarks, mid-Atlantic coastal plain, and Florida. Mollusks, mayflies, zooplankton, and many fishes are highly vulnerable to acidified waters. Christopher Schmitt of the U.S. Geological Survey provides a sweeping and depressing overview of the impacts of acid precipitation on biological diversity in *Status and Trends*. Trout and other fish species have been eliminated from lakes and streams from West Virginia to New England. This loss of fish has harmed ospreys, loons, kingfishers, mergansers, and other fish-eating ducks. Depression of benthic invertebrates may harm black ducks. Insectivorous birds suffer eggshell thinning because of the reduced availability of soil calcium to the insects on which they feed. Red spruce in the Appalachians is damaged by acid precipitation as well.[146] Two hundred lakes in the high country of the Adirondacks have lost all fish because of acid precipitation.[147]

Power plants also produce toxic heavy metals that harm fish and other wildlife.[148]

The blue pike became extinct in Lake Erie around 1974 partly because of pollution. It was once extremely abundant, producing over a billion pounds commercially caught between 1885 and 1962.[149]

The North American Arctic is part of the Arctic sink for air pollution from industrial nations. These pollutants have entered food chains and are being concentrated in animals at the top of the food chains. Pollution has also led to the thinning of the ozone layer over northern North America. Excessive ultraviolet radiation is harming plants and animals there.[150]

Marine Litter

According to *Status and Trends*, "waterborne litter entangles wildlife and masquerades as a food source, smothers beaches and bottom-growing plants, and provides a surface for colonizing small organisms that travel on marine debris to distant shores." Most sea turtle species, over 15 percent of seabird species, and over 25 percent of marine mammal species are known to get entangled in nets and other debris floating in the oceans. Furthermore, sea turtles eat plastic bags, thinking they are jellyfish, and birds eat plastic pellets, thinking they are fish eggs. Such ingestion can be deadly.[151]

Wound 7: Global Climate Change

Causes: Since the beginning of the industrial era, air pollution from cars, power plants, smelters; carbon dioxide releases from logging; and other human activities have increased the percentage of carbon dioxide, methane, and other greenhouse gases, leading to rises in the sea level, and changes in temperature and precipitation.

Climate experts Stephen Schneider and Terry Root write in *Status and Trends*, "In summary, no clear physical objection or direct empirical evidence has contradicted the consensus of scientists that the world is warming, nor has evidence emerged to contradict the substantial probability that temperatures will rise because of increases in greenhouse gases. . . . The consensus remains widespread that a global temperature increase of anywhere from 1°C to 5°C is reasonably probable in the next century."[152]

A full discussion of climate change and its widespread role in future extinctions is beyond the scope of this book. Schneider and Root's chapter on "Climate Change" in *Status and Trends*, cited in the previous paragraph, provides a good overview of the problem. Climate change will have a variety of impacts leading to increased extinctions. First, with sea-level rise, coastal habitats will be lost. All of the Florida Everglades, for example, may soon be under seawater. Second, changing temperatures and precipitation patterns will cause species to shift their ranges. Third, changes will have direct effects on certain species. These effects will be multiplied because modern civilization and high human populations have fragmented natural habitat, thus creating barriers to range shifts in response to climate change.

Climate change could hit reptiles and amphibians particularly hard because they disperse much more slowly than do birds and mammals and are even more hampered by habitat fragmentation.[153] Moreover, some reptiles, especially turtles, have their sex determined by temperature while they are in the egg. Some scientists predict that some "populations of turtles will regularly produce only females within 50 years."[154]

Other animals that will suffer earliest from "climate change are those in which populations are fairly small and limited to isolated habitats."[155] Even if trees shift their range in response to climate change while dying out in their previous range, it will take decades for them to become mature in their new range. Species dependent on mature trees, such as the red-cockaded woodpecker, may go extinct in the meantime. Moreover, "animals limited by vegetation will be able to expand their ranges only as rapidly as the vegetation changes. Consequently, the potential for significant disruption among communities is high. For instance, some animals may no longer be able to coexist because an invading species disrupts the balance between competing species or between predator and prey."[156]

Schneider and Root further warn that "it seems unlikely that all of the migrating species that survived the Ice Age would be able to safely reach refuges after migrating across freeways, agricultural zones, industrial parks, military bases, and cities of the twenty-first century. An even further complication arises with the imposition of the direct effects of changes in CO_2, which can change terrestrial and marine primary productivity as well as alter the competitive relations among photosynthesizing organisms."[157]

Climate change is expected to cause the most warming in Arctic areas.[158] Walrus and polar bear could lose habitat as pack ice melts away from Arctic shores. Permafrost could melt, pumping sequestered methane into the air, which will ratchet up the greenhouse effect. And so, the most pristine part of North America could become the hardest hit by climate change.

PART II

GOOD NEWS

The absence of top predators appears to lead inexorably
to ecosystem simplification accompanied by a rush of
extinctions.
—JOHN TERBORGH ET AL.

If you are still with me, you've slogged through a depressing, almost suicidal morass of mass extinction and ecological wounds. You may feel
battered and bloodied and damn near extinct yourself. Leopold's ecological education cuts with an awful sharpness. Even he did not know how
deep the wounds have been cut and how much they have bled—ecological wounds and psychological wounds alike.

The good news is this: Just as modern biological and historical
research has shown us clearly the ecological wounds of a mass extinction, so it can teach us how we might become ecological doctors and
heal those wounds by applying a few relatively simple principles to the
practice of conservation. Reed Noss is right. We do have the opportunity to halt a mass extinction.

We have two advantages over past generations of conservationists.
First, we understand that the overarching problem is human-caused
mass extinction. That understanding is the first and most crucial step to
solve the problem. Part 1 of *Rewilding North America* surveyed the topic
in sobering detail. We conservationists must set ourselves to the task of
halting the mass extinction we humans are causing. Second, we have the
knowledge to halt the mass extinction by (1) selecting, designing, and

establishing new protected areas; and (2) undertaking ecological restoration. That scientific and conservation knowledge is the stuff of Part 2.

Part 2 unfolds as follows:

Chapter 7, "Conservation Biology"—The lines of recent scientific inquiry—extinction dynamics, island biogeography, metapopulation theory, natural disturbance regimes, the ecological importance of large carnivores, and ecological restoration—that set the stage for rewilding and a North American Wildlands Network.

Chapter 8, "Rewilding North America"—Theory and practice of rewilding and how it leads to a North American Wildlands Network along a minimum of Four Continental MegaLinkages, with protected and restored populations of wolves, mountain lions, and other large native carnivores.

Chapter 9, "Selecting and Designing Protected Areas: The Early Days"—An overview of how recreational and ecological approaches to protected area selection and design have evolved over more than a hundred years.

Chapter 10, "Selecting and Designing Protected Areas: The Past Two Decades"—How recreational and ecological approaches to protected area selection and design have come together as wildlands networks—connected webs of protected areas.

Chapter 11, "The Importance of Wilderness Areas"—Why traditional protected areas—wilderness areas and national parks—are still the basic building blocks for a wildlands network and for protecting nature.

CHAPTER 7

Conservation Biology

The Dilemma

Two scenes, only months apart:

October 31, 1994. President Bill Clinton lifts his pen from the California Desert Protection Act, and the size of the National Wilderness Preservation System soars to over 100 million acres, nearly half of which is outside Alaska, and the size of the national park system jumps to almost 90 million acres, over one-third outside Alaska.[1] American wilderness areas and national parks—the world's finest protected-areas system—are a legacy of citizen conservationists from Barrow to Key West, of courageous federal agency employees, and of farsighted elected officials. One hundred million acres is more than I thought we would ever protect when I enlisted in the wilderness wars a third of a century ago.

February 14, 1995. The *New York Times* reports on a National Biological Service (now the Biological Resources Discipline within the U. S. Geological Survey) study done by three distinguished biologists. Reed Noss, editor of the widely cited scientific journal *Conservation Biology* and one of the report's authors, said, "We're not just losing single species here and there, we're losing entire assemblages of species and their habitats."[2] The comprehensive review shows that ecosystems covering—or formerly covering—half the area of the forty-eight contiguous states are endangered or threatened. The longleaf pine ecosystem, for example, once the dominant vegetation of the coastal plain from Virginia to Texas and covering more than 60 million acres, remains only in dabs and scraps making up less than 2 percent of its original sprawl. Ninety-nine percent of the native grassland of California has been lost. There has been a 90 percent loss of riparian forest ecosystems in Arizona and New Mexico. Of the various natural ecosystem types in the United States, fifty-eight have declined by 85 percent or more and thirty-eight by 70 to 84 percent.[3]

The dissonance between these two events is as jarring as chain saws in the forest, dirt bikes in the desert, the exploding of harpoons in the polar sea. How have we lost so much while we have protected so much—or at least what *seems* so much? This is the question biologists and conservationists alike were asking at the end of the twentieth century. Answers have rolled in from the applied science of conservation biology.

Ecological concerns—including protecting habitat for rare and imperiled species and protecting representative examples of all ecosystems—have long been at least minor goals in wilderness area and national park advocacy in the United States. In the 1920s and 1930s, the Ecological Society of America and the American Society of Mammalogists developed proposals for ecological reserves on the public lands. The eminent ecologist Victor Shelford was an early backer of protected wildlands big enough to sustain populations of large carnivores.[4] At the Sierra Club/Wilderness Society biennial wilderness conferences held from 1949 to 1973, scientists and others gave ecological justifications for wilderness preservation and discussed the scientific values of wilderness areas and national parks.[5]

Some of this country's greatest conservationists have been scientists, too. Two of the many hats John Muir wore were those of a botanist and a geologist. Aldo Leopold was a pioneer in ecology and wildlife management, and he saw wilderness areas as ecological baselines ("a picture of how healthy land maintains itself as an organism"[6]), as habitat for large carnivores, and as a means to protect representative ecosystems.[7] Wilderness Society founder Bob Marshall had a Ph.D. in plant physiology and explored the unmapped Brooks Range in Alaska seventy-five years ago not just for adventure, but to study tree growth in that extreme climate. Olaus Murie, president of The Wilderness Society in the 1950s and early 1960s, was an early wildlife ecologist and one of the first to study and defend the wolf.

In a practical way, however, aesthetic (scenic beauty), recreational (solitude and self-sufficiency), and utilitarian (watershed protection) arguments have dominated advocacy for wilderness areas, as well as for other protected areas. These values have had more influence on what areas were protected than have ecological reasons (although some conservation biologists and others have overstated this, and it is important to understand that this bias comes more from the Forest Service and other agencies than from citizen conservationists).[8]

In the last decade, however, ecological concerns have risen to the top in the conservation movement.[9] Scientists, particularly from the new discipline of conservation biology, have become more prominent in conservation groups. This is most obvious in the Wildlands Project, Wildlife Conservation Society, World Wildlife Fund, and The Nature Conservancy, but other groups, such as The Wilderness Society, Defenders of Wildlife, Endangered Species Coalition, American Lands, and Sierra Club, in their current campaigns to protect endangered species, wetlands, roadless areas, and ancient forests, have likewise emphasized ecological values. Smaller local and regional groups, such the Sky Islands Alliance, Southern Rockies Ecosystem Project, and Northwest Ecosystem Alliance, rely on ecological arguments. Hard-hitting groups like the Biodiversity Legal Foundation, Center for Biological Diversity, Forest Guardians, and Wildlaw have filed science-based lawsuits and appeals to protect endangered species and their habitats. More often than not, conservationists now defend wild places and wild things more for ecological reasons than for recreational and aesthetic reasons (although the latter remain valid and important). Wilderness protection groups such as the New Mexico Wilderness Alliance have adopted ecological criteria to guide their selection and design of proposed wilderness areas.[10] Conservation biologists have gained a foothold and an influence within federal and state land and wildlife management agencies, sometimes even high positions. Mike Dombeck, a biologist who became chief of the Forest Service in the last years of the Clinton administration, is an outstanding example.

Conservation Biology

Since 1991, the Wildlands Project and *Wild Earth* magazine have worked to bring together citizen conservationists and conservation biologists to craft an evolved idea of conservation and to apply science to the design and stewardship of protected areas.[11] This ecological renaissance in conservation has come about largely because of new research and theory in several branches of biology. Looking back over our shoulders, we see that six interrelated lines of scientific inquiry have led to the sort of wildlands networks now being proposed by the Wildlands Project and other conservation groups. They are also the basis for the North American Wildlands Network I propose in these pages. The six lines of inquiry are extinction dynamics, island biogeography, metapopulation theory, natural disturbance ecology, large carnivore ecology, and landscape-scale ecological restoration. Out of the application of these comes the conservation approach of *rewilding*, the focus of the rest of this book.

Extinction Dynamics

Ecological values came to the fore when we became aware of the shrill fury of the extinction crisis. Knowledge that we were living in—*and causing*—the greatest mass extinction since the end of the dinosaurs shook the daylights out of both biology and conservation. Biology could no longer be at arm's length from activism, if scientists wished their research subjects to survive. Conservation could no longer be about protecting outdoor museums and art galleries, and setting aside backpacking parks and open-air zoos. Biologists and conservationists all began to understand that species can not be brought back from the brink of extinction one by one. Nature reserves have to protect entire ecosystems, guarding the flow and dance of evolution. We have finally learned that wilderness is the arena of evolution.[12]

A new branch of applied biology was launched out of the scientific concern about mass extinction. "Conservation biology," population biologist Michael Soulé declared in 1985, "differs from most other biological sciences in one important way: it is often a crisis discipline. Its relation to biology, particularly ecology, is analogous to that of surgery to physiology and war to political science."[13]

Conservation biology came alive in September 1978, when Michael Soulé organized the first conference on conservation biology in San Diego. Following the conference was the 1980 publication of the anthology, *Conservation Biology: An Evolutionary-Ecological Perspective*, edited by Michael Soulé and Bruce Wilcox. The book, with contributions from leading biologists, focused on the extinction crisis through the lens of island biogeography. Contributors turned their attention to "the optimal design of nature reserves"—"the most valuable weapon in our conservation arsenal," according to Soulé and Wilcox.[14] A key question was: Why hadn't national parks, wilderness areas, and other reserves prevented the extinction crisis? Flowing from that question was another: How could reserves be better designed and managed in the future to shield biological diversity?

Soulé organized a second conservation biology conference at the University of Michigan in May 1985, the outcome of which included the organization of the Society for Conservation Biology, the Society's journal, *Conservation Biology*, and a new anthology edited by Soulé, *Conservation Biology: The Science of Scarcity and Diversity*.[15]

Island Biogeography

Conservation biologists first drew on a young, vigorous field of population biology called *island biogeography* for insights. In the 1960s, E. O. Wilson and Robert MacArthur studied colonization and extinction rates in oceanic islands like the Hawaiian chain. They hoped to craft a mathematical formula for the number of species that an island can hold, based on factors such as the island's size and its distance from the mainland.[16]

Soon after MacArthur and Wilson crafted their theory of island biogeography, Jared Diamond, John Terborgh, and Michael Soulé applied island biogeography to *land-bridge* islands.[17] Land-bridge islands are different from oceanic islands, which have never been part of the continents. Hawaii, for example, is a string of volcanic peaks rising from the sea floor to thousands of feet above the waves. Any plants or animals had to get there from somewhere else—by flying, blowing, or floating across several thousand miles of open ocean.

However, land-bridge (or continental) islands, like Borneo or Vancouver or Ireland, were once parts of nearby continents. When the glaciers melted ten thousand to eighteen thousand years ago and the sea level rose some 400 feet, these high spots were cut off from the rest of the continents and became islands. Over the years, land-bridge islands invariably lose species of plants and animals that remain on their parent continents, a process called *faunal relaxation*.[18] Island biogeographers developed mathematical formulas for the rate of species loss and for future colonization, and to determine whether equilibrium of the number of species would someday be reached.

Certain generalities leaped out at the researchers. The first species to vanish from land-bridge islands are the big guys. Tigers. Rhinos. Bears. The larger the island, the slower the rate at which species disappear. The farther an island is from the mainland, the more species it loses; the closer, the fewer. An isolated island loses more species than does one in an archipelago.

Closely tied to island biogeography is the *species-area relationship*, discussed in chapter 4. In 1979, Michael Soulé and his students Bruce Wilcox and Claire Holtby used the species-area relationship to predict the loss of large mammals in East African reserves.[19]

Usable habitat also can be reduced by fragmentation of forest ecosystems. Ornithologists have become increasingly alarmed by the role of forest fragmentation in the decline of songbirds. For years, it has been known that many warblers, flycatchers, vireos, thrushes, and other songbirds have been declining in the more fragmented parts of the central and eastern United States and Canada. These *Neotropical migrants* winter in Central America and Mexico but fly north in the spring to take advantage of the long days and plentiful insects for breeding and for rearing young. Their decline was first blamed on destruction of their winter habitat in the tropics. Research later showed that a large piece of the puzzle was fragmentation of their forest habitat in North America. Many of the Neotropical migrants need interior forests for habitat. This interior forest is especially important for nesting because it protects against nest parasitism.

The brown-headed cowbird is a species hard to love. Formerly a denizen of the plains and prairies, where it followed herds of bison and elk to scoop up insects in their wake (it was known as the *buffalo bird*), the cowbird spread east with the clearing of the great eastern forest and with the growing number of cattle in settlements. The cowbird is a nest parasite—it lays its eggs in the nests of other birds and leaves them to be hatched and raised by the unknowing builders of the nest. Cowbird eggs generally hatch sooner than do those of warblers, vireos, and other songbirds. The young cowbird often pushes the other eggs out of the nest, and the poor little warbler parents work themselves to a frazzle feeding the big, ugly, demanding cowbird chick.

Songbirds need interior forest habitat for nesting partly because brown-headed cowbirds will usually venture only a few hundred yards into a forest. But when road corridors, power-line rights-of-way, clearcuts, housing developments, and the like break up a forest, the interior forest habitat is greatly reduced or eliminated, allowing songbirds no refuge from cowbird brood parasitism.[20] In other words, these edge effects reduce the effective size of the remaining forest patches. Martha Groom and Nathan Schumaker write, "As habitat patches become smaller and are increasingly surrounded by habitats favorable to competitors, predators, and parasites, the quality of the habitat fragment decreases for interior species."[21]

In 1985, as Soulé and other top biologists were forming the Society for Conservation Biology, University of Michigan ecologist William Newmark (now with the Utah Museum of Natural History) looked at a map of the western United States and Canada and realized that our national parks were islands. As the sea of settlement and logging had swept over North America, national parks had become islands of ecological integrity surrounded by human-dominated lands. Did island biogeography apply?

Newmark found that the smaller the national park and the more isolated it was from other wildlands, the more species it had lost. The first species to go had been the large, wide-ranging critters—such as lynx, wolverine, and grizzly bear. Relaxation had occurred, *and was still occurring*. Newmark predicted that all national parks would continue to lose species (as Soulé had previously predicted for East African reserves). "Without active intervention by park managers, it is quite likely that a loss of mammalian species will continue as western North American parks become increasingly insularized."[22] Even Yellowstone National Park is not big enough to maintain viable populations of all the large wide-ranging mammals native to it. Only the total area of the connected complex of national parks in the Canadian Rockies is substantial enough to ensure their survival.

Metapopulation Theory

While Newmark was applying island biogeography to national parks, Reed Noss and Larry Harris at the University of Florida were using the *metapopulation* concept to design reserves for the Florida panther, an endangered subspecies, and the Florida black bear, a threatened subspecies. According to Andy Dobson, a "metapopulation can be defined as a collection of subpopulations of the same species, each of which occupies a separate patch of a subdivided habitat."[23]

A small isolated population of bears or panthers faces all sorts of genetic weirdness—inbreeding depression causes a chronic loss of fitness; genetic drift causes progressive loss of genetic variation; and natural selection becomes less effective because of the previous two.[24]

Furthermore, a small population is more vulnerable than is a large one to local extinction (*winking out*, in ecological jargon). For example, weather extremes, an exotic predator, or reproductive chance (few females born) can cause a local extinction more readily in a small population—it simply has less margin for trouble. If those animals (now extinct) were isolated, their habitat cannot be recolonized by members of the species from another population. But if habitats are connected so that animals can move between them—even if it's only one horny adolescent male every ten years—then inbreeding is usually avoided, and a habitat whose population winks out can be recolonized by dispersers from a nearby population.[25]

Bruce Wilcox and Dennis Murphy wrote in 1985 that "habitat fragmentation is the most serious threat to biological diversity and is the primary cause of the present extinction crisis."[26] Noss acted on their warning by designing a conceptual nature reserve system for Florida consisting of core reserves surrounded by buffer zones and linked by habitat corridors. Most of the core reserves were big chunks of existing federal land. In a paper presented to the 1986 Natural Areas Conference, Noss said, "The problems of habitat isolation that arise from fragmentation can be mitigated by connecting natural areas by corridors or zones of suitable habitat."[27] In other words, protecting and restoring connective habitat in a fragmented landscape can mitigate the problem of island-like nature reserves. (I used to give a slide show on island biogeography and wildlands network design a couple of dozen times a year. The most common response I got was, "Why did it take so long to figure out something so obvious?") From the Noss proposal, we can trace a new approach to protected area design that now dominates the field of nature reserve planning. At first, however, it was not recognized as such.

Florida's human population growth rate is one of the fastest in the nation. When the Noss proposal, calling for 60 percent of Florida to be protected in a nature reserve network, was first published in 1985, it was considered, well, impractical. Even laughable. However, over the next decade his visionary application of conservation biology was adapted and refined by the state of Florida. In 1994, the Florida Game and Fresh Water Fish Commission published a 239-page document, *Closing the Gaps in Florida's Wildlife Habitat Conservation System*. Using geographic information systems (GIS) computer mapping technology, *Closing the Gaps* identified Biodiversity Hot Spots for Florida. The study looked in detail at range occurrences and habitat needs for thirty-three sensitive species, from the Florida panther to the pine barrens treefrog, and at twenty-five thousand known locations of rare plants, animals, and natural communities. Existing conservation lands in Florida then covered 6.95 million acres. The hot spots—called Strategic Habitat Conservation Areas—encompassed an additional 4.82 million acres.[28] Florida began to work with private landowners to protect identified areas and appropriated $3.2 billion to purchase Strategic Habitat Conservation Areas and other conservation lands by the year 2000—a program called Preservation 2000. Where it was once a new doctoral student's "pie in the sky," a conservation-biology-based reserve system is now the master plan for land protection in Florida. So mainstream was this program that Republican Jeb Bush, elected governor of Florida in 1998, campaigned on appropriating additional money after Preservation 2000 ran its course. Unfortunately, Bush's program, called Florida Forever, has targeted more land for urban parks and "less toward wildlands with higher biodiversity values";[29] even so, that Bush touts a Preservation 2000 successor is testament to the program's popularity.

Natural Disturbance Ecology

Another piece in conservation biology's big-picture puzzle is the importance of natural disturbances. Caribbean forests are adapted to periodic
hurricanes and eastern temperate North American forests to tornadoes,
blowdowns, and ice storms. Many plant communities in North America
evolved with wildfire. Floods are crucial to establishment of new trees in
riparian forests. Carnivores exercise *top-down regulation* of prey species
numbers and behaviors. Such disturbances help maintain the natural
mosaic of landscapes and natural vegetation types. If a wildland is too
small and isolated, a disturbance can affect or perturb all of it, thus eliminating a habitat type for a long time. To be viable, habitats must be large
enough to absorb major natural disturbances (types of *stochastic events*). As
early as 1978, ecologists S. T. A. Pickett and J. N. Thompson argued that
nature reserves needed to be big enough for natural disturbance regimes.
They termed this a *minimum dynamic area.*[30] When Yellowstone burned
in 1988, there was a great hue and cry over the imagined devastation, but
researchers have found that the fire was natural and beneficial. Because
Yellowstone National Park covers 2 million acres and is abutted by several million acres more of national forest wilderness areas, the extensive
fires affected only a portion of the total reserve area and were well within
the bounds of historical natural disturbance.

Things did not turn out so well when The Nature Conservancy's
Cathedral Pines Preserve in Connecticut was hammered by tornadoes in
1989. In this tiny patch of remnant old-growth white pine forest (some
trees were 150 feet tall), 70 percent of the trees were knocked flat, devastating the entire forest patch. Had the tornadoes ripped through an
old-growth forest of hundreds of thousands of acres, they instead would
have played a positive role, by opening up small sections to new forest
growth.

Large Carnivore Ecology

While metapopulation dynamics and island biogeography theory were
being applied to conservation area design, biologists were beginning to
acknowledge the worth of large carnivores to all sorts of ecosystems.
Before, scientists tended to see wolves and jaguars as somewhat unimportant species perched on top of the food chain (though Aldo Leopold,
prescient as ever, recognized their keystone role in the 1940s[31]). They
had little influence on the overall functioning of the natural system,
biologists thought.

Recent field research, however, shows that ecosystem integrity is often dependent on the functional presence of large carnivores. John Terborgh of Duke University (in my mind, the dean of tropical ecology) has studied the ecological effects of eliminating large carnivores (jaguars, pumas, and harpy eagles) from tropical forests. He tells us that big cats and eagles are major regulators of prey species numbers—the opposite of the once-upon-a-time ecological orthodoxy that saw them as unimportant. He has also found that the removal or population decline of large carnivores can alter plant species composition, particularly the balance between large- and small-seeded plants, due to increased seed and seedling predation by superabundant herbivores that are normally regulated by large carnivores. This is called *top-down regulation*.[32] Terborgh and his coauthors in *Continental Conservation* write, "'Top-down' means that species occupying the highest trophic level (top carnivores) exert a controlling influence on species at the next lower level (their prey) and so forth down the trophic ladder."[33]

In contrast, *bottom-up regulation* is driven by energy moving up the food web (*trophic levels*) from plants to herbivores to carnivores. Although bottom-up regulation is a part of the big picture, those wildlife managers who stress it may be influenced by political considerations to keep "carnivore numbers artificially low or eliminate them altogether."[34] Top-down or bottom-up, however, is not an either-or situation, but a both-and, as David Brower liked to say. Brian Miller, a conservation biologist at the Denver Zoo and a fellow of The Rewilding Institute, and his colleagues point out that "forces flow in both directions simultaneously and interact while doing so."[35] Because top-down regulation has been so slighted by wildlife managers in the past, we now need to appreciate and celebrate its proper role in maintaining and restoring ecosystem health.

Chapter 3 in *Continental Conservation*, by Terborgh and other top carnivore biologists, is the authoritative summary of the ecological importance of wolves, big cats, and other carnivores.[36] Terborgh and his fellow researchers recently discussed a classic example of top-down regulation in *Science*.[37] In 2001, Brian Miller and his Wildlands Project colleagues offered an up-to-date summary of the evidence in *Endangered Species Update*.[38]

There are "two fundamentally different ways" in which the consequences of the loss of top-down regulation occur: competitive exclusion and trophic cascades.[39]

Competitive exclusion: Through predation, carnivores can moderate competition among similar species so that more species are able to use a certain habitat. On the other hand, when freed from control by its predators, one species in a guild of species may be able to outcompete and thus eliminate the others. As Brian Miller and company write, "Removing the predator will dissolve the ecological boundaries that check competition."[40]

Trophic cascades: In top-down regulation, different trophic levels are limited by the next level up. For example, in a simple system of three trophic levels—plants, herbivores, and carnivores—plants are limited by herbivores, which are limited by predators.[41] A classic example of a trophic cascade has been described from years of research on the relationship between wolves, moose, and balsam fir on Isle Royale National Park in Lake Superior. When the wolf population is low, growth in the firs is depressed because of heavy browsing by moose.[42]

Michael Soulé sees trophic cascades, when top-down regulation of ecosystems is truncated by the loss of large carnivores, playing out in four ways:

1. Numerical release of prey species. Predators can control population growth of prey species. When big hunters disappear, their prey species may boom in numbers and degrade their habitat.
2. Behavioral release of prey species. In the presence of their predators, prey species wisely behave timidly. When large carnivores disappear, prey species may act more boldly and hence cause harm to their habitat.
3. Numerical release of mesocarnivores. Populations of smaller carnivores are often held in check by larger carnivores. When large carnivores disappear, smaller predators may have population explosions, thereby increasing their predation on other species. Soulé calls this phenomenon, midsized predators multiplying in the absence of large predators, *mesopredator release*.
4. Behavioral release of mesocarnivores. Smaller carnivores are very careful when larger carnivores are out and about. In the absence of large carnivores, smaller carnivores may act more boldly and prey more heavily on vulnerable species.[43]

The following well-researched examples show these kinds of effects. Note that the elimination of large carnivores often leads to more than one of the effects.

Coyotes were removed on a Texas grassland where twelve species of burrowing rodents coexisted. Twelve months later, only Ord's kangaroo rat was found. Without predation by coyotes, it was able to outcompete and exclude the other burrowing rodents.[44]

Sea otters were a top predator in the kelp forests of the North Pacific. When they were hunted out, sea urchin populations exploded. Because urchins graze on kelp, this critical habitat was largely lost and species using it—raptors, shorebirds, fish, and invertebrates—declined. With the return of sea otters under strict protection, sea urchin populations dropped and kelp forests began to recover—along with the diversity of species associated with kelp.[45] Recently, however, sea otter populations in the Aleutians have crashed again. This time the crash is not due to direct human hunting but to a small rogue pod of killer whales that have turned from their old prey to sea otters. Jim Estes and his team of researchers find evidence that the killer whales have been preying on increasingly smaller species for sixty years. They originally preyed on whales, which provided huge amounts of meat on the fluke. Human whalers took a heavy toll on the whales and their populations dropped like a rock. Killer whales then turned to the next largest source of meat—harbor seals. Their population crashed, so the killer whales went after Steller's sea lions. They, too, crashed, and now the killer whales are scarfing up the appetizer-sized sea otters.[46]

The eastern United States is overrun with white-tailed deer. Their predation on trees and herbs is preventing forest regeneration and altering species composition, according to University of Wisconsin botanists William Alverson, Don Waller, and Steve Solheim way back in 1988, but consistently reaffirmed since then.[47] If wolves and mountain lions were allowed to return, they would scatter deer from their concentrated wintering yards and reduce their numbers, thereby allowing the forest to return to more natural patterns of succession and species composition.

With the extermination of wolves and the near extermination of mountain lions sixty years ago in Yellowstone National Park, elk populations built up. Lacking their predators, elk grew lazy and lackadaisical, loafing in large herds in river meadows. Their behavior changed so much, it was hard to call them elk. Not only did they overgraze the grasslands, their browsing of willow shoots hampered beavers from reestablishing themselves in Yellowstone. However, with the recent reintroduction of wolves to Yellowstone, elk have become elk again. They're awake! They're moving. They're looking over their shoulders. They aren't loafing in big herds in open river valleys. Wolves have changed elk behavior for the better—to a more natural set of behaviors—and are thereby bringing integrity back to the ecosystem. For example, willows are again growing along streams, and researchers expect beavers to return. In addition, wolf-killed elk are a smorgasbord for many species, ranging from grizzly bears to insect-eating song-birds.[48] Between 1921 and 1999, there was "no significant recruitment of new stems into the aspen overstory" in Yellowstone. Oregon State University researchers William Ripple and Eric Larsen write, "We hypothesize that disturbance to predator/prey relationships, especially between wolves and elk, has been a major factor in [Yellowstone National Park] aspen decline."[49] Similarly, without wolves and grizzlies, moose in parts of the Greater Yellowstone Ecosystem are overbrowsing willows, which has led to a decline of Neotropical songbirds.[50]

Michael Soulé and his graduate students have shown that native songbirds survive in remnant coastal sage scrub habitats surrounded by suburban San Diego where there are coyotes; songbirds disappear when coyotes disappear. Coyotes eat foxes, opossums, and prowling house cats. Foxes, opossums, and cats eat quail, cactus wrens, thrashers, gnat-catchers, and their eggs and nestlings. When coyotes are present, the smaller predators skulk off to vacant lots and backyards, and the native scrub birds breathe a sigh of relief.[51]

Likewise, in the East, David Wilcove has found that songbirds are victims of the extirpation of wolves and cougars. As we have seen, the population decline of songbirds because of forest fragmentation is well documented, but Wilcove has shown that songbird declines are partly due to the absence of large carnivores in the East. Cougars and gray wolves do not eat warblers or their eggs, but raccoons, foxes, skunks, and opossums do, and the cougars and wolves eat these midsize predators. When the big guys were hunted out, the populations of the middling guys shot up—with dire results for the birds.[52]

Filling of Venezuela's Lago Guri reservoir behind a huge hydroelec-tric dam inadvertently started one of today's most important ecological experiments. The water covered an area of formerly hilly rain forest 72 miles by 42 miles. For years, water surrounded islands ranging from tiny to over 2,500 acres. John Terborgh and his fellow researchers doc-umented swift changes in resident species. For the smaller islands (less than 25 acres), 75 to 90 percent of terrestrial vertebrate species disap-peared within seven years. What remained were hyperabundant popu-lations of a few species filling two roles: seed eaters and generalized herbivores.[53]

Without large predators (jaguar, puma, and harpy eagle), howler monkeys have shot up to more than ten times their typical densities on many islands. Iguana and leaf-cutter ant populations have also exploded. This Venezuelan rain forest has seventy species of trees in the canopy. But on the predator-free islands with these three species of herbivores cheek to jowl, five or fewer tree species are able to reach the sapling stage: although the mature trees are able to reproduce, their seeds and seedlings are gobbled up by herbivores. These ecosystems "have spun out of control," and it "seems inevitable that most of the plant and animal species that survived the initial contraction in area will go extinct within one or two tree replacement cycles."[54]

As Terborgh and his coauthors point out, "Both top-down and bottom-up regulation can operate concurrently in the same system."[55] Nonetheless, solid research by top biologists has shown and continues to show that when large cats, canids, weasels, raptors, and other predators are removed from an ecosystem—marine, tropical, or temperate—the ecosystem is deeply wounded. *Continental Conservation* puts it bluntly: "The absence of top predators appears to lead inexorably to ecosystem simplification accompanied by a rush of extinctions."[56]

Brian Miller and his colleagues write, "In short, management policies based on reducing carnivore numbers have caused, and will continue to cause, severe harm to many other organisms."[57]

Moreover, the "removal of a top predator enables prey densities to increase such that epizootics may occur."[58] In other words, loss of carnivores can lead to devastating epidemics among their prey.

In an important 2003 article in *Conservation Biology*, Michael Soulé, Jim Estes, Joel Berger, and Carlos Martinez del Rio propose that top carnivores and other "highly interactive species" need to be present in an ecosystem in "ecologically effective densities." The point at which such species fall below the densities needed to regulate their ecosystem is called the "breakpoint." For example, there is a breakpoint in sea otter density after which otters can no longer control the sea urchins overgrazing the kelp community, or, as Soulé and company write, "Abrupt phase shifts between kelp-dominated and deforested states thus occur with changing abundance of sea otters." The breakpoint may vary for the same species depending on the presence of other predators or different ecological conditions, or "ecological effective densities will depend on context: they are not the same everywhere and under all circumstances."[59]

Restoring large carnivores begins to heal ecosystems. It's that simple.

Wildlands Restoration

In chapters 5 and 6, I outlined the seven ecological wounds humans have caused and are causing in North America. Recognizing and understanding the damage we have done to wild nature and then organizing this knowledge into the seven ecological wounds allows us to take a more thorough and systematic approach for healing the wounds and, just possibly, to save ourselves through our action. The whole point of using the wound categories is to guide us to more effective protection and restoration of biological diversity. Just as it has in categorizing the wounds, the Wildlands Project has followed a medical model and has proposed various *therapies* to heal land wounds and illnesses.

A hallmark of recent conservation is ecological restoration. Unfortunately, much of what is called ecological restoration falls far short of the mark. Michael Soulé warns against "restoration" that seeks only to put back the process, but not the community. He writes that "it is technically possible to maintain ecological processes, including a high level of economically beneficial productivity, by replacing the hundreds of native plants, invertebrates and vertebrates with about 15 or 20 introduced, weedy species."[60] *Continental Conservation* cautions that "process and function are no substitute for species."[61] Without native species, the land is domesticated or feral, not wild. Unmanaged land without native species is not a wilderness, but a wasteland.

In setting goals for wildlands restoration, we must answer the question "the full range of native species and ecosystems when?" Dan Simberloff, a noted ecologist at the University of Tennessee, is the lead author for the chapter "Regional and Continental Restoration" in *Continental Conservation*. He and his coauthors explain that restoration can "never achieve an exact reproduction of a system" that existed at some previous time.[62] Instead, we should seek to put all the pieces (species) back into an ecosystem instead of trying to recreate a poorly understood ecosystem as it was at some arbitrary point before significant human disruption. Another argument for this approach is that ecosystems have been steadily changing since the retreat of the ice began eighteen thousand years ago.[63] To try to go back to AD 1500 would be trying to recreate ecosystems that probably would have changed by now even without the heavy hand of humans mucking things up.

Much restoration has focused on small sites—a patch of tallgrass prairie, a salt marsh, a suburban creek. These efforts are vital for protecting and recovering imperiled species with narrow habitat requirements, but we also need to practice restoration on a landscape level, for three reasons: (1) wide-ranging species require large areas; (2) ecological disturbance (such as fire) can only be restored in large areas; and (3) the "dynamic, nondeterministic character of natural communities requires restoration of large areas in order to promote the long-term viability and adaptability of populations and communities."[64]

Less than landscape-scale restoration produces "ecological museum pieces—single representatives of communities that, although present because of unusually large restoration and maintenance investments, do not exist in any ecologically meaningful way."[65] A medical analogy would be that of keeping a patient alive on life-support indefinitely and at great expense when there is no hope that she will ever be able to survive on her own.

Healing the Wounds: Goal-Setting

To rewild North America, we must have a vision that is bold, scientifically credible, practically achievable, and hopeful. The practically achievable part requires specific goals and action steps—organized to heal the specific wounds.

Although ecological restoration is essential for an overall conservation strategy, it is painfully clear that, in the twenty-first century, wildlands and wildlife will continue to be imperiled by human activities. A frontier approach to exploiting nature still rules in much of Canada, the United States, Mexico, and Central America. Restoration will come to naught if further wounding of the land is not stopped. Therefore, each of the seven healing-the-wounds goals is twofold: (1) to prevent additional wounding, and (2) to heal existing wounds. The following goals are adapted from the *New Mexico Highlands Wildlands Network Vision*.[66]

Goal 1: Permanent protection of extant native species from extinction or endangerment, and recovery of all species native to the continent except those already extinct.

Goal 2: Permanent protection of all habitat types from further degradation and loss, and restoration of degraded habitats.

Goal 3: Protection of the land from further fragmentation, and restoration of functional connectivity for all species native to the region.

Goal 4: Restoration and permanent protection of the functioning of ecological and evolutionary processes.

Goal 5: Prevention of the further spread of exotic species (including pathogens), and elimination or control of exotic species already present.

Goal 6: Prevention of the further introduction of ecologically harmful pollution into the region, and removal or containment of existing pollutants.

Goal 7: Management of landscapes and wildlife to provide opportunities for adaptation and adjustment to climate change.

These are heady goals. With nearly half a billion people living in North America (including Central America), they can be gained in the near term only in part or even in small part for much of the continent. They apply completely only to wildlands networks in regions still wild or suitable for major restoration.

Moreover, these goals are comprehensive and should be embraced in principle by the whole conservation movement and land managers. No one organization can tackle them all, but all who love nature should adopt them as overarching goals for twenty-first-century conservation. They must be carried out on local, regional, and continental scales.

Rewilding Focus

In the chapters that follow, rather than discuss in detail the comprehensive healing-the-wounds approach, I instead will focus on a specific piece of the conservation pie that is particularly essential to continental-scale conservation. This vital piece—called *rewilding*—is often overlooked in restoration ecology and biodiversity protection efforts. Rewilding as a conservation strategy is based on three key points: (1) healthy ecosystems need large carnivores, (2) large carnivores need big, wild roadless areas, and (3) most roadless areas are small and thus need to be linked. I will offer a vision for a North American Wildlands Network based on rewilding by using the most obvious and suitable wildlands to tie the network together from south to north and west to east.

This vision of an enduring wilderness coexisting alongside civilization is achievable in twenty years—if only we have the will. I choose a time span of twenty years because I believe we can reasonably plan twenty years into the future but beyond that we are limited in what we can foresee.

CHAPTER 8

Rewilding North America

Rewilding

The lesson from the science presented in chapter 7 is this: *Nature reserves must be big and connected.*

The six areas of recent ecological research—extinction dynamics, island biogeography, metapopulation theory, natural disturbance ecology, top-down regulation by large carnivores, and landscape-scale ecological restoration—are the foundation for all informed protected area design. They are brought together in the idea and scientific approach of *rewilding*, developed by Michael Soulé in the mid-1990s. Rewilding is "the scientific argument for restoring big wilderness based on the regulatory roles of large predators," according to Soulé and Reed Noss in their landmark 1998 article in *Wild Earth*, "Rewilding and Biodiversity."

> Three major scientific arguments constitute the rewilding argument and justify the emphasis on large predators. First, the structure, resilience, and diversity of ecosystems is often maintained by "top-down" ecological (trophic) interactions that are initiated by top predators. Second, wide-ranging predators usually require large cores of protected landscape for foraging, seasonal movements, and other needs; they justify bigness. Third, connectivity is also required because core reserves are typically not large enough in most regions; they must be linked to insure long-term viability of wide-ranging species....In short, the rewilding argument posits that large predators are often instrumental in maintaining the integrity of ecosystems. In turn, the large predators require extensive space and connectivity.[1]

If native large carnivores have been killed out of a region, their reintroduction and recovery is the heart of a conservation strategy. Wolves, cougars, lynx, wolverines, grizzly and black bears, jaguars, sea otters, and other top carnivores need to be restored throughout North America in ecologically effective densities in their natural ranges where suitable habitat remains or can be restored. (Obviously, large areas of North America have been so modified by humans and support such large human populations or intensive agriculture that rewilding is not feasible.) Without the goal of rewilding for large areas with large carnivores, we are closing our eyes to what conservation really means—and demands. Disney cinematographer Lois Crisler, after years of filming wolves in the Arctic, wrote, "Wilderness without animals is dead—dead scenery. Animals without wilderness are a closed book."[2]

Soulé and Noss "recognize three independent features that characterize contemporary rewilding: (1) large, strictly protected core reserves (the wild), (2) connectivity, and (3) keystone species."

In shorthand, these are "the three C's: Cores, Corridors, and Carnivores."[3]

Although Soulé and Noss state, "Our principal premise is that rewilding is a critical step in restoring self-regulating land communities," they claim two nonscientific justifications: (1) "the ethical issue of human responsibility," and (2) "the subjective, emotional essence of 'the wild' or wilderness. Wilderness is hardly 'wild' where top carnivores, such as cougars, jaguars, wolves, wolverines, grizzlies, or black bears have been extirpated. Without these components, nature seems somehow incomplete, truncated, overly tame. Human opportunities to attain humility are reduced."[4]

Healing-the-wounds ecological restoration and rewilding are tightly linked. When we kill off big cats, wolves, and other wild hunters, we lose not only prominent species, but also the key ecological and evolutionary process of top-down regulation. Restoring large carnivores is essential for landscape-level ecological restoration, as is the restoration of other highly interactive species, and natural processes such as fire and flood.

Because many conservation groups, scientists, and agencies are involved in small-scale restoration and local biodiversity protection, my emphasis is on rewilding as the means for landscape and continental restoration.[5]

Rewilding is a landmark for the wilderness conservation movement as well as for those primarily concerned with protecting biological diversity. Soulé and others have crafted the *scientific basis* for the need to protect and restore big wilderness-area complexes. Here science buttresses the wants and values of wilderness recreationists. Big wilderness areas are not only necessary for inspiration and a true wilderness experience,[6] they are necessary for the protection and restoration of ecological integrity and native species diversity.

Continental-Scale Conservation

The six lines of scientific inquiry discussed in chapter 7 give us guidance in our work. Our knowledge of the Sixth Extinction tells us what the problem is—the mass extinction of species caused by humans—and what our task is—to stop it. Island biogeography tells us that we can't practice successful conservation in isolated areas but rather that we must look at the whole landscape. Metapopulation theory further warns us that when an isolated, small population of wildlife blinks out, it is unlikely to be reestablished by dispersers from another population. Understanding the necessary role of large disturbance events (such as fire, windstorms, and flood) makes it clear that our goal must be big, self-regulating ecosystems. The role of large carnivores and other highly interactive species in top-down regulation of ecosystems tells us that we need wolves and big cats, and that they need vast, unroaded habitat. And ecological restoration argues that it is not enough to protect wild places—we need to restore their health as well.

Together, these six areas of research unmistakably warn us that to halt mass extinction and to have an enduring resource of wilderness we need to protect and restore sprawling wild landscapes with linked populations of keystone species, where natural ecological and evolutionary processes can roll on unhindered into wilderness-forever. In other words: *To practice serious conservation in North America, we must practice conservation on the scale of North America.*

The same holds true for other continents.

The North American Wildlands Network

I offer the following as a mission statement for continental-scale conservation: "To establish a North American Wildlands Network along Four Continental MegaLinkages—Pacific, Spine of the Continent, Atlantic, and Arctic-Boreal—that will provide secure core habitat and landscape permeability for ecologically effective populations of gray wolves, red wolves, mountain lions, lynx, jaguars, ocelots, grizzly bears, black bears, polar bears, wolverines, and other wide-ranging or highly interactive species in their native habitats." Real recovery of gray wolves and mountain lions, the leading partners in top-down regulation in temperate North America, demands a vision for the wolf and for the mountain lion.

A North American Wolf Vision

In 1600, wolves lived in North America from the high Arctic islands to just north of the Valley of Mexico, and from the Atlantic Ocean to the Pacific Ocean. Beginning with the earliest European settlements, colonists declared war against wolves. By the middle of the twentieth century, wolves were essentially extirpated from the United States and Mexico.

We now know that the fear of wolves was based on myths, and that wolves are a vital and necessary part of healthy, functioning North American ecosystems. With this new knowledge, tentative efforts have been made to restore wolves in the most out-of-the-way parts of temperate North America. However, these restoration efforts by the U.S. Fish and Wildlife Service endeavor only to recover small, geographically isolated populations encompassing a relatively insignificant proportion of their historic range. Furthermore, the Fish and Wildlife Service has no plans for restoring wolves to substantial areas of potentially suitable habitat (the southern Rocky Mountains, New England, and the Pacific Northwest, for example).

We call for the recovery of wolves across North America. Such recovery means

- Restoration of wolves in suitable habitat throughout their former range in North America, from the northern Sierra Madre Occidental in Mexico to the Canadian Rockies and Coast Range, and from the U.S. Pacific Northwest to the Upper Great Lakes and to upstate New York and New England.
- Restoration of potentially suitable habitats and crucial linkages between patches of suitable wolf habitat, where wolves are free to behave like wolves.
- Restoration of wolves in ecologically and evolutionarily effective populations so that they may fulfill their natural keystone role of ecosystem regulation, aiding the persistence of native flora and fauna.
- Restoration of wolves throughout this expanse, so that all wolf populations are connected by a continuum of functioning dispersal linkages.

In short, we envision the return of the wolf to its rightful place in North American wildlands, to a community where humans dwell with respect and tolerance for wild species.

A North American Mountain Lion Vision

In 1600, mountain lions (also called pumas, cougars, panthers) lived in North America from the southern edge of the boreal forest south into South America, and from the Atlantic Ocean to the Pacific Ocean. Beginning with the earliest European settlements, colonists declared war against mountain lions. By the beginning of the twentieth century, mountain lions were essentially extirpated from east of the Rocky Mountains in temperate North America. Continuing through the first half of the twentieth century, mountain lions were ruthlessly hunted in the West and in Mexico until their populations were heavily depleted.

We now know that the fear of mountain lions was based on myths, and that mountain lions are a vital and necessary part of healthy, functioning North American ecosystems. Mountain lions gained some protection during the last half of the twentieth century through the efforts of conservationists, ethical hunters, and progressive wildlife managers. Some fifty to one hundred Florida panthers hold on, now augmented genetically and numerically with the release of Texas mountain lions into their habitat. Mountain lions are back in small numbers in northern Minnesota, the Upper Peninsula of Michigan, and likely the Ozarks, but federal and state agencies have refused to undertake serious restoration efforts in the East.

We call for the conservation of mountain lions in the West and the recovery of mountain lions east of the Rockies. Such recovery means

- Restoration of mountain lions in suitable habitat throughout their former range in North America, from Florida up through the Appalachian Mountains to the Canadian Maritimes, from New England through Ontario to the Upper Great Lakes to the Rockies, from Texas across to Florida, and up through the Ozarks to the Upper Great Lakes.
- Restoration of potentially suitable habitats and crucial linkages between patches of suitable mountain lion habitat where mountain lions are free to behave like mountain lions.
- Restoration of mountain lions in ecologically and evolutionarily effective populations so that they may fulfill their natural keystone role of ecosystem regulation, aiding the persistence of native flora and fauna.
- Restoration of mountain lions throughout this expanse, so that all mountain lion populations are connected by a continuum of functioning dispersal linkages.
- Restoration of a tolerance and appreciation for the mountain lion among local and regional human populations.

In short, we envision the return of the mountain lion to its rightful place in North American wildlands, to a community where humans dwell with respect and tolerance for wild species.[7]

There are four key points in these recovery visions. First, wolf and mountain lion recovery means the presence of wolf packs and big cats in all suitable habitat that remains or can be restored in their former ranges in temperate North America, not just in a few remote areas. Today, wolves are radio collared, tracked, recaptured, and even killed if they show interest in livestock. Mountain lions are heavily hunted for "sport" and for killing livestock in every state and province in Mexico and the western United States and Canada, except for California, and even there they are killed if they behave too much like cats. Second, we need big areas where wolves and mountain lions are left alone and where public lands livestock grazing, if it is allowed at all, is compatible with large carnivores. In other words, management should not try to reshape wolves and cats into "wee, sleeket, cowran, tim'rous beastie[s]."[8] Third, wolves and mountain lions need to be present in large-enough populations that they exercise top-down regulation of their prey and smaller carnivores, not just in tiny populations where they are an insignificant force. And, fourth, wolves and mountain lions must be present across the landscape in suitable recovery areas so that they are not genetically isolated. Dispersing wolves must be able to safely travel from the central Idaho wilderness to the Oregon coast, from Durango to Arizona, from New Mexico to Yellowstone, and from Maine to the Adirondacks. In addition to wide-open connectivity throughout the western United States and Canada, mountain lions need to be able to safely travel from the Everglades up the Appalachians to the Canadian Maritimes and across to the Upper Great Lakes region and then to the Rockies.

These points are based on recent work by Michael Soulé and three leading carnivore biologists, Jim Estes, Joel Berger, and Carlos Martinez del Rio. Their 2003 article in *Conservation Biology*, "Ecological Effectiveness: Conservation Goals for Interactive Species," is a big step forward for conservation science and practice. They propose two goals for the "laws and policies that apply to the conservation of biodiversity":

> The first is the goal of geographic representation of interactions, which calls for extensive geographic persistence of highly interactive species. Conservation plans and objectives (design, management, and recovery) should provide for the maintenance, recovery, or restoration of species interactions in as many places as feasible, both within the historic range of

highly interactive species or in other sites where the consideration of climate change and other factors is appropriate.

The second goal concerns ecological effectiveness within
ecosystems, communities, or landscapes: Conservation plans
should contain a requirement for ecologically effective
population densities; these are densities that maintain critical
interactions and help ensure against ecosystem degradation.
This goal replaces the de facto nonecological practice of
requiring only the attainment of minimum viable populations.[9]

To move toward these wolf and mountain lion visions, we need a
vision for the landscape—their habitat.

How do we protect and restore connected habitat so that wolves,
mountain lions, and other wide-ranging species that do not prosper in
close proximity to humans have populations linked throughout North
America?

How do we do this in the simplest, most practical way?

In other words, what is the minimum required to rewild North
America? Aldo Leopold warned that the first rule of intelligent tinkering is to keep all the cogs and wheels.[10] For rewilding North America,
we need to find or restore some of the cogs and wheels we've already
tossed into the dust bin. We also need to redraw the lost blueprint of a
wild North America so we know how to put the cogs and wheels back
together again.

Rewilding on the Ground: Landscape Permeability

Continental planning for rewilding also tweaks the way we see connectivity and fragmentation on the land. For continental rewilding, the
classic model of core-corridor-core becomes general *landscape permeability* in which large core habitats are embedded. Peter Singleton and his
Forest Service colleagues considered landscape permeability for wolf,
lynx, grizzly, and wolverine in the state of Washington and in extreme
southern British Columbia. They explain the shift as follows:

> The early theoretical work in [the field of habitat fragmenta-
> tion] was largely based on island biogeography theory, which
> emphasized perceptions of "islands" of suitable habitat in a
> "hostile sea" of nonhabitat. Concepts of habitat corridors pro-
> viding linear connections through this "hostile sea" developed
> from the application of island biogeography theory to conser-
> vation problems. Several more recent discussions of this issue

have pointed out that these approaches focusing on "suitable" corridors through "hostile" landscapes may be overly simplistic, and have proposed that different conditions on the landscape create different levels of resistance to movement for different species. Landscapes between patches may encompass either habitats through which an animal can move easily or barriers that prevent or redirect movement. It is the composition and configuration of these characteristics that define the permeability of a landscape.[11]

Singleton and company define landscape permeability as "the quality of a heterogeneous land area [a landscape] to provide for passage of animals." They explain the shift in how they view the landscape as, "In contrast to focusing on the identification of corridors or connected habitat patches, the evaluation of landscape permeability should provide a broader measure of resistance to animal movement and give a consistent estimate of the relative potential for animal passage across entire landscapes."[12] In another publication, they explain that "the broader evaluation of landscape permeability provides an estimation of relative potential for animal passage across the entire landscape, including the identification of potential barriers to animal movement."[13]

Let me add a caveat: I believe the core-corridor (linkage) model applies in more fragmented regions and through barriers in a generally permeable landscape. I don't see landscape permeability as a replacement for cores and linkages; rather I see it as a complementary approach. Nor is it something entirely new. In 1992, for example, Reed Noss wrote that "multiple-use zones" could often serve a corridor function.[14]

Animal movements can be either *intraterritorial*, within a home range for daily or seasonal travel, or *interterritorial*, "long-distance dispersal or exploratory movements outside of an established home range." Intraterritorial movement affects "individual survival and reproduction." Interterritorial travel "influences the level of gene flow between groups (subpopulations) of animals, the ability of animal populations to become established in unoccupied suitable habitat, and other metapopulation functions."[15]

Certain species are more particular about permeability than others. Singleton and company explain:

> Some species, e.g., wolves and lynx, are able to move long distances through diverse habitats. For these species, maintaining landscape linkages that have relatively few landscape barriers but do not support breeding individuals may be adequate to

provide for movement between areas where populations of those species persist. However, other species (e.g., grizzly bears) have not been documented to make long distance movements through marginal habitat areas. For those species that are not inclined to make long-distance interterritorial movements, maintaining breeding habitat for at least a few individuals in the linkage area may be necessary to achieve a functional linkage between blocks of habitat supporting larger groups of animals.[16]

For these reasons and because different species have different habitat needs for travel, evaluating landscape permeability needs to be on a species by species basis—which is what Singleton and his fellow researchers do in their study.[17]

Areas "of reduced landscape permeability between habitat concentrations" are called "fracture zones."[18] Fracture zones can be relatively small such as an interstate highway and associated development between wild mountain ranges, or moderately sized such as the agribusiness-dominated Central Valley of California. Singleton and company write of Washington, "fracture zones between . . . blocks of habitat generally correspond to developed valley bottoms where forest cover is often discontinuous, where human population centers are usually located, and where road densities are often high."[19]

Of course, fracture zones can also be huge, such as the Midwest (not including the Upper Great Lakes region). One does not need to be a professional geographer or carnivore biologist to know that large areas of North America are simply not suitable for rewilding, at least not in the foreseeable future. Dense human populations, intensive agriculture, and a domesticated landscape make rewilding highly unlikely for much of the East, Midwest, and South. Large areas in the West are also unsuitable. Other highly settled and domesticated areas unsuitable for rewilding are in southern Canada and in much of Mexico and Central America.

From the standpoint of continental conservation and rewilding, I propose that we look at North America in shades of landscape permeability: the degree to which the land is open and safe for the movement of large carnivores and other wide-ranging and sensitive species between large core habitats.[20] In much of the tundra and boreal forest of Alaska and northern Canada, the land is mostly wild, with essentially undisturbed native vegetation, landscape permeability, and all native species, including carnivores and large ungulates, in something close to their natural populations. However, even here, poorly regulated trapping, wolf extermination programs, and excessive subsistence hunting have altered the natural system over wide areas. Moreover, oil and gas exploitation, mining, and boreal-forest clearcuts as far as the eye can see have ripped away the wildness of the land in many places. Indeed, Alberta's nineteenth-century-style resource looting is being carried out today with head-spinning gusto and could largely fracture landscape permeability in the northern (boreal) half of that province.

South of the boreal forest, most of western Canada and a good bit of the western United States retain landscape permeability to a fair degree. For example, mountain lions are able to move through the majority of the region north to south and east to west, as research by Ken Logan and Linda Sweanor suggests.[21] Were they not shot on sight by wannabe frontiersmen, wolves could similarly travel over the same territory. Permeability is not so good for grizzlies, wolverines, and bighorn sheep. To a lesser degree, parts of the Upper Great Lakes region, Florida, Appalachians, northern New England and New York, and the Canadian Maritimes retain some landscape permeability and could have it restored to a higher degree. Some mountainous and tropical forest regions of Mexico and Central America also retain fair landscape permeability. Throughout these places, however, there are large domesticated regions and major barriers to wildlife movement. Nearly everywhere, wildness wanes: the land becomes more domesticated and less permeable to wildlife movement. Nonetheless, the regions above are the parts of North America that could realistically be considered for rewilding (or kept wild). Public lands or large private landholdings, ruggedness of terrain, natural vegetation, low road density, and low human population density generally characterize the areas most suitable for rewilding.[22]

This does not mean that conservationists should ignore the more domesticated and fragmented parts of North America. The existing approach to nature reserve protection and restoration must continue, with an emphasis on ecosystem representation and special elements of biodiversity, and a more ambitious vision. Domesticated regions of North America, such as the Tennessee River system, hold much of the most imperiled biological diversity on the continent. I think the concept of habitat corridors through a hostile sea remains highly applicable to such areas. The approaches for conservation area design shift from areas of high domestication and low permeability to areas of low domestication and high permeability. Additionally, there may be other areas, such as the northern Great Plains, that could be rewilded in the future. But, it is simply common sense to acknowledge that wolves are not soon going to be chasing bison across Iowa or north Texas, no matter how much we may dream.

I believe that the minimum requirement for rewilding North America is protection and restoration of Four Continental MegaLinkages as shown in figure 8.1.

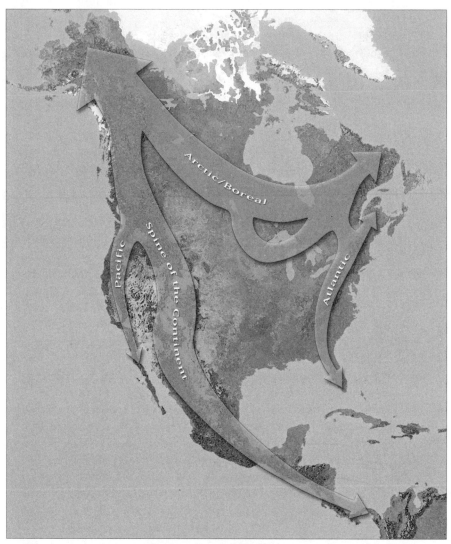

FIGURE 8.1. Four Continental MegaLinkages are the basis for a rewilding vision for protecting and restoring landscape permeability in North America. These MegaLinkages represent broad areas in which more detailed wildlands networks should be designed and protected. (Wildlands Project map by Todd Cummings; revised by Kurt Menke.)

Pacific MegaLinkage: From the high mountains of northern Baja California up the southern Coast Range to the Sierra Nevada and Cascades, and then up the Coast Range of British Columbia into southern Alaska.

Spine of the Continent MegaLinkage: From the volcanic cordillera of Central America up the Sierra Madre Occidental to the Rocky Mountains of the United States and Canada, then into the MacKenzie Mountains of the Yukon and across the Brooks Range of Alaska.

Atlantic MegaLinkage: From the Everglades to Okefenokee, and then to the Appalachians (including the geologically distinct Adirondacks) into the Canadian Maritimes.

Arctic-Boreal MegaLinkage: Northern North America from Alaska across to Quebec and Labrador with a dip down into the Upper Great Lakes.

I have drawn a schematic map of the Pacific and Spine of the Continent Megalinkages in the western United States by linking the largest wild cores and core complexes (see figure 8.2). These existing and proposed protected areas are made up of wildlands of 500,000 acres or more with relatively insignificant internal fragmentation; lightly traveled roads, campgrounds, national park facilities, ranch headquarters, and the like may be present. Separate core complexes are shown adjacent when more troublesome barriers—such as heavily traveled roads, villages, agricultural landscapes, intensive timber cutting—lie between them. The linkages include many smaller cores and core complexes. These linkages seem the most logical method of connecting the cores: the lands are reasonably permeable with mostly natural vegetation, they comprise a high percentage of public land or private land in conservation ownership, and they are of continental importance. The Rewilding Institute, which I now head, works with regional biologists and conservation groups to draft detailed and well-researched maps of the Mega-Linkages, including less-critical linkages and the landscape permeability on public lands that provides essential connectivity. These maps will be available on our website as they are produced. This planning of the MegaLinkages is explained in Part 3 of *Rewilding North America*.

The Atlantic MegaLinkage is similarly designed but not yet mapped. It uses cores and core complexes of 100,000 acres or more. In general these cores are less wild than those in the West and will require more restoration, as will linkages between them. Possible cores for the Pacific, Spine, and Atlantic MegaLinkages are listed on the Island Press Web site at http://www.islandpress.org/appendix/rewilding/index.html.

The Arctic-Boreal Megalinkage is currently unmapped. Canadians are working to protect the boreal forest and to add to the acreage of protected tundra.

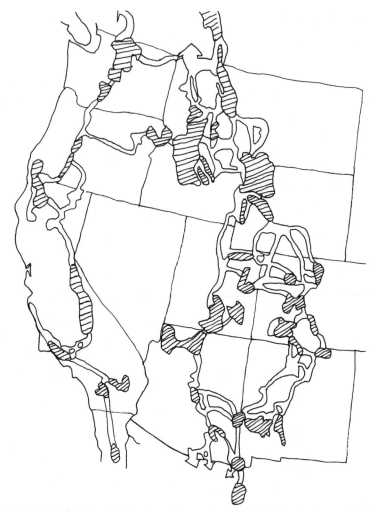

FIGURE 8.2. This simplified map of the western United States shows the skeletons on which the Pacific and Spine of the Continent MegaLinkages will be fleshed out. Crosshatched areas show wild complexes of 500,000 acres or more with minimal core fragmentation. The parallel lines between the cores show important wildlife movement linkages. General areas of landscape permeability are not shown. (Map by Dave Foreman.)

Because the Pacific, Spine of the Continent, and Atlantic MegaLinkages run south-north, they not only follow the natural lay of the land but also allow for species movement north in response to climate change.

Although the tundra and the boreal forest are the wildest and most intact components of the North American Wildlands Network, they may not be so for much longer. The planned destruction and domestication of Canada's boreal forest by vast and widespread timber mining (it isn't forestry) and by oil, gas, and oil sand extraction is one of the most important conservation issues in the world. Boreal forests are particularly vulnerable to industrialization because they have very low productivity and take a long time to grow to maturity. The Arctic tundra of the Northwest Territories and Nunavut are wide open for a diamond-mining frenzy. As we conservationists work on rewilding other parts of North America, we must also work to keep Canada's—and Alaska's—north wild.

Reality And Vision

"But wait," I can hear some hard-bitten and scarred conservation campaigners say. "We're in a crisis now. Oil and gas drilling, mining, logging, road building, and a thousand other things threaten wildlands today. It's silly—even counterproductive—to talk about big dreams. Conservationists need to focus 100 percent on immediate threats and stave them off."

I understand this viewpoint, but I believe it is dead wrong. We must have vision, we must have hope, if we are to defend wild nature today. It has been so in the past; it is so today.

Let me return to a passage by Doug Scott I quoted in the introduction to this book. Scott begins his inspiring and authoritative *A Wilderness-Forever Future: A Short History of the National Wilderness Preservation System* with a vision: "Here is an American wilderness vision: the vision of 'a wilderness-forever future.' This is not my phrase, it is Howard Zahniser's. And it is not my vision, but the one I inherited, and that you, too, have inherited, from the wilderness leaders who went before." Scott quotes Zahniser, "The wilderness that has come to us from the eternity of the past we have the boldness to project into the eternity of the future."[23]

During the twentieth century, most conservation work was defensive. Citizen conservationists, scientists, dedicated agency staffers, and some members of Congress fought to protect wildlands and wildlife from dams, logging, mining, road building, development, off-road vehicles, and bad grazing practices. The 1964 Wilderness Act clearly states that its purpose is to protect natural areas from development: "In order to assure that an increasing population, accompanied by expanding settlement and growing mechanization, does not occupy and modify all areas within the United States and its possessions, leaving no lands designated for preservation and protection in their natural condition, it is hereby declared to be the policy of the Congress to secure for the American people of present and future generations the benefits of an enduring resource of wilderness.[24]

Samuel Hays, a great conservation historian turned citizen conservationist who campaigned for the 1975 Eastern Wilderness Areas Act, writes that "wilderness proposals are usually thought of not in terms of perpetrating some 'original' or 'pristine' condition but as efforts to 'save' wilderness areas from development."[25]

Without the dedicated effort of citizen conservationists to stop the looting of wild places, dams would have flooded the Grand Canyon, Gila Wilderness Area, Dinosaur National Monument, and other "protected" areas; oil and gas wells and pipelines would crisscross the Arctic National Wildlife Refuge and Bob Marshall Wilderness Area; scarce ancient forest would be left anywhere on the public lands; DDT may have brought the bald eagle and peregrine falcon to extinction; and miles and miles of paved scenic highways would tear along ridgetops in the wildest national parks. Without citizen suits to protect endangered species, dozens of species of native fishes, birds, amphibians, mammals, invertebrates, and plants would be no more. Without books, articles, photographs, films, music, scientific papers, and public educational materials, hardly anyone would be aware of the threats to nature.

Some naively criticize conservationists for these defensive actions, for fighting "brush fires," and for "doom-and-gloom" prophesizing. But without them, Earth would fast become unlivable for many more species—including humans. The state of nature would be far bleaker than it now is. Nonetheless, it is not enough for conservationists to only react to urgent threats against nature. Too much talk of the looming dark of mass extinction, global climate change, and a thoroughly domesticated Earth leaves people depressed, distraught, and without hope—and thus without the spark to take action.

Fortunately, as Doug Scott shows us in his evocation of Howard Zahniser, throughout twentieth-century conservation, citizens, scientists, members of Congress, and land managers have also worked positively for a future where humans and wild nature can coexist. Arm in arm with defensive actions is a vision of a wilderness-forever future. Inherent in the statement of purpose for the Wilderness Act is a hopeful vision for the future—of an enduring resource of wilderness.

We conservationists need to recognize, as Howard Zahniser did before us, that conservation needs a bold, *hopeful* vision. Moreover, we now know that it is not enough to slow the war on nature—we need to heal the ecological wounds we have already caused.

This was the theme of the 1992 Wildlands Project mission statement: "Our vision is simple: we live for the day when Grizzlies in Chihuahua have an unbroken connection to Grizzlies in Alaska; when Gray Wolf populations are continuous from New Mexico to Greenland; when vast unbroken forests and flowing plains again thrive and support pre-Columbian populations of plants and animals; when humans dwell with respect, harmony, and affection for the land; when we come to live no longer as strangers and aliens on this continent."[26]

The vision for a North American Wildlands Network along Four Continental MegaLinkages evolved from this mission. Such a rewilding vision does not shoulder aside nor downplay the need for vigilant and uncompromising defenses against schemes to domesticate the whole earth, but it adds a positive blueprint for all conservation work, a context for wildlands and wildlife defense. This vision stands out because it is bold, scientifically credible, practically achievable, and hopeful.

The joining of these four characteristics in a conservation vision is what makes it powerful. It is bold because it offers a plain alternative to business as usual and is unflinching in daring to say what actually needs to be done to stop our war on nature. By using the best ecological research to set goals and to guide the selection, design, and restoration of protected areas, it is scientifically credible. Now, one can easily smith a bold and scientifically credible vision that has no hope of success. In taking advantage of the vast experience of the citizen conservation movement to weave a strategy for implementation of the vision, the vision becomes practically achievable. Of particular note is the combination of hopefulness with a realistic blueprint of how to achieve the vision. Human beings—conservationists are no exception—need hope to carry on. The vision to rewild North America offered in this book is both hopeful and doable as well as bold and scientifically credible. My hope is that this vision rouses citizen conservationists across the continent and provides them the means to make the future better.

CHAPTER 9

Selecting and Designing
Protected Areas: The Early Days

Since the late 1980s, I've worked with Michael Soulé and others to bring the traditional wilderness conservation movement together with conservation biology. We've made much progress, but misunderstandings yet dance around the edges. In this chapter and the next two, I will continue to try to play matchmaker. I wish to persuade citizen conservationists that the insights and guidelines of conservation biology are necessary if wilderness is to endure, and that an ecological approach will make wilderness areas and the National Wilderness Preservation System wilder: untrammeled, self-willed, and self-regulating for all of us—human, big cat, warbler, or spider. I wish to convince conservation biologists that without wilderness areas and national parks the state of wild nature would be far grimmer and that our traditional protected-area systems remain the best tool for halting the extinction crisis.

In previous chapters, I've discussed science. This chapter is about history. It differs from most other historical studies of the conservation movement and the wilderness idea, because it is specifically a history of protected-area selection and design. What further distinguishes the history in this chapter is that I tie in my own direct experience of working on protected-area selection and design for the past thirty years. This gives me a different vantage point. Moreover, I have a theory (or theories) of the evolution of protected-area selection and design.

I remember my thoughts upon first reading Leopold's question, "Of what avail are forty freedoms without a blank spot on the map?"[1] All my life, even as a little kid, I had been drawn to maps and especially to the blank spots. What wildness lurked there? Whatever it was, it beckoned me, as did the far horizons as my family drove around the West. I read Leopold in 1971 as I explored the works of conservation: Leopold, Sears, Shepard, Nash, Abbey, Carson, and Ehrlich. In those days, I worked for a subcontractor of the U.S. Air Force. With a crew of hard-drinking ne'er-do-wells, I'd bounce around the Southwest in an unruly, big truck—The Beast—and spread out a couple of acres of canvas at specified coordinates and aligned on given azimuths at certain times. We didn't know why we were doing what we were doing (except for the stingy paychecks) or where the directions were coming from. I soon reckoned it was for high-resolution satellite and spy-plane photography, after the voice on the phone told me not to leave t-shirts on the canvas again.

We used U.S. Geological Survey (USGS) 1:250,000-scale topographic maps to find our lay-down sites. I poured over those maps in the down time, looking for the blank spots. Back in the office, I traced the outlines of the big roadless areas on onion-skin paper. Later that year, I found out from the U.S. Forest Service that it was conducting an inventory and evaluation of roadless areas to determine if any should be recommended for wilderness designation. I also found out that I wasn't the only one in New Mexico interested in protecting additional wilderness; there were others and they called themselves the New Mexico Wilderness Study Committee (NMWSC).

In 1972, while at the University of New Mexico, I started a wilderness study group and tried to work with the rather aloof Sandia Lab scientists and engineers who largely made up the NMWSC. Because none of them were much drawn to the Gila National Forest in southwestern New Mexico (it was too "dry" and "hot"), they let me be the "honcho" for roadless area field work there. The Gila National Forest was also studying the Gila Primitive Area that year to decide what portion of it should be added to the Gila Wilderness Area. I honchoed that for the NMWSC, too. I dropped my biology classes at the university and spent much of the year hiking roadless areas and drawing lines on maps. I had to shoe horses and spread canvas now and then to get a little money, but my unpaid job drawing proposed wilderness area boundaries was the best work I've ever had. I've spent the last thirty years drawing proposed wilderness area boundaries on maps—and I've helped some of them become law. I've watched how the philosophy of selecting and designing protected areas has changed. I'll even take a little credit for helping it change. In this chapter, I'll discuss protected area selection and design through 1980. In chapter 10, I'll discuss conservation area design after 1980.

Protected Areas

Yellowstone National Park was established in 1872, and we can see two distinct pathways to selecting and designing protected areas that have emerged since that time. The first approach was followed by government agencies and citizen conservationists to draw boundaries for candidate national parks, wilderness areas, wildlife refuges, and such. This approach was often based on values such as landscape beauty and outdoor recreational potential (and all too often on the lack of resource extraction value), and also to protect habitat for favored species—waterfowl and game animals. However, criticism of this approach has been overplayed by some critics of the traditional conservation movement, as I shall show later. The second path was blazed by scientists with the goal of selecting and configuring ecologically important areas for protection and restoration. But in fact the historical record (and my personal experience during the last third of a century) shows more back-and-forth between these two ways than is commonly realized. It also shows that what some may think is new is, in fact, based on ideas and strategies from long ago. For these reasons, I believe knowing the history of protected areas is important for today's conservation biologists and citizen conservationists alike. If you don't know whose shoulders you're standing on, you are standing in a void.

Note that each approach requires two steps: (1) identify areas to be protected, and (2) decide how much is to be protected by walking a boundary on the ground and drawing it on a map. I'll refer to these steps as, respectively, *selection* and *design*. Both are key to how well the land is protected. I'll also use *protected area* and *nature reserve* interchangeably for national parks, wilderness areas, wildlife refuges, and other federal, state (or provincial), local government, and private reserves. The term *conservation area*, when I use it, will refer to protected areas based on the theory of island biogeography and other ecological concepts after about 1970. I use the term *wildlands network* for the specific web of core wild areas, linkages, and compatible-use lands proposed by the Wildlands Project, The Rewilding Institute, and cooperating groups.

Early Protected Area Selection and Design

Organized conservation efforts in North America began only about a century and a half ago. I've used the metaphor of the "River Wild" to show that today's conservation movement is the blend of about a dozen currents flowing together during that time. Those currents and (roughly) the decade each began are

Wildlife protection, 1840s

Stewardship, 1860s

National park (scenic beauty) protection, 1870s

Forest protection, 1880s

Wilderness area protection, 1910s

Ecological representation, 1910s

Carnivore protection, 1920s

Endangered species protection, 1960s

Landscape connectivity, 1970s

Ecological restoration, 1980s

Rewilding, 1990s

These currents feeding the River Wild have not replaced one another but rather complement one another and add to the whole.[2] All of them have influenced protected area selection and design, but those that have had the strongest roles are wildlife, national park, forest, and wilderness area protection, and representation, connectivity, and rewilding. The others have more strongly shaped land management, both inside and outside protected areas.

The first national park in the world—Yellowstone—was set aside by Congress and President Ulysses S. Grant in 1872. Additional national parks were established in 1890 and thereafter. In 1891, Congress authorized the president to withdraw forested headwaters in the West from disposal to private interests in order to protect watersheds and forests from despoilment. (The state of New York was similarly protecting state lands in the Adirondacks at the same time.) Selection and boundary design of these national parks and forest reserves often were done hastily and far away in Washington, D.C.[3] Protection was more on paper than on the ground. (The cavalry had to be sent into Yellowstone to stop poachers in the 1890s, for example. There had been little to no on-the-ground stewardship during the previous twenty years.) Early citizen conservationists such as John Muir and Edward Sargent saw national parks and forest reserves as ways to protect wilderness and to keep out destructive extractive uses, including livestock grazing and logging. That early hope for wilderness was dashed when legislation in

1897 opened forest reserves (soon to be called *national forests*) to timber cutting, cattle and sheep grazing, and other kinds of ecologically damaging resource extraction and management.[4] In 1911, the Forest Service was authorized to buy private land in the East (where the public domain had passed into private ownership) to protect watersheds.

National parks began to be developed with roads, lodges, and other facilities for tourism. Extermination campaigns against predators were key to wildlife management in the parks.[5] Over the strong objections of John Muir and his allies, a major dam was built in Yosemite National Park. Such disappointments marked America's first wilderness movement.

A second, largely independent wilderness protection effort began after World War I. This campaign was sparked and led not by citizen conservationists but by professional foresters and other resource managers working for federal agencies, including Aldo Leopold, Arthur Carhart, Elers Koch, Benton MacKaye, and Bob Marshall. In 1924, Aldo Leopold convinced the Southwest Regional Office of the U.S. Forest Service to set aside three-quarters of a million acres in the headwaters of the Gila River in New Mexico as a wilderness area. His goal, and that of Forest Service employees who followed him, such as Bob Marshall, was not to prevent resource extraction such as livestock grazing and logging but to bar automobiles and roads from large areas. In a 1925 article urging the Forest Service to establish more areas like the Gila Wilderness, Leopold made this plain: "The term wilderness, as used here, means a wild, roadless area where those who are so inclined may enjoy primitive modes of travel and subsistence, such as exploration trips by pack-train or canoe . . . . Generally speaking, it is not timber, and certainly not agriculture, which is causing the decimation of wilderness areas, but rather the desire to attract tourists."[6]

Leopold was painfully aware of the spread of roads in the national forests because, as chief of operations for the Southwest Region of the Forest Service from 1919 to 1923, he had been in charge of road building and maintenance. He asked: "Who wants to stalk his buck to the music of a motor? Or track his turkey on the trail of the knobby tread? Who that is called to the high hills for a real *pasear* wants to wrangle his packs along a graveled highway? Yet that is what we are headed for, at least in the Southwest. Car sign in every canyon, car dust on every bush, a parking ground at every waterhole, and Fords on a thousand hills!"[7]

Leopold's call for more wilderness areas was fought by many in the Forest Service,[8] but in 1926, Forest Service Chief William Greeley generally endorsed protecting "Wilderness Recreation Areas."[9] The Forest

Service (and later the federal Bureau of Land Management [BLM]) put wilderness under the care of its recreation division, and there it stayed until recently.

During the 1920s, as the wilderness area movement gained ground with the Forest Service in the West, professional forester and regional planner Benton MacKaye in Massachusetts proposed an Appalachian Trail for foot travel from Georgia to Maine.[10] In 1925, the Appalachian Trail Conference was organized to create the trail on the ground.[11] In 1926, after reading Leopold's landmark article, "Wilderness as a Form of Land Use,"[12] MacKaye wrote that he hoped the Appalachian Trail would protect "a series of what Aldo Leopold would call 'wilderness areas.'"[13] By 1929, MacKaye's thinking had evolved further to calling for "wilderness ways"—linked wilderness areas—and to advocate for restoration of the "primeval forest" in the East.[14] Mark this well: MacKaye was ahead of his time—he was more or less proposing the Wildlands Project's vision more than seventy years ago.

In 1930, Bob Marshall wrote his first major article on the need for wilderness areas, "The Problem of the Wilderness."[15] Like Leopold, he saw wilderness areas as large primitive recreation areas without roads and vehicles, as places that demanded self-sufficiency on the part of the traveler.

The second pathway for protected area selection and design had begun in 1917, as a separate effort led by ecologist Victor Shelford for the Ecological Society of America's Committee on Preservation of Natural Conditions. Its goal was to protect reserves representing ecological communities where succession and climax conditions were unaltered by civilization.[16] Unlike wilderness areas, which advocates believed should be vast, these areas could be smaller.[17]

The wilderness area and natural area movements were seen as distinct but complementary. Marshall, a forester with a doctorate in plant physiology, and a famed wilderness explorer and hiker, at first believed that wilderness areas would need to be logged on very long rotations to prevent forests from becoming "senile" and unattractive,[18] and Leopold first thought that wilderness ranching would add pioneer charm to the visitor experience.[19] Paul Sutter, in his pathfinding study of the early wilderness movement, *Driven Wild*, writes that this showed Leopold "hoped to preserve frontier conditions, not ecologically pristine conditions."[20] The 1929 Forest Service Regulation L-20 reflected this attitude: it established vague protection guidelines for what were now to be called *primitive areas* on the national forests (logging was not prohibited), and encouraged forest supervisors to also establish smaller "research reserves" for science.[21] In 1932, Marshall wrote, "The difference between primeval and wilderness areas is that the primeval area exhibits primitive conditions of growth whereas the wilderness area exhibits primitive methods of transportation." However, wilderness areas could have primeval areas within them, thought Marshall.[22] (The Forest Service over the years designated a few "research natural areas" (RNAs) within some wilderness areas, or established wilderness areas or primitive areas over existing RNAs.) Victor Shelford understood this difference. In his 1932 listing of "Classes of Nature Sanctuaries," he defined "primitive area" as "an area in which human transportation and conditions of living are kept primitive. Some of the areas are to be cut over periodically."[23]

In the 1920s, leading boosters of national parks, such as Robert Sterling Yard, began to shift from an insistence that only areas with monumental scenery qualified as national parks to a view that would "laud the parks as museums and universities."[24] Yard, who had been Horatius at the bridge in limiting national park status only to areas of nationally significant scenery, where awe-inspiring forces of geology and evolution were displayed,[25] became convinced by Victor Shelford and other ecologists to allow areas of lesser scenic value but of world-class biological value—such as the Everglades—into the National Park System, as well as areas of high primitive value—such as the Great Smoky Mountains.[26]

An often overlooked piece of North American protected areas strategy began in 1903 when President Theodore Roosevelt withdrew Pelican Island in Florida as a wildlife refuge to protect the brown pelican. He soon "established throughout the country a host of bird sanctuaries."[27] In 1908, Klamath Lake, in South Central Oregon, was set aside for waterfowl migrating along the Pacific flyway.[28] In 1913, Congress authorized migratory bird refuges and set penalties for killing protected migratory birds.[29] A migratory bird treaty between the United States and Britain (acting for Canada) in 1918 helped to overcome constitutional objections to a federal role in bird protection.[30] From then on, through the decades, national wildlife refuges were established, many for the purpose of protecting stepping-stone habitats for migrating birds, especially ducks and geese. These refuges were strongly pushed by the Audubon societies and by ethical duck hunters like Ding Darling, an editorial cartoonist and later the director of the Bureau of Sport Fisheries and Wildlife for President Franklin Delano Roosevelt. Insofar as I can tell, national wildlife refuges were the first example of trying to protect avenues of connectivity for migrating species—*flyways*.

A surprisingly large number of biologists and conservationists—

including organizations such as the American Society of Mammalogists, New York Zoological Society, and the Boone and Crockett Club—came to oppose the extermination of predators during the 1920s and early 1930s. Accordingly, the Ecological Society of America grew its view of nature sanctuaries beyond small areas protecting original vegetation to include areas large enough to maintain "all their native animals"— including large carnivores such as the wolf and mountain lion. The Society's 1932 "Nature Sanctuary Plan" (written by Shelford) stated, "Biologists are beginning to realize that it is dangerous to tamper with nature by introducing plants and animals, or by destroying predatory animals or by pampering herbivores."[31]

In 1935, the founders of The Wilderness Society, including Marshall, MacKaye, Yard, and Leopold, proposed five classes of protected areas:

Extensive wilderness areas—large areas "free from all mechanical disturbances" and requiring self-sufficiency from the visitor.

Primeval areas—"virgin tracts in which human activities have never modified the normal processes of nature."

Superlative scenic areas—national parks and similar areas.

Restricted wild areas—smaller, less-wild areas near cities.

Wilderness zones—"strips along the backbone of mountain ranges . . . along rivers which, although they may be crossed here and there by railroads and highways, nevertheless maintain primitive travel conditions along their major axes."[32]

Thus we find—eureka!—that wildlands networks combining the ecological, recreational, and aesthetic values of wild nature as proposed by the Wildlands Project and others today are not a wholly new idea but are grounded in the original vision of The Wilderness Society founders.

In addition to prohibitions on roads and vehicles, The Wilderness Society called for no logging "in any sort of wilderness."[33] A few years later in his call-to-arms article, "The Universe of the Wilderness Is Vanishing," Marshall emphatically changed his earlier view about logging: "All types of commercial land use conflict fatally with primitive values. The commercial activities that today most frequently invade the wilderness are irrigation, waterpower development, mining, grazing, and logging."[34]

After forming the organization, the leaders of The Wilderness Society began to incorporate ecological concerns more fully into their wilderness area idea. Leopold's writing increasingly emphasized the scientific values of wilderness areas, although he certainly did not turn his back on recreational values.[35] In the first issue of *The Living Wilderness*, he wrote, "I suspect, however, that the scientific values [of wilderness] are still scantily appreciated, even by members of the [Wilderness] Society. These scientific values have been set forth in print, but only in the studiously 'cold potato' language of the ecological scientist. Actually the scientific need is both urgent and dramatic."[36]

Clearly, Shelford and other ecologists were influencing wilderness advocates, particularly Leopold, who later was elected president of the Ecological Society of America and worked on the Committee on Preservation of Natural Conditions.[37] Forest Service regulations U-1 and U-2 in 1939 reflected this change. These regulations ordered the national forests to study their primitive areas and to propose permanent boundaries. Areas over 100,000 acres would be called *wilderness areas*, and those under 100,000 acres would be called *wild areas*. Logging was prohibited, along with roads and motor vehicles.

In *A Sand County Almanac*, Leopold wrote, "A science of land health needs, first of all, a base datum of normality, a picture of how healthy land maintains itself as an organism. . . . The most perfect norm is wilderness."[38] Compare that view of wilderness with his earlier views in the 1920s. Within Leopold's philosophy and policy recommendations, the two paths to protected area selection and design had merged.

After World War II, the mission of the Committee for the Preservation of Natural Conditions became increasingly advocacy-oriented—too much so for the Ecological Society of America, which eventually became a nonactivist scientific society. Those pursuing the protection of natural areas split off from the Society to form the Ecologist's Union in 1946, which became The Nature Conservancy in 1950.[39] The Conservancy's strategy was to identify and purchase important natural areas outside the public domain, restoring and protecting them as private preserves. Through this work, priceless ecological hotspots not on the public lands were saved from development. (I served on the founding board of trustees of the New Mexico Chapter of The Nature Conservancy from 1976 to 1980 and saw its work as a crucial complement to my work on public lands as The Wilderness Society's Southwest Representative.)

Also after World War II, the priorities of the Forest Service radically shifted from that of custodial management of the national forests to aggressive promotion of timber sales and road building.[40] Roadless wildlands around primitive areas fell to saws and bulldozers. The Forest Service proposed paring away primitive areas to get the sawtimber. The

Wilderness Society and Sierra Club sadly concluded that congressional protection of wilderness areas was necessary to counter the Forest Service's logging frenzy, and Howard Zahniser of The Wilderness Society thereupon led an eight-year campaign, from 1956 to 1964, to pass a wilderness act.[41]

The post–World War II protected areas movement was again led by citizen conservationists (although a number of them had worked for agencies), unlike the between-the-wars effort led by agency folks.

Besides protecting all existing wilderness areas within national forests, the 1964 Wilderness Act directed the National Park Service and the U.S. Fish and Wildlife Service to study their roadless areas over 5,000 acres for wilderness area recommendation and for the Forest Service to study its remaining primitive areas, but nothing was said about national forest roadless areas. The Bureau of Land Management (BLM) was not required to study or designate wilderness areas on its lands until mandated to do so by the 1976 Federal Lands Policy and Management Act. The Wilderness Society's Harry Crandell was largely responsible for the wilderness review section.

The post-1964 generation of conservationists grew steadily more ambitious. They looked at de facto wilderness on the national forests, including recovering areas in the East. In 1965, Montanans persuaded their congressional delegation to introduce legislation to create the Lincoln-Scapegoat Wilderness from land not formerly designated as primitive. The Forest Service was outraged at this churlishness. Conservationists in other states, including eastern ones like Alabama, followed suit.[42] Citizens' promotion of "wildcat" wilderness area proposals pushed the Forest Service to undertake an inventory of national forest roadless areas and make additional (but puny) wilderness area recommendations in the 1970s—the first and second Roadless Area Review and Evaluations (RARE I and RARE II).[43]

Wilderness lovers in the East, fed up with the Forest Service's refusal to even consider recovering areas in that part of the country for wilderness area recommendation, appealed to Congress under the leadership of Ernie Dickerman of The Wilderness Society. The resulting 1975 Eastern Wilderness Areas Act, which designated fifteen wilderness areas in national forests east of the Rockies, was a milestone in the history of protected areas.[44]

By this time, the National Park Service recognized ecosystem representation as a legitimate criterion in identifying candidate national park units (a decision encouraged by citizens). Canyonlands and Redwoods National Parks, and the national seashores and lakeshores are examples of parkland designated using these criteria. It was in the 1970s, however, that the wilderness stew bubbled over as conservationists brought stronger ecological values into wilderness area advocacy. During the RARE I and II processes and the BLM wilderness review,[45] agency biologists and citizen conservationists encouraged the use of ecological representation as a selection criterion for proposed wilderness areas. Ecological representation was a major argument used by conservationists and members of Congress to pass the 1975 Eastern Wilderness Areas Act. Ecological and landform representation were specific criteria for wilderness area recommendations by the Forest Service in RARE II.[46] George Davis of the Forest Service's RARE II team championed ecological representation during that process. Protection of previously unprotected ecosystems has since become a solidly mainstream goal of the conservation movement. Moreover, as early as 1972, citizen conservationists were crafting wilderness area proposals to protect connectivity between areas.[47] Even before the scientific development of the core-linkage-compatible-use model, wilderness groups were calling for the protection of wilderness area complexes—groups of proposed areas close together.

These new ideas did not have smooth sailing, however. Many in the Forest Service, including most of the agency leadership, opposed designating much more wilderness, and what designations they favored all too often conformed to their rocks-and-ice aesthetic stereotype. The BLM also sought to limit the acreage considered for wilderness and generally signed off on only the most scenic areas—flat areas were simply not acceptable to the aesthetic chaperones in the agency. Even some conservationists fought against wilderness area designation for lands they considered unappealing for recreation. For example, the founder of the New Mexico Wilderness Study Committee (NMWSC) planned to publicly oppose wilderness designation for proposed areas in Bosque del Apache National Wildlife Refuge ("cow pasture" is how he described them), but Clifton Merritt, western regional director of The Wilderness Society, browbeat him into silence on the issue.[48] As the Wilderness Society's New Mexico Field Representative, I went back to Washington, D.C., and testified in favor of the Bosque wilderness units, which were passed quickly by Congress in 1975. During this time, several NMWSC founders were concerned that only a certain number of acres of additional wilderness would ever be protected in New Mexico. Wanting those acres to be in the spectacular high country of northern New Mexico, they suggested that I minimize the amount of wilderness The Wilderness Society proposed for the Gila National Forest. Well, shucks,

I guess I just didn't really understand what they wanted me to do, so I ignored their request, and during the 1970s, the size of our wilderness area proposals on the Gila National Forest (and elsewhere) steadily grew. In 1980, wilderness legislation for New Mexico established new wilderness areas and additions to existing wilderness areas in national forests throughout the state. We certainly didn't get everything we wanted but we did better than expected.

Throughout the twentieth century, fighting proposals to dam wild rivers has been a leading cause of conservationists. Taken aback by the dam-building frenzy of the federal government's Army Corps of Engineers and the Bureau of Reclamation in the 1950s and 1960s, conservationists became more stalwart by the mid-1960s in fighting dam construction. For some visionaries, such as pioneer grizzly bear researchers Frank and John Craighead, the defensive action of fighting dams was not enough. They looked at the 1964 Wilderness Act and asked why similar protection couldn't be given to rivers. After proponents waged a grassroots campaign, Congress passed the National Wild and Scenic Rivers Act. The 1968 act protected free-flowing rivers by prohibiting dams, water diversions, rip-rapping, and channelization on river stretches placed in the National Wild and Scenic Rivers System. Wild and scenic rivers remain under the jurisdiction of the federal agencies who manage the land around them or by states. Depending on the degree of development along them, river stretches can be designated as wild, scenic, or recreational. Generally, only one-quarter mile on each side of the river is protected from incompatible development.[49]

Adding more rivers to the system by acts of Congress has been controversial. I received my first death threat in 1973 when I convinced New Mexico Congressman Harold Runnels to introduce legislation to merely study stretches of the Gila and San Francisco Rivers in southwestern New Mexico.

Although conservation biologists have not given the system much heed, wild and scenic river designation can be an effective way of protecting aquatic and riparian habitat and connectivity.

Also in 1968, Congress passed the National Trails System Act, which immediately designated the Appalachian and Pacific Crest Trails as National Scenic Trails. Since then, several other long trails, particularly the Continental Divide National Scenic Trail, have been added to the system. The national trails have been largely overlooked by conservationists because they are primarily recreational designations, but they are the backbones of the Pacific, Spine of the Continent, and Atlantic MegaLinkages.

The 1980 Alaska National Interest Lands Conservation Act (ANILCA) remains the high point for visionary protected area designation, using ecological criteria to guide selection and design of protected areas. Championed by Ed and Peggy Wayburn of the Sierra Club, Celia Hunter and Mardy Murie of The Wilderness Society, dedicated National Park Service staff, and other wilderness warriors, the many-year battle for ANILCA was a Brobdingnagian clash between farseeing Alaskans and their friends in the lower forty-eight states, and short-sighted resource looters in Alaska and Houston. Those of us who worked hard on the Alaska Lands Act in the 1970s were guided by a vision of protecting whole ecosystems with all native species, of protecting representative areas of all ecosystems throughout Alaska, and of doing the job right in the first place. Though necessary and unnecessary compromises alike crept in as congressional champions dickered with the Alaskan politicians, President Carter decided to sign a weakened bill after Ronald Reagan was elected president in November of 1980. Imperfect though the Alaska Lands Act was, the 100-million-plus acres of new national parks, wildlife refuges, wilderness areas, and wild and scenic rivers in Alaska remain the finest protected areas system in the world. Some current advocates of a scientific approach to land protection do not realize how ecologically based ANILCA was. With a few proposed additions to ensure landscape permeability between units, the Alaska conservation model serves as an inspiration for the Four Continental MegaLinkages. It was a great honor for me to work on the Alaska lands legislation and to work with committed visionaries such as Celia Hunter, Ginny Wood, and Mardy Murie. Nothing, anywhere in the world, has matched the achievement of the Alaska National Interest Lands Conservation Act in the quarter century since.[50]

However, I must emphasize that despite these advances of the 1970s, ecological values did not replace or shortchange the traditional wilderness values of solitude, peace, inspiration, challenge, and freedom. Ecological values were additional criteria for the selection and design of protected areas, not new or competing ones. There is nothing wrong or outdated about traditional wilderness values. They stand as strong today as they ever did. Ecological values only increase their eloquence.

CHAPTER 10

Selecting and Designing Protected Areas: The Past Two Decades

Conservation Area Design

As we saw in chapter 7, during the 1970s, biologists began to develop more sophisticated ecological approaches to protected area selection and design. That chapter emphasized the science behind the process. This chapter continues the discussion by examining the history of *conservation area design*—applying the science to protected area selection and design. Chapter 7 also described how, in the mid-1970s, John Terborgh, Jared Diamond, E. O. Wilson, Michael Soulé, and other biologists drew from the theory of island biogeography to propose ecological guidelines for conservation area design.[1] These principles were used in the 1980 World Conservation Strategy by the International Union for the Conservation of Nature and Natural Resources (IUCN).[2] Reed Noss and Allen Cooperrider later explained that "the rules state that, all else being equal,"

- Large reserves are better than small reserves
- A single large reserve is better than a group of small ones of equivalent total area
- Reserves close together are better than reserves far apart
- Round reserves are better than long, thin ones
- Reserves clustered compactly are better than reserves in a line
- Reserves connected by corridors are better than unconnected reserves[3]

As we shall see, these principles from a quarter century ago or more have survived the fiery furnace of academic debate. At first, this ecological approach to protected areas guided international conservation more than it did conservation in the United States. Nonetheless, conservation biology influenced a wing of the U.S. conservation movement early in the 1980s—specifically, the activist group, Earth First! From its beginning, Earth First! advocated an uncompromising *ecological* approach to wilderness area and species protection. Although later overshadowed by the wild and woolly practices of direct action (nonviolent civil disobedience) and "monkeywrenching," this ecological emphasis continued until the original Earth First! disbanded in 1990.[4] During the decade of the 1980s, the Earth First! movement made at least five major intellectual or policy contributions in the turn to an ecological approach for protected area selection and design. These were to (1) protect all roadless areas, (2) restore landscape-level ecosystems, (3) propose very large areas for protection, (4) protect all old-growth forests, and (5) educate conservationists about conservation biology.

Earth First! cofounders Bart Koehler, Howie Wolke, Susan Morgan, Ron Kezar, and I had all been active in the RARE II campaign for The Wilderness Society, Friends of the Earth, or Sierra Club. Conservation groups had proposed that only 35 million acres of 62 million acres of Forest Service roadless areas be designated as wilderness areas. The final Forest Service proposal was a stingy 15 million acres. We were stung by this slap in the face. We also knew that many conservationists (including us) had believed that all 62 million acres should be protected but were afraid to propose so much because we would be thought radical. Thus, one of Earth First's first proposals was to designate all 62 million acres as wilderness.[5] Ecological arguments were key to this position. Although the proposal was denounced as extremist at the time, in January 2001 (only twenty years later), Forest Service Chief Mike Dombeck and President Clinton, with massive citizen support, protected nearly all roadless areas in national forests from road building—largely for ecological reasons.[6] The Clinton ruling is perhaps the best example of how a continually evolving concept of wilderness has influenced on-the-ground policy and management.

In March 1981, Earth First! staged its famous "Cracking of Glen Canyon Damn" stunt and proposed that the dam be torn down and 180 miles of the Colorado River be liberated and restored. Such a idea was considered preposterous at the time, but today discussion about dam removal is common and has attracted more widespread support. In July of 1997, for example, Boise's *Idaho Statesman* editorialized in favor of tearing down four dams on the lower Snake River that block upstream migration of salmon.[7] Arizona Public Service (APS) and the Federal Energy Regulatory Commission (FERC) are planning the removal of a one-hundred-year-old dam on Fossil Creek and two hydroelectric plants, and restoration of the stream by 2009.[8] In 1997, FERC ordered the removal of 162-year-old Edwards Dam on the Kennebec River in Maine so that salmon, sturgeon, shad, and other migratory sea fish could once again spawn in the river.[9] Edwards was torn down in 1999. Dams have also been demolished in North Carolina, California, and Oregon.[10] Congress held a hearing in 1997 as a forum to bash the proposal to remove Glen Canyon Dam on the Colorado River—"a certifiable nut idea," according to Colorado Senator Ben Nighthorse Campbell. However, the former Commissioner of the Bureau of Reclamation, Daniel Beard, noted that "by holding the hearing in the first place, the panel gave legitimacy to the option of removing dams because it tacitly admitted that dams are not permanent fixtures of the landscape."[11] Clearly dam removal is no longer nutty but is rather a serious policy for ecological restoration of rivers.

Another early project Earth First! undertook was to produce the "Earth First! Wilderness Preserve System" proposal. Howie Wolke, Bart Koehler, Shaaron Netherton, and I published this map with huge proposed wilderness preserves in *The Earth First! Journal* in 1983.[12] Although nothing much happened with the proposal, it inspired many conservationists with the idea of restoring vast tracts of land and water to wilderness, and thereby blazed the trail that leads to the North American Wildlands Network.

During the early 1980s, conservation groups had generally decided not to push for wilderness area designation for roadless areas that had economically valuable old-growth forest (there were exceptions, of course). The timber industry's clout with politicians in both parties was just too strong. In early 1983, Mike Roselle, Bart Koehler, and I found that Oregon conservation groups were not going to continue to fight Forest Service plans to build a major logging road between a large roadless area and the Kalmiopsis Wilderness in southwestern Oregon. Legislation and lawsuits to protect the area had failed. Combined, the wilderness and the roadless areas next to it were the largest block of old-growth forest left on the U.S. Pacific Coast. Mike Roselle organized local residents to blockade the construction of this Bald Mountain Road in April, May, and June of 1983. Andy Kerr, with the Oregon Wilderness Coalition, now the Oregon Natural Resources Council, seized the opportunity to sue the Forest Service over National Environmental Policy Act (NEPA) violations in the RARE II final environmental impact statement. He convinced Neil Kagan, a new lawyer who had never appeared in federal court, to file the suit, naming Earth First! and several individuals as plaintiffs. That summer, federal judge Redden enjoined the Forest Service from building the road; the lawsuit (*Earth First! v. Block*) later froze Forest Service development plans in all roadless areas in Oregon and Washington.

We had received under-the-table support from Forest Service wildlife and watershed scientists, including research data suppressed by the Forest Service brass. Other Forest Service researchers soon published their findings, which showed that old-growth forests, far from being the biological deserts claimed in forestry mythology, were actually swarming with life—life that was largely lost after clearcutting. All of these events encouraged Andy Kerr, and Brock Evans of the Sierra Club, to begin the national effort to protect ancient forests, which continues today and which has prevented logging on hundreds of thousands of acres. Influenced by the ancient forest campaign, conservation groups began including more old-growth forest in their wilderness area proposals. In fact, since the mid-1980s, ancient forest has been one of the most prominent values behind wilderness area protection efforts.

Also in 1983, Reed Noss began to write articles about conservation biology theory and practice for *The Earth First! Journal*, which I edited. I offered Michael Soulé and Bruce Wilcox's *Conservation Biology* anthology for sale through the *Journal* (I was later told by the publisher that we sold more copies than any other single outlet). During the early Earth First! era, Howie Wolke was a tireless advocate for an ecological approach. Our book, *The Big Outside*, and Howie's book, *Wilderness on the Rocks*, represented our 1980s ecological ideals for wilderness.[13]

It was not until the late 1980s and early 1990s, however, that mainstream U.S. conservation groups began to fold conservation biology selection and design principles more explicitly into wilderness area protection and management proposals. I believe that the key step behind this embrace of conservation biology by conservation groups was the 1985 proposal by Reed Noss (with the help of Larry Harris) of the University of Florida for a *network* of conservation areas in Florida that would protect and restore movement linkages for panthers and bears across the state. Noss's proposal was published in both the *Natural Areas Journal* and the *Earth First! Journal*, which underscores how Earth First! followed conservation biology in the 1980s.[14]

During the 1990s, leading scientists summarized the broad scientific consensus on conservation area design in several forms. Michael Soulé and his graduate students studied bird losses in fragmented chaparral habitats in the San Diego metropolitan area in the 1980s. Based on those studies, Soulé offered these simple conservation area design principles in 1991:

• Bigger is better
• Single large is usually better than several small
• Large native carnivores are better than none
• Intact habitat is better than artificially disturbed
• Connected habitat is usually better than fragmented[15]

Note how similar Soulé's guidelines were to the 1980 IUCN principles.

Inspired by Noss's and Soulé's work, conservationists in the northern Rockies, led by Mike Bader and the Alliance for the Wild Rockies, applied conservation biology principles there as early as 1990. Alliance leaders, including pioneer grizzly bear researcher John Craighead and former Wilderness Society executive director Stewart Brandborg, reckoned that if Yellowstone National Park was not large enough to maintain viable populations of grizzlies and wolverines, then it should be linked with the big wilderness areas of central Idaho, the Glacier National Park/Bob Marshall Wilderness complex (also called the Northern Continental Divide Ecosystem) in northern Montana, and the Banff/Jasper National Park complex in Canada. To maintain healthy populations of wide-ranging species, landscape connectivity had to be protected and restored throughout the northern U.S. Rockies and north into Canada. The Northern Rockies Ecosystem Protection Act (NREPA), which would designate 20 million acres of new wilderness areas and wilderness recovery areas in the United States and protect linkages between areas, was first introduced in Congress in the early 1990s as the first wilderness area legislation to reflect the new conservation biology landscape model.[16] It has been reintroduced in every succeeding Congress, drawing over one hundred bipartisan cosponsors in 2003. Scores of grassroots wilderness groups have helped to promote the legislation, although local members of Congress, beholden to entrenched resource extraction industries, continue to oppose it. The Sierra Club was the first major national conservation organization to endorse NREPA.

Inspired by NREPA, scientists and conservationists in Canada and the United States proposed a visionary "Yellowstone to Yukon" (Y2Y) conservation network, which would protect habitat and wildlife movement linkages from Yellowstone National Park in the south through the Canadian Rockies to the southern Yukon.[17]

A core lesson learned from conservation biology is that ecosystems and wildlife ranges do not follow political boundaries, and effective conservation systems often need to cross international borders, as the Y2Y conservation network does. A noteworthy effort to follow biological, not political, boundaries for networks can be seen in a project in Central America, where in the early 1990s government agencies, scientists, and local conservationists worked with the Wildlife Conservation Society to propose a network that would link existing national parks and other reserves from Panama to Mexico's Yucatan. This proposed network, originally called *Paseo Pantera* (Path of the Panther) but now more often referred to as the Meso-American Biological Corridor, would allow jaguars, mountain lions, and other wide-ranging species to move between core reserves throughout Central America.[18]

The Forest Service's 1990 *Conservation Strategy for the Northern Spotted Owl* set out five reserve design principles "widely accepted among specialists in the fields of ecology and conservation biology."[19] In 1992, Reed Noss updated those five with a key sixth principle in *Wild Earth*:

1. Species well distributed across their native range are less susceptible to extinction than species confined to small portions of their range.
2. Large blocks of habitat, containing large populations of a target species, are superior to small blocks of habitat containing small populations.
3. Blocks of habitat close together are better than blocks far apart.
4. Habitat in contiguous blocks is better than fragmented habitat.
5. Interconnected blocks of habitat are better than isolated blocks; corridors or linkages function better when habitat within them resembles that preferred by target species.
6. Blocks of habitat that are roadless or otherwise inaccessible to humans are better than roaded and accessible habitat blocks.[20]

The similarity of these principles to those of Terborgh and Diamond (mid-1970s), the IUCN (1980), and Soulé (1991) show how well established and enduring are the ecological guidelines for conservation area selection and design.

Marine Protected Areas

Oceans have been largely ignored in the discussion about protected areas. Recently, however, scientists, conservationists, and commercial fishers worried about the collapse of fisheries and other ecological wounds to marine ecosystems have acknowledged the importance of protected areas for ocean conservation. Maxine McCloskey, as a citizen conservationist, has advocated marine protected areas since the 1960s. She summarized the history of marine reserves in a 1997 article for *Wild Earth*. In 1966, a Panel of Oceanography of the President's Science Advisory Committee recommended, "Establishment of a system of marine wilderness preserves (would be) an extension to marine environments of the basic principles established in the Wilderness Act of 1964 that would provide ecological baselines, preservation of unmodified habitats for research and education, and marine wilderness recreation." Since then, the idea of ocean wilderness areas has continued to be discussed in the United States and internationally. McCloskey lists sixteen kinds of marine features that should be protected.[21]

Bradley Barr of the National Oceanic and Atmospheric Administration (NOAA) and James Lindholm of the National Undersea Research Center at the University of Connecticut propose that management of U.S. waters in the Exclusive Economic Zone, which extends 200 miles from shore, follow the current range of management for federal lands—from "multiple-use" BLM lands to wilderness areas. They proposed that NOAA be added to the agencies covered by the Wilderness Act.[22]

There is growing recognition that for marine conservation areas to be effective, bottom trawling and fishing (commercial and recreational) must be prohibited in large areas. Such "no-take" areas provide secure habitat for many species to breed and grow larger populations, which then disperse into fished areas for the long-term benefit of fishers. Because oceans are "open" in that larvae can disperse as plankton for over 100 miles, "marine reserves could be designed as networks linked by these dispersal currents, helping to make sure that the various protected populations replenish each other."[23]

A marine version of a MegaLinkage has been sparked by the Canadian Parks and Wilderness Society: called the Baja California to Bering Sea Marine Conservation Initiative, it uses the Pacific gray whale as the overarching focal species. Conservationists, marine biologists, and government agencies are working together on this vision.[24]

Wildlands Network Design

In December 1990, John Davis and I planned *Wild Earth* magazine as a voice for a visionary, ecological approach to conservation. A few months later, in the spring of 1991, Michael Soulé suggested a meeting to discuss the vision of what we wanted North America to be like in a hundred years. Doug Tompkins, then owner of Esprit sportswear, hosted that meeting in San Francisco in November 1991. Out of that meeting came the Wildlands Project.[25]

As Wildlands Project founders, we explicitly sought an approach to wildlands conservation that combined traditional wilderness and wildlife conservation with conservation biology; in other words, we wanted to integrate the two approaches to protected area selection and design. Our specific mission was to offer a vision for a North American Wildlands Network—a system of core wild areas, wildlife movement linkages, and compatible-use lands. For us, it was not enough to protect just what was left wild—because we knew that such small, isolated areas would lose their ecological integrity over time.

We chose the word *wildlands* instead of *wilderness* to show our commitment to a landscape network instead of just to isolated protected areas. Wildlands include designated wilderness areas, other protected core areas, and wildlife movement linkages. (These categories are described in chapter 12.) The goal for these areas is to protect and restore will-of-the-land (i.e., self-regulating ecosystems) and the *wildeor* (i.e., self-willed beasts). Wildlands also include compatible-use areas (previously called *buffers*) on public lands, where sensible, conservative resource use[26] and motorized recreation on roads is allowed, and on private lands, where landowners are voluntarily learning to live with the *wildeor* while supporting their families.

The Wildlands Project took conservation area design to a new level—that of *wildlands network design*—by considering the whole landscape.

In 1992, *Wild Earth* published a special issue devoted to the recently formed Wildlands Project. In it, Reed Noss wrote a landmark article on ecologically based reserve selection and design. He described what is now the widely accepted model for conservation area design and what has become the template for regional wildlands networks and the North American Wildlands Network:

> A regional reserve system consists of three basic ingredients: core reserves, multiple-use (buffer) zones, and corridors. Select your core reserves first, then interconnect and buffer them across the landscape. For many species, properly managed multiple-use zones will function as corridors. An archipelago of core reserves in a matrix with low road density and low-intensity human activities will function well for most native species. Multiple-use zones at a landscape scale can be corri-

dors at a regional scale. Whenever possible, however, significant core reserves should be linked by corridors containing roadless interiors.[27]

The publication of the book, *Saving Nature's Legacy*, by Noss and Cooperrider in 1994 gave conservationists the most comprehensive and accessible discussion up to that time about using conservation biology for a range of land and wildlife protection and management questions, including the selection and design of protected areas.[28] It remains an essential reference for conservationists.

In November of 1997, Michael Soulé and John Terborgh of the Wildlands Project convened a workshop of thirty top conservation biologists to work out remaining issues of conservation area design. Workshop participants formed teams to write chapters for a 1999 volume edited by Soulé and Terborgh, *Continental Conservation*, which gives state-of-the-art guidelines for conservation area design, ecological restoration, and land protection.[29]

The Wildlands Project and its partners approach landscape conservation through a closely intertwined two-part process for individual ecological regions. The first part involves designing and establishing a wildlands network of protected core areas, wildlife and riparian linkages, and compatible-use lands based on rewilding and focal species planning—the *wildlands network design*. The second part involves developing and implementing a plan to heal the wounds across a whole landscape—the *wildlands network conservation vision*.

In the mid- to late-1990s, I coordinated planning by the Wildlands Project, Sky Island Alliance, and other groups for a rewilding-based conservation vision for the Sky Islands region, where New Mexico, Arizona, Sonora, and Chihuahua come together. In an effort to distinguish our approach from other conservation area designs, our consortium of conservation groups called this approach the *wildlands network design*.[30] We built the Sky Islands Wildlands Network (SIWN) on the 1992 Noss model of cores, corridors, and buffers (see fig. 10.1). We further refined these units for the New Mexico Highlands Wildlands Network (NMHWN), where we used four classes of *core wild areas*, three classes of *wildlife movement linkages* (originally called *corridors* by Noss), and four classes of *compatible-use areas* (called *multiple-use zones*, or *buffers*, by Noss). (Linkages are also important for plant migration in response to global climate change.) Because so-called multiple-use as practiced by the U.S. Forest Service and the Bureau of Land Management has not led to responsible land management, we used the

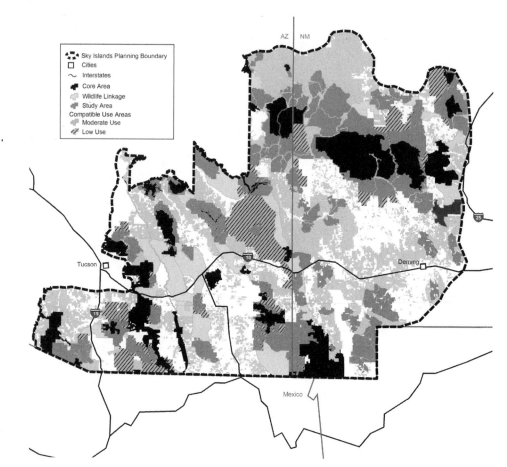

FIGURE 10.1. A simplified map of the Sky Islands Wildlands Network showing cores, wildlife linkages, study areas, and moderate- and low-use compatible-use lands. Classes within the units are not shown. (Adapted by Kurt Menke from the Sky Islands Wildlands Network Plan.)

term "compatible-use lands" instead of "multiple-use zone." The Southern Rockies Wildlands Network (SRWN) also uses these classes of units (see chapter 12).

The Sky Islands Wildlands Network offers a vision for how self-willed land and civilization can coexist. However, even a landscape-wide vision like the Sky Islands Wildlands Network will remain an island unless further tied to wildlands networks around it. After the Sky Islands proposal was published, conservationists began work on the adjacent New Mexico Highlands Wildlands Network, published in 2003. Published in 2004 were wildlands network designs and proposals for the regions dubbed Southern Rockies and Heart of the West. Together, these detailed proposed wildlands networks stretch from the Mexican border to just south of Yellowstone National Park along a 1,000-mile stretch of the Spine of the Continent—the Spine being the North American cordillera of the Central American volcanoes, Sierra Madre Occidental, Rocky Mountains, MacKenzie Mountains, and Brooks Range.

CHAPTER 11

The Importance of Wilderness Areas

Conservation biology began with the recognition that protected areas were conservation's most valuable tool and that a primary task for conservation biology was how to best design them.[1] More recently, however, sustainable development advocates and postmodern-deconstructionist academics have questioned the effectiveness of protected areas for safeguarding biodiversity. This criticism has particularly targeted the value of traditional protected areas, such as national parks. While much of this criticism has been directed at protected areas in Latin America, Africa, and Asia, learned potshots have also been taken at wilderness areas in North America.[2] In this, even a few conservation biologists have joined in.

John Terborgh and other leading field researchers have steadfastly defended protected areas in the so-called "developing world."[3] I've taken on the postmodern deconstructionists' distortion of the wilderness idea and their limited knowledge of wilderness area history and policy elsewhere.[4] Here, however, I mostly want to convince conservation biologists and other biodiversity advocates that wilderness areas in North America are still our best tool to protect and restore nature—and that they can be made even more effective.

In general, wilderness area critics, including some conservation biologists, have failed to acknowledge the tremendous successes of traditional American conservation and international national parks. Some claim that an ecological approach doesn't fit with a traditional conservation approach. Many of these critics just don't know what they are talking about. Others have overstated their case in typical human fashion to make their point. I was guilty of this in the early days of the Wildlands Project. Arguing that networks should be designed based on ecological principles, I and others exaggerated the "rocks and ice" nature of wilderness areas and national parks.

Conservation biologists generally need to know more about wilderness areas and the history of the conservation movement. Some are as unschooled in the citizen conservation movement and its accomplishments as are some citizen conservationists of conservation biology. In this chapter I will show that wilderness areas and national parks are the bedrock underlying protection of biodiversity and rewilding.

Furthermore, because of criticism of wilderness areas and national parks, some conservation leaders view conservation biology with suspicion. I want to convince them that rewilding and biodiversity protection goals are compatible with recreational and aesthetic values in wilderness areas and that rewilding will only make traditional protected areas better for nature and for recreation.

Reed Noss and his colleagues write in *Continental Conservation*, "Experience on every continent has shown that only in strictly protected areas are the full fauna and flora of a region likely to persist for a long period of time." What are these strictly protected areas? "A distinguishing characteristic of core areas is limited human access—that is, low road density or, ideally, roadlessness."[5] *Wilderness.*

Existing wilderness areas, national parks, national wildlife refuges, and roadless or lightly roaded areas on the U.S. public lands (and on comparable lands elsewhere in the world) are the building blocks for an ecologically oriented wildlands network.[6] Far from tossing aside existing protected areas and the wilderness and park systems, we conservationists must expand such areas and reconnect them. Nor should we see traditional and responsible wilderness recreation as incompatible with a wildlands network.

From the perspective of conservation biology, we can look closely at existing wilderness areas and national parks in the United States and answer the question, "Why has the world's greatest protected areas system not prevented biological meltdown?" By identifying the specific reasons why existing wilderness areas and national parks have not fully protected biodiversity, we can see that these shortcomings are not inherent in the ideas behind traditional protected areas, but rather are results of politics and history, and of limited ecological theory and knowledge in the past century. Possible reasons include the following:

- Because of historic patterns of settlement and the giveaway of public land to lumber corporations, railroads, and land speculators, many ecosystems were gobbled up into private or corporate ownership and were thus not available to be protected as parks, refuges, and wilderness areas. Eastern deciduous forests, longleaf pine/wiregrass forests, tallgrass prairies, lush river valleys in the West, and the grandest forests of the Pacific Northwest became corporate and private lands before representative samples of these ecosystems could be included in federal or state conservation systems.

- Within national forests and other public lands, the most productive sites, including the richest forests and riparian bottomlands, were often settled with small towns and ranches on private inholdings before protected area withdrawals were first made (even in some national parks). Moreover, the most productive and accessible areas of the public lands were heavily logged, overgrazed, and roaded before wilderness areas were established.

- The political power of cut-and-run industries and local boomers has also prevented most public lands with rich forests, fertile valleys, or flowing grasslands from being set aside. This has led to the "rocks-and-ice" situation: We have done a pretty good job of protecting alpine, subalpine, and some harsh desert ecosystems, but not so good with ecologically more productive ecosystems.

- Through habitat destruction, species-cleansing of large carnivores, and greedy market hunting, many species were eliminated or severely depleted before wilderness areas and national parks could be established (and some wildlife slaughter, especially of predators, has continued even in protected areas). Such species in the United States include passenger pigeon, Carolina parakeet, thick-billed parrot, ivory-billed woodpecker, California condor, beaver, bison, grizzly bear, gray wolf, red wolf, mountain lion, lynx, jaguar, wolverine, prairie dogs, bighorn sheep, woodland caribou, elk, pronghorn, gopher tortoise, desert tortoise, sea turtles, American manatee, American crocodile, and sea otter. These species, now extinct, locally extirpated, or reduced in numbers, all play (or played) important ecological roles in their ecosystems. Their loss degrades the ecological integrity of national parks and wilderness areas, as well as other lands.

- Our longtime failure to understand the keystone role of natural fire has upset fire-dependent ecosystems. Zealous firefighting in national parks and wilderness areas, inspired by the cult of Smokey Bear, has led to changes in forest and grassland species composition, loss of habitat for plants and animals, and buildup of fuels that lead to unnaturally destructive fires.

- Eighty years ago, Aldo Leopold wrote about the ecologically harmful effects of cattle and sheep grazing in the Southwest.[7] Four generations later, many folks still don't get it. Livestock grazing in national parks, national wildlife refuges, and wilderness areas before and after establishment has hurt streams and riparian forests, degraded grasslands, changed forest composition, and harmed wildlife through habitat destruction (southwestern willow flycatcher), fencing (pronghorn), competition for forage (elk), transmission of exotic diseases (bighorn sheep), and predator "control" (gray wolf and mountain lion).

Aldo Leopold long ago voiced many of these same warnings when he wrote that "most of these remnants [wilderness areas and national parks] are far too small to retain their normality" and "[t]he irruption of elk following the loss of carnivores has damaged the plant community [in Yellowstone] in a manner comparable to sheep grazing."[8]

The interplay of these factors has led to a protected areas system that has not protected representatives of all ecosystems, native wildlife, and ecological processes. However, the fault is with American land-use history and the political process of protected-area designation, not with the idea of wilderness areas and national parks as means of protection. (As I look back over conservation history, I am amazed that conservationists have protected so much given the powerful opposition.) Nor is it the fault of the values of and decades of hard work by the conservation movement. The extinction crisis is not caused by banking on wilderness areas. If these areas have not fully protected biodiversity, it is because of the political forces working at every step of the way to weaken and pare away such proposed reserves, and because conservationists in the past did not have the science we do today. The biodiversity crisis is worsening in large part because not enough land has been protected as wilderness areas and national parks.[9] This is true worldwide; it is true for North America. I believe most conservation biologists understand this. Those few biodiversity advocates who dismiss traditional protected areas for these problems are simply demonstrating their ignorance of conservation history as well as their political naiveté.

We can condense these points to the following seven "wounds" as they apply to protected areas.

• *Direct killing*. Some native species of animals have been extirpated from nearly all of our protected areas. Few if any protected areas outside Alaska and northern Canada hold ecologically effective populations of all their native species. Moreover, many species are not found in protected areas because their habitats have been left out.

• *Ecosystem degradation*. Functional examples of many types of ecosystems have never been protected in nature reserves. Moreover, many ecosystems in protected areas are degraded from prior or ongoing human abuse.

• *Ecosystem fragmentation.* Many wilderness areas and national parks are cut off from other protected areas. Often, the land between protected areas is degraded and fragmented and therefore does not provide either habitat or safe dispersal ways for wildlife between protected areas.

• *Loss of natural processes.* Natural ecological and evolutionary processes, particularly fire, flooding, predation, and natural insect and disease outbreaks, have been eliminated or weakened in protected areas. Many protected areas are far too small and isolated to be "minimum dynamic areas," that is, too small to support large-scale natural disturbances without loss of ecological integrity.

• *Exotic species.* Disruptive exotic species have become established in many protected areas; more are poised to invade.

• *Pollution.* Air, water, and land pollution harms plants and animals in protected areas.

• *Climate change.* Protected areas have not been designed to facilitate movement by plants and animals in response to climate change.

It is *not*, however, legitimate to blame the conservation movement for these problems, many of which the best scientists did not understand until recently. It *is* legitimate to use this knowledge to guide us in ecological restoration and in the selection and design of protected areas in the future.

The vision I offer in these pages of designing and protecting a North American Wildlands Network begins with existing national parks and wilderness areas as core protected areas. The next step is the protection of roadless areas and largely roadless areas on the public lands as additions to cores and as linkages between cores. Yes, we need careful scientific mapping and data analysis to identify biodiversity hot spots, unrepresented ecosystems, habitats of rare or imperiled species, and likely restoration areas on both public and private lands, but we should begin with designated and de facto wilderness on the public lands.

Let me now outline some reasons why wilderness areas, national parks, and national wildlife refuges are the heart of the North American Wildlands Network:

In the United States, over 106 million acres are protected in the National Wilderness Preservation System (about half of this is in Alaska), 90 million acres in the National Park System (about two-thirds of this in Alaska), and a little over 90 million acres in the National

Wildlife Refuge System (about four-fifths in Alaska). These figures do not add up to a grand total of 280 million acres, though, because 40 million national park acres and almost 21 million wildlife refuge acres are also protected as wilderness. The total acreage protected in these three systems is about 220 million acres, almost 100 million acres of which are in the contiguous forty-eight states. This acreage is already publicly owned, it is generally protected for its ecological integrity, and it is off-limits to most commercial exploitation—a pretty good foundation for protecting biodiversity, I would say. Furthermore, this does not include well-protected state lands, such as the New York and California state wilderness systems.

Wilderness areas and national parks *do* protect areas of great value for biological diversity. For example, former Sierra Club executive director Michael McCloskey points out that the 1930s battle for Kings Canyon National Park won an area wanted for a dam site by California Central Valley irrigators. He writes, "While commercial interests often succeeded in getting some areas they coveted dropped from park proposals, this does not mean that conservationists got nothing, or that parks got only worthless lands." McCloskey gives as another example the $1.3 billion worth of timber that went into Redwood National Park.[10]

One of America's most experienced conservationists, Brock Evans of the Endangered Species Coalition, writes:

> [I]t is wrong to say . . . that [existing parks and wildernesses] have no valuable natural resources in them. Have you ever hiked up the 15 miles of ancient forests in the Suiattle River Valley inside the Glacier Peak Wilderness Area? Or the valleys of Buck Creek, Downey Creek, Sulfur Creek, Agnes Creek; have you ever hiked up French Pete Creek, the valleys of the Minam or Little Minam in the Eagle Cap Wilderness, through Moore Flat, Maggie Creek in the Norse Peak Wilderness— just to name a few areas that come immediately to mind in the Northwest battles? Every one of these places, and a lot more . . . have trees in them—big trees, low elevation trees; every one of them was bitterly opposed by the timber industry.[11]

These areas, along with the Hoh and Quinalt Valleys in Olympic National Park, are the finest remnants of ancient forest in the Pacific Northwest. Conservationists fought hard for these places for ecological reasons and won, over the strident opposition of the timber industry.

The finest and most natural old-growth ponderosa pine forest in the world is protected in New Mexico's Gila Wilderness Area only because conservationists have worked since 1952 to prevent the Forest Service, which would like to see the forest logged, from moving the wilderness area boundary to exclude it. State and federal wilderness areas, wildlife refuges, and parks in the East hold many of the ancient forest remnants there and much of the best recovering forest. The Five Ponds Wilderness in New York's Adirondack Park alone has 50,000 acres of ancient forest. Some of the best remaining wetlands and a few sizable grasslands are preserved in wilderness areas, national parks, and national wildlife refuges.

These areas also protect prime habitat (albeit not enough) for imperiled and sensitive species such as wolverine, fisher, grizzly bear, gray wolf, mountain lion, and bighorn sheep. Were it not for these areas, protected through the blood, sweat, and tears of *recreational* wilderness conservationists,[12] those species would be in greater danger today—if they still existed in the lower forty-eight states at all. Wilderness areas, national parks, and national wildlife refuges are prime areas for repatriation of extirpated species—the more charismatic of which include the gray wolf, red wolf, lynx, wolverine, bighorn sheep, mountain lion, jaguar, woodland caribou, California condor, and thick-billed parrot.

Not all national parks were protected primarily for their scenery. Mount McKinley National Park (now Denali National Park) was set aside in 1917 not for the stunning mountain itself but as a wildlife reserve. Everglades National Park, established in 1947 (but authorized in 1934), was specifically protected as a wilderness ecosystem. As we've seen, the Forest Service used ecosystem representation to recommend areas for wilderness in the second Roadless Area Review and Evaluation (RARE II) in 1977–1979. A goal behind the 1980 Alaska National Interest Lands Conservation Act was to protect functioning representative ecosystems throughout the state.

In many regions of the United States, existing protected areas can be linked together with other public lands, many of them roadless or near-roadless. Such areas of de facto wilderness already have a strong and knowledgeable constituency. Furthermore, early in 2001, President Clinton protected roadless areas on national forests from future road building, logging, and other development, although since then the Bush administration has tried to undo that protection. Conservation groups are generally willing to expand their long-standing wilderness area proposals with ecological criteria, as later explained in chapter 13. In many areas of the United States, a wildlands network designed for large carnivores can be largely established on existing federal and state lands, although some key linkages are on private lands.

National parks, wildlife refuges, and wilderness areas are the only proven effective public protected areas. In 1993, President Clinton trumpeted a plan to protect ancient forests in the Pacific Northwest. But many of the proposed spotted owl reserves and old-growth conservation areas were clearcut during the "logging without laws" orgy of the mid-1990s. Wilderness areas and national parks, in contrast, are still off-limits to commercial logging.

Conservationists and hikers already know the public lands, often better than do land managers or even biologists. Where do rare birds nest? Ask your local birders. Where are the remaining native forests? Train some local hikers and they will find them. What are the existing uses, where are the roads, where are the proposed timber sales? Check with the local conservation group. The field inventories of local wilderness groups are far more accurate sources of road presence than official computerized databases.

We have national parks, wildlife refuges, and wilderness areas because conservationists have been able to sell the idea of wilderness, refuges, and parks to the American public. The venerable arguments of natural beauty, physical challenge, spiritual inspiration, wildlife protection, and *wilderness* resonate deeply in the American soul. The concept of biodiversity does not yet have that power. Those of us who wish to protect the diversity of life need to figure out how to market the idea. Piggybacking onto the popular wilderness preservation movement is a good way to do it. Conservation biologists and others pushing for the protection of ecological values can learn much from experienced citizen conservationists about how to implement new wildlands network proposals through the political process. Citizen conservationists are a mobilized, effective, and knowledgeable group of political fighters who will do most of the heavy lifting and strategizing for the conservation action needed for eventual success. In most cases, responsible wilderness recreation is compatible with protecting biodiversity. Many of the leading conservation biologists are also wilderness lovers who recognize the value and role of wilderness areas in protecting nature and acknowledge the importance of wilderness recreation. Some are backpackers, river runners, and backcountry hunters (Michael Soulé is a noteworthy example).

Describing a scientific study and preliminary reserve design for the Klamath-Siskiyou region on the California-Oregon coast, Reed Noss writes, "Somewhat to our surprise, roadless areas on public lands turned out to function well as the basic 'building blocks' of our reserve design."[13] Elsewhere, Noss and his coauthors write, "A surprisingly large number of conservation goals for the [Klamath-Siskiyou] region can be met through protecting and linking key roadless areas with high biological values. . . . Important habitats and other natural features not represented in roadless areas can be protected through conservation actions on a relatively small area of additional public and private lands."[14]

Wilderness area designation is the tried and true way to protect roadless areas and to restore ecologically important areas that currently have some roads or other human intrusions. A wildlands network without wilderness areas is incomplete and doomed to failure. *Continental Conservation* puts it this way: "Conservation strategies that lack meaningful core areas are naïve, arrogant, and dangerous. Such approaches assume a level of ecological knowledge and understanding—and a level of generosity and goodwill among those who use and manage public lands—that are simply unfounded."[15]

If we are to protect biological diversity, we must build on national park, wildlife refuge, and wilderness area systems already in place within the United States, and also on comparable areas outside the United States.

PART III

TAKING ACTION

We have an opportunity unique to our generation: to halt a mass extinction.

—REED NOSS

So. In Part I, I ladled out the gory bad news of mass extinction. In Part II, I gathered good news from conservation science, history, and policy to show that we know much of what we need to know to slow or stop the Pleistocene-Holocene Event. Now we finally come to the fitting back together of Leopold's cogs and wheels. In Part III, I want to tinker and cobble with the real work of selecting, designing, restoring, and protecting a North American Wildlands Network. I propose in these final chapters a sketch of a vision and an agenda for twenty-first-century conservation. Of course, what I offer isn't all that's needed to heal the ecological wounds. But it is an essential part without which we cannot ultimately protect the diversity of life. As in the rest of the book, I focus here on solutions that are continental in scale and look first to the wild.

The final four chapters go like this:

Chapter 12, "Putting the Pieces Together: Building a North American Wildlands Network"—How to design regional wildlands networks and the North American Wildlands Network from a rewilding point of view.

Chapter 13, "An Ecological Approach to Wilderness Area Selection and Design"—Guidelines from conservation biology for the selection and design of wilderness areas that will better protect and rewild nature.

Chapter 14, "Land Management Reforms for Implementing the North American Wildlands Network"—Relatively simple, straightforward, and inexpensive land protection, restoration, and management reforms that will help to quickly establish the North American Wildlands Network on the ground.

Chapter 15, "Hope for the Future"—How do we turn a land ethic into deeds to heal the land?

And then it's all up to you.

CHAPTER 12

Putting the Pieces Together: Building a North American Wildlands Network

Over the last several years, conservationists in the Southwest have developed a practical approach for designing wildlands networks that will protect and restore healthy core wild areas and the permeable landscapes between them. The science behind such design is not difficult. I would, in fact, argue that proper design consists for the most part of straightforward conservation land zoning based on a few key scientific principles as discussed in previous chapters, and that it relies on the best scientific studies of the region in question. As Craig Allen, a top-notch researcher with the U.S. Geological Survey in New Mexico, said at the 2003 George Wright Society conference, "While good science is necessary, it is not paramount or sufficient" for good conservation.[1]

A simplified approach to the design of regional wildlands networks and the North American Wildlands Network is three-part:

First, identify existing and potential large core wild complexes on public and private land. The distinguishing characteristic of core complexes is roadlessness or near roadlessness on public lands and roadlessness or tightly controlled road access on private lands.

Second, identify the most likely and easily achievable wildlife movement linkages or areas of landscape permeability on public and private lands between the core wild complexes. These major linkages will comprise existing and proposed smaller core wild areas (public land wilderness areas and private lands managed for conservation), proposed

179

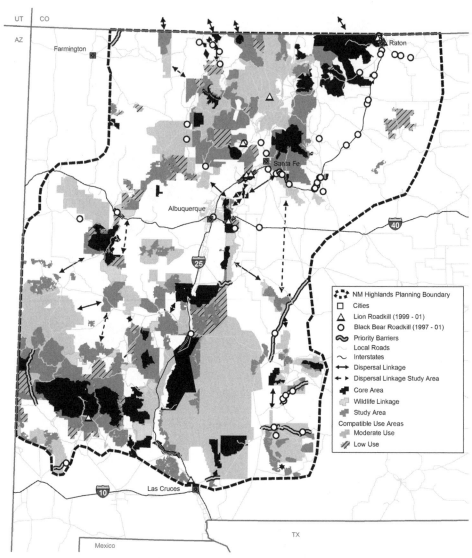

FIGURE 12.1. Map of the New Mexico Highlands Wildlands Network, showing cores, linkages, and compatible-use lands. Major barriers and roadkill data
for black bear and mountain lion are also shown. (Adapted by Kurt Menke
from the New Mexico Highlands Wildlands Network Vision.)

wildlife linkage units, and compatible-use lands on public and private
ownerships.

Third, identify fracture zones and barriers to landscape permeability
within the wildlands network, and seek practical solutions for mitigating
them (see fig. 12.1).

Wildlands Network Unit Classification and Management Guidelines

In 1992, Reed Noss offered a recipe for what is now called *wildlands network design*.[2] That recipe included descriptions and management/ restoration guidelines for different kinds of units in a protected network. During the Sky Islands planning process, we revised and expanded the types of units to better fit with existing conservation area categories and landownership types. Bob Howard, Matt Clark, and I made additional minor changes for the New Mexico Highlands Wildlands Network.[3] I'll briefly describe the different units here. For a detailed discussion of these units, see the section "For More Information" at the end of the book.

Since the publication of the New Mexico Highlands Wildlands Network in 2003, I've added a new category of barriers. Identifying barriers should become an integral part of wildlands network design.

Traditional conservation areas, such as national parks, wilderness areas, and national wildlife refuges, generally have guidelines for management that have been developed over decades. However, management guidelines for ecologically based wildlands network units are still in the discussion stage. These management and restoration approaches are further explored in chapter 14.

Core Wild Areas

Core wild areas are roadless or have motorized access tightly controlled. Resource extraction is prohibited or limited. They are the highest level of protected area and the heart of a wildlands network.

Study areas. Public land areas that need additional fieldwork to determine final wilderness area boundary recommendations. Not all of a study area will necessarily be proposed as Wilderness.

Core wilderness. Existing or proposed wilderness areas on national forests, Bureau of Land Management (BLM) lands, national park units, national wildlife refuges, and state lands. Also included are wilderness recovery areas, where significant restorative management is needed.

Core agency. National park units, national wildlife refuges, some BLM-managed national monuments and national conservation areas, and some state parks, wildlife areas, city and county open space, and other protected public lands that are not designated or proposed as wilderness areas. Resource extraction and off-road vehicle use are not permitted.

Core private. Private nature reserves managed by The Nature Conservancy, other conservation groups, and land trusts, and large private holdings managed for nature protection.

Core private wilderness. Private or tribal lands managed essentially as wilderness.

Landscape Linkages

The Spine of the Continent wildlands networks propose three classes of linkages: riparian, wildlife movement, and dispersal. The first two are lands that would be managed primarily for enhanced landscape permeability or as specific travel routes through developed landscapes or barriers, particularly for highly sensitive species. Dispersal routes allow genetic interchange within and between metapopulations. Increasingly important is protection of south to north and low-elevation to high-elevation linkages as suitable habitat for plant and animal range shifts because of climate change.

Riparian linkage. Linkages along rivers, including both the national wild and scenic rivers system and state wild and scenic rivers systems.

Wildlife movement linkage. Terrestrial linkages managed for specific species for seasonal movement, dispersal, and travel between core wild areas.

Dispersal linkage. Generally permeable areas of federal, state, private, and mixed land ownership that may not provide good habitat but that are generally safe for wildlife dispersal between core habitats.

Compatible-Use Lands

Lands managed prudently and carefully for resource extraction or road-accessible recreation around core protected areas are important for wildlands networks. Although they are not strict nature reserves, compatible-use lands are an essential part of regional and continental conservation planning for the simple reason that in today's fragmented landscape, politically feasible core areas cannot protect enough habitat for sensitive species. On regional and continental scales, compatible-use lands provide much of the necessary landscape permeability for wide-ranging species.

Low-use compatible-use public lands. Public lands with low road density (no more than 0.5 mile per square mile) and low-intensity use, managed for permeability.

Moderate-use compatible-use public lands. Public lands with no more than 1 mile of road for every square mile and moderately intensive use, but still managed for permeability.

Transportation compatible-use lands. The lands along roads dividing adjacent core wild areas. Management of these lands should be primarily guided by preventing and modifying barriers to wildlife movement.

Private compatible-use lands. Private lands voluntarily managed to protect wildlife habitat and permeability, and to restore ecosystems. These include ranches and timberlands under ecologically oriented management.

Barriers

From a standpoint of landscape permeability, barriers can be specific structures, such as freeways or dams, or mortality sinks of agricultural or residential areas. Identifying such barriers generally needs more attention in wildlands network design.

Terrestrial barriers. Roads and other specific constructions that are barriers to wildlife movement.

Aquatic barriers. Dams and other river constructions or dewatered stream sections that prevent movement by aquatic and riparian wildlife.

Landscape barriers. Fracture zones (residential, agricultural, and clearcut expanses) that are barriers to movement by specific species.

Focal Species Planning

The rewilding approach to wildlands network design uses the habitat needs of *focal species* to select and design proposed protected areas. In an overview of focal species planning in a 1998 issue of *Wild Earth*, Brian Miller and his colleagues explained, "Focal species are organisms used in planning and managing nature reserves because their requirements for survival represent factors important to maintaining ecologically healthy conditions."[4]

A number of categories of focal species have been suggested for conservation planning, depending on the goals of the particular effort. The Wildlands Project and its cooperators have experimented with different categories of focal species and with different species in the categories in the Spine of the Continent wildlands networks.[5] The

North American Wildlands Network now uses three categories:
(1) highly interactive (formerly called keystone), (2) flagship, and
(3) wilderness quality indicator.

Keystone species "enrich ecosystem function in a unique and significant manner through their activities, and the effect is disproportionate
to their numerical abundance," according to Miller and company.[6] As
we saw in chapter 7, large carnivores are keystone species because of
their role in top-down regulation of ecosystems. Beavers and prairie
dogs, through their shaping of ecosystems, are also keystone species,
although they are properly called *foundation species*, because they affect
the landscape in part because they are so abundant. However, beavers
need not always be numerous to positively affect ecosystems. And, as
we saw in chapter 8, Michael Soulé now prefers the term *highly interactive species* to cover keystone and foundation species. He and his coauthors of "Ecological Effectiveness" write that "a species is highly interactive when its virtual or effective absence leads to significant changes
in some feature of its ecosystem(s). Such changes include structural or
compositional modifications, alterations in the import or export of
nutrients, loss of resilience to disturbance, and decreases in native
species diversity."[7] The Rewilding Institute has replaced the term "keystone" with "highly interactive" for the North American Wildlands
Network.

Flagship species are popular wild animals, such as wolves, jaguars, and
bighorn sheep. They help build public and political support for a wildlands network. Conservation campaigns have effectively used flagship
species for more than a century. Less charismatic species benefit from
the habitat protection for flagship species. Three leading southeastern
U.S. carnivore biologists, Dave Maehr, Tom Hoctor, and Larry Harris,
write, "Large carnivores are logical flagships for large-scale landscape
restoration because viable populations require large areas and the effects
of their selective pressure—feedback loops—require long time periods."
For Florida, they propose the Florida panther "as an excellent tool for
restoring species, processes, and evolution to an ecologically fragmented
region."[8]

Wilderness Quality Indicator species are those that are highly sensitive
to human activities or presence (wolverines are a good example) or those
of whom humans are highly intolerant (wolves are a good example).
These are the beasts that need large roadless areas if they are to prosper.
Although some require remote, wilderness habitat, others can live in
less-wild lands, but are often killed there by people. For example, some
seventeen Mexican wolves have been shot from roadsides in Arizona and

New Mexico between their reintroduction in 1998 and the fall of 2003. Between March and September 2003, seven Mexican wolves were killed near roads.[9]

For each MegaLinkage in the North American Wildlands Network, we need to use appropriate highly interactive, flagship, and wilderness quality indicator focal species. Focal species will change for the three south-to-north MegaLinkages with latitude. Candidate focal species for each MegaLinkage include:

Pacific MegaLinkage: Mountain lion, California condor, wolverine, fisher, gray wolf, salmon, grizzly bear, beaver, lynx, bighorn sheep, caribou.

Spine of the Continent MegaLinkage: Jaguar, ocelot, mountain lion, beaver, gray wolf, American marten, wolverine, lynx, grizzly bear, bighorn sheep, pronghorn, northern goshawk, caribou.

Atlantic MegaLinkage: Mountain lion, black bear, beaver, fisher, red wolf, gray wolf, lynx, wolverine, river otter, Atlantic salmon.

Arctic-Boreal MegaLinkage: Wolf, caribou, lynx, polar bear, grizzly bear, wolverine, musk ox.

However, a single species may serve as an overarching focal species for all or part of a MegaLinkage. For example, Dave Maehr, of the University of Kentucky and a leading expert on the Florida panther, proposes that the cougar is "the most logical flagship for rewilding eastern North America."[10]

Network Design

By carefully selecting focal species in the three categories of highly interactive, flagship, and wilderness quality indicator, conservationists and scientists can design effective wildlands networks of cores, linkages, and compatible-use areas (also called *permeable landscapes*). Selected focal species generally qualify in several of these categories. There are two complementary methods of using focal species to select and design a wildlands network: *expert judgment* and *computer modeling*.

The first method, expert judgment, is based on field research and knowledge of an animal's habitat needs. I define "experts" here to include those who are very familiar with the region and those who know the focal species and their ecological interactions. On-the-ground experts include citizen conservationists, outdoor recreationists, hunters, agency staff, landowners, and biologists. These people know the details of potential wilderness areas, land ownership, ecological condition of the land, road presence or absence, and other human impacts. Species experts are naturalists and biologists who specialize in the different focal species and understand their habitat needs in the region. Through group meetings and individual comments, such experts designed and planned the Spine of the Continent wildlands networks. The best information to use to identify wildlife habitat and travel routes comes from field research involving long-term tracking and monitoring of focal species.

A key part of focal species planning is in-depth literature review and discussions with experts for each focal species' history and status, ecology and habitat, population structure and viability, movements, sensitivities and threats, and justification and focal value. For example, Dave Parsons, retired Mexican Wolf Recovery Team leader for the U.S. Fish and Wildlife Service, completed state-of-the-art focal species analyses for gray wolf, mountain lion, black bear, American marten, bighorn sheep, elk, and beaver for the New Mexico Highlands Wildlands Network. In these analyses, he made specific management and land protection recommendations for each species. University of New Mexico biologist Paul Polechla prepared a river otter analysis for this study. A summary is included in the *New Mexico Highlands Wildlands Network Vision* and the comprehensive report is available on CD as *Natural History Characteristics of Focal Species in the New Mexico Highlands Wildlands Network*.[11] It is an important reference for any kind of conservation planning.

Based on my knowledge of the Southwest, I drafted the New Mexico Highlands Wildlands Network design on a 1:500,000-scale land-ownership and topographic map of New Mexico. Kurt Menke, a GIS (geographic information systems) expert, then converted the map to digital form. Parsons and other experts, both scientists and conservationists, reviewed and helped revise the wildlands network design through several iterations.

The second method of using focal species in wildlands network design is through computer modeling. Three kinds of computer modeling of focal species' habitat needs—*least-cost path*, *SITES*, and *PATCH*—have been used and are being refined for practical wildlands network design. Of course, such modeling needs to be used in common with expert judgment and field research. Least-cost path analysis identifies the safer and more attractive routes that an individual species would probably use to get from one core habitat to another.[12] Originally developed by The Nature Conservancy to identify representative ecosystems and biodiversity hot spots, SITES selects "the smallest overall area needed to meet target goals," according to Reed Noss and his fellow researchers writing in *Conservation Biology*.[13] SITES also can control the level of geographic clustering or contiguity of neighboring core areas. PATCH is "a spatially explicit, dynamic model of population viability for focal species."[14] In other words, it models what the habitat for a species may be in the future, given various scenarios.

To be most useful, the data used in these models should be reviewed by species, ecosystem, and conservation land-use experts because of the widespread inaccuracy, bias, and incompleteness in available computerized data sets. For example, Jim Strittholt and Dominick DellaSala, who have done much computer modeling for conservation, caution, "We also suspect that many more rare species are present in roadless areas than are presently known because of the remoteness of roadless areas, a lack of organized biological surveys, and a current sampling bias toward areas with road access."[15] Peter Singleton and his fellow Forest Service researchers, whose computer models identify and evaluate landscape permeability for large carnivores in Washington, warn that "the actual functionality of the linkage areas we identify can only be tested through empirical field studies."[16]

Wildlands network design differs somewhat in "frontier" regions, which are still largely wild but are now threatened by large-scale resource exploitation (Canada's boreal forest, for example) from regions already settled (the U.S. Rocky Mountains, for example). The best case of protected areas selection and design in a frontier region is the 1980 Alaska National Interest Lands Conservation Act discussed in chapter 9. Its methodology and process would be a good model for selecting conservation areas in the Canadian arctic tundra and boreal forest. Canadian conservationists and government agencies should study the history of the Alaska Lands Act.

Fieldwork

Without fieldwork—lots of fieldwork—wildlands network design is an abstraction on a map or in a computer. Because many information sources and maps are outdated, biased, incomplete, or partially inaccurate, extensive ground-truthing of land conditions and proposed protected area boundaries must be done for a wildlands network to have defensible boundaries and management recommendations for each unit. Fieldwork is needed for inventorying and assessing road systems, potential wilderness boundaries, ecological conditions, focal species presence, linkage barriers, and special elements to improve the accuracy of the wildlands network design. I learned the value of fieldwork at the very beginning of my conservation work when I hiked around RARE (Roadless Area Review and Evaluation) I areas and proposed additions and deletions to the Gila Wilderness. I found that inaccuracies were rife in the Forest Service maps and descriptions. Computerizing data can worsen this problem because people tend to accept computerized data more readily and don't go back to original sources as often as they did before computerization.

In the New Mexico Highlands Wildlands Network Vision, Matt Clark discusses the kinds of fieldwork used in the Southwest.[17] *Wilderness surveys*, as conducted by the New Mexico Wilderness Alliance, Sky Island Alliance, and other groups, will be described in chapter 13.

Linkage surveys evaluate landscape permeability and identify barriers to movement for different focal species. The best example here is the Missing Linkages effort coordinated by the South Coast Wildlands Project, which has identified fifteen important wildlife linkages that are threatened with development and additional barriers in Southern California.[18]

Underpass surveys study road barriers by inventorying and measuring the dimensions of underpasses, culverts, and other structures that may allow different species to bypass major barriers, such as interstate highways. Identifying animal tracks determines what species, if any, are using each. For example, Matt Clark and his crew found that black bears were crawling through culverts under Interstate 25 east of Santa Fe, New Mexico. Roadkill data are also studied. Such studies show where barriers stop wildlife movement and where linkage restoration is needed.

Ecological conditions surveys are carried out by biologists and trained volunteers to assess ecological values, wounds, and health in proposed cores and linkages.

Tracking surveys, such as those carried out by the Sky Island Alliance, use trained volunteers covering regular routes to find out what species are using a particular terrain. Tracking is an excellent way to judge landscape permeability.

Not only do these various kinds of fieldwork provide essential information for drafting and revising a proposal, they also build a strong constituency of committed conservationists to organize in support of the proposal.

Conservation on Private Lands

Despite the large acreage of public land in the Spine of the Continent and Pacific MegaLinkages in the United States, some of the ecologically most important areas and essential linkages between public land blocks are in private ownership. This is even more true for the Atlantic Mega-Linkage and the Upper Great Lakes section of the Arctic-Boreal Mega-Linkage. Some private lands are managed by their owners in such a way that they function as cores, linkages, or compatible-use areas. Others are not so well managed. Private lands, therefore, play a key role in the North American Wildlands Network. Private lands included in wildlands networks are

- Lands owned by The Nature Conservancy, Audubon Society, and land trusts.
- Large private ranches, hunting and fishing club lands, and timberlands managed for conservation purposes, including large carnivore protection.
- Smaller tracts of private land in important ecological locations, such as riparian areas, owned and stewarded by conservation-friendly and conservation-savvy people.
- Key private inholdings and public lands grazing allotments that need to be purchased by conservation groups or conservation-friendly individuals.

It is important to note that inclusion of private lands on wildlands network maps does not mean that conservationists are trying to dictate to landowners what to do with their property. Rather, identification of such lands is often recognition that outstanding stewardship by the landowners currently protects these lands as vital habitat and linkage areas for focal species. In some cases, private ownership better protects land for sensitive species than would public ownership. Such landowners often undertake innovative ecological restoration and species recovery projects. A wildlands network's endorsement of outstanding private land management does not necessarily mean that such landowners have participated in planning or endorse the wildlands network. Private lands also may be shown that are important ecologically or for landscape permeability, but that are not under conservation management. Such lands should be high priorities for willing-seller acquisition or conservation easements by private groups or government so they can be restored and rewilded.

Because of the general absence of public lands in Mexico, private lands are even more important for wildlands networks there. In the Northern Sierra Madre Occidental Wildlands Network in Mexico, for example, the Wildlands Project and other U.S. conservation groups are strongly committed to helping Naturalia, the Northern Jaguar Project, and other Mexican groups with the purchase of important core areas as habitat for jaguar, black-tailed prairie dog and black-footed ferret, thick-billed parrot, and other focal species. Many of these core areas will protect source populations of these species for recolonization of U.S. portions of the network. In Mexico, as in the United States, conservation easements and long-term use agreements are useful tools to protect private lands for their natural values.[19]

CHAPTER 13

An Ecological Approach
to Wilderness Area
Selection and Design

Wilderness area selection and design based on rewilding goals and for protection and restoration of biodiversity uses somewhat different criteria than that of wilderness area selection and design for primitive-recreation purposes. A rewilding approach enhances recreational and aesthetic values. Selection and design for rewilding and biodiversity goals simply apply knowledge from conservation biology to determine what is required to protect an enduring resource of wilderness. An ecological approach is solidly in the tradition of the wilderness area movement.

Rewilding is not just science; it is conservation—the blending of traditional wilderness values of beauty, inspiration, and pioneer travel with ecological values. Nor is planning for rewilding only a scientific exercise. It is ecologically informed, muddy-boots conservation aimed at flesh-and-blood, root-and-leaf, fire-and-flood upshots in the political world as well as the wild world.

Working with Jack Humphrey and Andy Holdsworth of the Sky Island Alliance, Barbara Dugelby, Rod Mondt, and Kathy Daly of the Wildlands Project, and Bob Howard of the New Mexico Wilderness Alliance (NMWA), I put together practical rewilding guidelines for wilderness area selection and design during planning for the Sky Islands Wildlands Network from 1994 to 2000. I've further polished the guidelines here after working with the crackerjack New Mexico Wilderness Alliance inventory team on their comprehensive study of potential wilderness areas on Bureau of Land Management (BLM) lands in New Mexico.[1] Matt Clark of NMWA took the lead on incorporating these guidelines for use in the field. These guidelines are grounded in conservation biology but are practical and easy to use by citizen wilderness groups. One does not need to be a scientist to use them. Applying these principles to the hundreds of wilderness area proposals being framed by citizen groups across the United States and elsewhere in North America is an essential step toward passing on to future generations an enduring resource of wilderness.

Understanding Wilderness Areas

Since the days of Thoreau and Muir, conservationists have crafted inspiring, convincing arguments for the protection of wilderness. Some of the most eloquent work in the English language comes from celebrating the values of wilderness. However, literary and popular-culture ideas of wilderness are scattered and often fuzzy. This leads to confusion about wilderness areas—what they are, how they are managed, and what can be done in them. Moreover, the anticonservation crowd of resource extraction industries and motorized recreationists, some agency managers, and now postmodern-deconstructionist academics have deliberately or ignorantly fogged the meaning of wilderness and the purposes and protection of wilderness areas. If we go back to Old English and earlier, "wilderness" literally means "self-willed land,"[2] or "place of wild beasts."[3] These literal translations hold the essence of the idea of wilderness. The Wilderness Act uses the word "untrammeled," meaning unhobbled or unnetted, to describe the ideal of wilderness. Wilderness opponents huff and puff that wilderness areas are "human exclusion zones" or that only areas "where the hand of man never set foot" (in Dave Brower's priceless phrase) qualify for wilderness area designation. Even many conservationists are unclear about the Wilderness Act and what it permits or requires. Before we can apply ecological criteria to the selection and design of wilderness areas, we need to understand what the Wilderness Act really says and how it has been applied in picking new wilderness areas. This is particularly important for conservation biologists.

I emphasize two key points about the Wilderness Act necessary for understanding its meaning. First, the Wilderness Act strongly acknowledges ecological as well as recreational values. Second, it does not require, or even expect, candidate wilderness areas to be pristine or untouched.

The Wilderness Act permits and encourages nonmotorized and nonmechanized recreational activities, including hunting and fishing. However, the Act also makes it clear that wilderness areas are more than recreational areas or places for solitude. In 1941, Leopold wrote, regarding wilderness areas, "The important thing is to realize that recreation is not their only or even their principal utility."[4] In the several definitions of wilderness areas in the Wilderness Act, both experiential and ecological values are recognized and held to be compatible. Scientific research is acknowledged as a value and use of wilderness areas.

The Wilderness Act has different standards for candidate wilderness areas than for management of wilderness areas after designation. This distinction is the cause of much confusion about what qualifies for protection as a wilderness area. For example, contrary to popular perception, there is no requirement that an area must be pristine or even roadless to be designated as wilderness.[5] "Pristine," which is an ultimate word like "unique," does not appear in the Wilderness Act. However, after designation, no permanent roads or use of mechanized equipment may be allowed (except for certain administrative needs, usually of the emergency kind). This befuddlement between the entry criteria and the post-designation management criteria has sometimes led to cutting back wilderness area proposals, usually by agencies, but sometimes by conservationists.

Section 2(c) of the 1964 Wilderness Act confirms both of the above points:

A wilderness, in contrast with those areas where man and his works dominate the landscape, is hereby recognized as an area where the earth and its community of life are untrammeled by man, where man himself is a visitor who does not remain. An area of wilderness is further defined to mean in this Act an area of undeveloped Federal land retaining its primeval character and influence, without permanent improvements or human habitation, which is protected and managed so as to preserve its natural conditions and which (1) generally appears to have been affected primarily by the forces of nature, with the imprint of man's work substantially unnoticeable; (2) has outstanding opportunities for solitude or a primitive and unconfined type of recreation; (3) has at least five thousand acres or is of sufficient size as to make practicable its preservation and use in an unimpaired condition; and (4) may also contain ecological, geological, or other features of scientific, educational, scenic, or historical value.[6]

Note that this definition uses the phrases "earth and its community of life" and "protected and managed to preserve its natural condition" before the phrase "has outstanding opportunities for solitude or a primitive and unconfined type of recreation." Ecological values were clearly on the minds of the drafters of the Wilderness Act. Furthermore, the wording "which *generally* appears to have been affected *primarily* by the forces of nature, with the imprint of man's work *substantially* unnoticeable" unmistakably shows that Congress did not think that candidate areas had to be pristine (emphasis added).

Designation of an area as wilderness is consistent with the restoration of natural ecological conditions, such as reintroduction of wolves or beavers, restoration of natural fire, control of exotic species, or planting willow and cottonwood wands along degraded streams ("protected and *managed* so as to preserve its natural conditions"). Some wilderness designation legislation has specifically called for restoration measures. The 1999 Dugger Mountain (Alabama) Wilderness Act, for example, directs the U.S. Forest Service to use mechanized equipment and an existing road to remove a fire tower. After removal of the tower, the road is to be permanently closed. The National Park Service has recommended certain areas be designated as "potential wilderness additions" in order to allow ecological restoration and removal of nonconforming structures or uses. After restoration, the area would automatically become wilderness, with roads closed and mechanized equipment banned.

Conservationists should not be shy about proposing less-than-pristine areas for wilderness designation so long as they acknowledge the intrusions.[7] Since 1965 with the introduction of the Scapegoat Wilderness bill, conservationists throughout the United States have been doing just that. Conservationists have proposed and Congress has designated wilderness areas containing roads, small dams, past logging, old farms, abandoned cabins, and other human intrusions that have faded or that can be removed and the land restored. Even experienced wilderness backpackers would be surprised at how much human sign has been included in wilderness areas (and how much that sign has faded). Of course, ecological and experiential (recreational and aesthetic) justifications need to be made for proposing such areas. The goal of wilderness designation is not only to prevent destruction of untrammeled places, but also to help ecosystems become self-regulated (self-willed, untrammeled) again.

Traditional Selection Criteria

Land managing agencies have traditionally used varying standards of quality and purity to pick candidate areas for protection and for drawing boundaries around such areas. For example, candidate national parks had to be of "national-park quality"—possessing world-class scenery or natural wonders. Candidate wilderness areas needed to be of "wilderness quality"—scenic and inviting for nonmechanized recreation. Boundary selection by agencies and Congress has often carved out scenically "lower quality" portions of such areas. Sometimes these "lower quality" areas had greater ecological value than the areas protected but also had exploitable timber or other resources. In the first Roadless Area Review and Evaluation (RARE, 1971–1972), the Forest Service used a "quality index" to numerically rate and rank areas for their wilderness area value. An area with many lakes, for example, got a 6, while an area with "no lakes and few streams" got a 1. An area with lots of trails rated a 3, while an area with few trails was stuck with a 0.[8] Recreational values in keeping with the old alpine landscape esthetic were thus highly rated by the Forest Service, whereas areas with natural vegetation, rare species, and other ecological values did not gain points for these qualities. We conservationists strongly criticized this biased rating system at the time. We also damned the flawed notion of being able to quantitatively rate and rank the natural values of areas as the Forest Service was doing.

Purity has been a standard used by federal agencies ostensibly to limit protection of areas to only those that appear to be without human blemishes. More often, however, purity has been used as a subterfuge by the agencies to drop areas with timber, minerals, potential dam sites, or other resources industry wished to exploit. Both the Forest Service and BLM have set standards of wilderness purity not required by the Wilderness Act.[9] For example, in RARE 1971–1972, the Southwest Regional Forester decreed that areas had to be truly roadless. As a result, tire tracks that remained visible into the next season excluded thousands of acres from being identified as roadless and considered for wilderness area study.[10] In 1972, the Forest Service proposed to remove several thousand acres of the Gila Primitive Area on Aeroplane Mesa from protection because of the faint sign of a long-abandoned airstrip.[11]

In the early 1970s, the Forest Service stridently opposed designating wilderness areas east of the Rockies because of their purity dogma. Members of Congress, including the champions of the 1964 Wilderness Act, made it clear that purity had not been their intent.[12] Senator Frank Church, the floor manager of the Wilderness Act, said that the Forest Service

> would have us believe that no lands ever subject to past human impact can qualify as wilderness, now or ever. Nothing could be more contrary to the meaning and intent of the Wilderness

Act. The effect of such an interpretation would be to automatically disqualify almost everything, for few if any lands on this continent—or any other—have escaped man's imprint to some degree.

This is one of the great promises of the Wilderness Act. We can dedicate formerly abused areas where the primeval scene can be restored by natural forces.[13]

Senator Henry Jackson agreed with Church, saying, "It is my hope to correct this false so-called 'purity theory' which threatens the strength and broad application of the Wilderness Act."[14]

Republican Senator James Buckley (brother of William F. Buckley and now a senior federal judge) quoted Aldo Leopold, who wrote, "In any practical program the unit areas to be preserved must vary greatly in size and degree of wildness." Buckley then said, "The distortion of this approach by efforts to straitjacket the Wilderness Act into some kind of 'purer-than-driven-snow' standard has no merit at all."[15] Republican Congressman John Saylor, the prime sponsor of the Wilderness Act in the House, said, "The act they [the Forest Service] tell us, is too narrow, too rigid, and too pure in its qualifying standards. Very frankly, those who take this position are wrong."[16]

There are many examples of less-than-pure areas being designated as wilderness—even in the West. In New Mexico, several miles of constructed dirt roads were closed and the land incorporated into the Sandia and Manzano Wildernesses in 1978. Part of the Gila Primitive Area with two gas-powered water wells and over 1,000 acres of juniper chaining was added to the Gila Wilderness in 1980.

To further illustrate, my old friend Jim Eaton, who has worked on wilderness area protection in California for over thirty-five years, tells me that, in completing wilderness boundary studies, he has driven or walked on roads suitable for passenger vehicles in the following now-designated California wilderness areas: Siskiyou, Snow Mountain, Point Reyes, Dome Land, Death Valley, Mojave National Preserve, Joshua Tree, Sheephole Valley, Palen/McCoy, Mecca Hills, Orocopia Mountain, Whipple Mountain, Russian, Lava Beds, Lassen, Yolla Bolly-Middle Eel, Ishi, Bucks Lake, Desolation, Mokelumne, Carson-Iceberg, Emigrant, Ansel Adams, John Muir, South Sierra, Kiavah, and Sheep Mountain.[17] Must proposed wilderness areas be roadless? No. Must they become roadless after designation? Yes.

Sometimes, under political pressure to appear "credible," conservation groups have taken a more "purist" view than required by the

Wilderness Act on what qualifies for wilderness. Some conservationists have taken this approach due to their lack of knowledge about the meaning and history of the Wilderness Act. One way this happens is for conservation groups to use "wilderness quality" to identify areas proposed as wilderness and then use human intrusions (particularly roads and vehicle tracks) to determine proposed boundaries. This cautious approach is understandable. Anticonservation politicians and extractive industry flacks love nothing more than to point out some human intrusion in a citizen wilderness area proposal that conservationists have overlooked. In response, some groups rigorously exclude past signs of human activity from their proposals.

In other cases, because agencies have inventoried roadless areas for suitability for wilderness area recommendation, conservation groups follow suit. For example, a wilderness group staffer in a western state instructed field workers to exclude roads passable to a passenger car. Another western wilderness group instructed its field volunteers that, under the criteria of the 1964 Wilderness Act, a qualifying area "must be at least 5,000 contiguous roadless acres." Both statements are in error, as we've seen. Under these purist misinterpretations, crafting a wilderness area proposal can become a technical exercise of determining if a vehicle route is a "road" or a "way." Under federal definitions, a "road" has been constructed and maintained, while a "way" has been created merely by the passage of motor vehicles. Of course, we still need to begin with roadless areas to identify potential wilderness areas, and it is important that wilderness groups continue to document, using field-intensive methods, roads and other intrusions. But they should not feel bound in what they can propose by such intrusions if there are reasonable ecological or other arguments to include less-than-pristine lands in their proposals.

Ecological Selection and Design Criteria

Protecting a wild place for its ecological value, in addition to its scenic or recreational opportunities, requires looking at an additional set of characteristics and seeing how an area fits into the larger natural landscape. How should the concepts of quality and purity be played now?

Quality. Inspiring scenery, high-country lakes, splendid campsites, interesting trails, and good fishing were qualities once sought in candidate wilderness areas. Important qualities today include habitat for sensitive species (including large carnivores), natural forests, unusual plant communities, plant communities not well represented in protected areas, winter range, migration routes, and hot spots of biodiversity.

Purity. In the past, the appearance of naturalness was more important than naturalness. Signs of an abandoned airstrip were thought a
greater intrusion on the wilderness character of an area than were
sheet and gully erosion from livestock grazing or doghair thickets of
pine resulting from fire suppression. A highly engineered, constructed
pack trail did not detract from the purity of an area, but a fading truck
trail did. Today, naturalness is more important than the appearance of
naturalness.

These new views of quality and purity are now leading conservationists to select and design wilderness areas. The following specific guidelines now used in boundary selection by the New Mexico Wilderness
Alliance, Sky Island Alliance, and other citizen groups are based on the
general conservation area design principles discussed in earlier chapters.

Human Intrusions

Human intrusions, including constructed roads and unconstructed vehicle ways, grazing facilities (stock tanks and corrals), logged areas, power
lines, and old mines, should be inventoried, photographed, and carefully
mapped and described. If intrusions are little used or substantially unnoticeable, the land should be included in a wilderness area proposal. If an
intrusion is noticeable or currently in use, its visual impact, level of use,
purpose, and importance should be weighed against the ecological values that would be protected or restored by closing or mitigating the
intrusion and including the land in a wilderness area or other protective
classification.

Size

The larger a wilderness area, the better. Size helps to buffer the interior of wilderness areas from edge effects and road impacts, provides
greater habitat, protects a more diverse area, and makes it more likely
that an area can be returned to natural disturbance regimes (especially
fire, flood, and predation). A small, isolated area needs more human
intervention for a longer time to maintain natural processes of disturbance, top-down regulation, and so forth. Large carnivores, many
other shy, wide-ranging, or sensitive species such as interior-nesting
songbirds, keystone processes (like natural fire), and natural vegetation
need large core areas. However, this is not cause to ignore protection
for smaller areas.

The relationship between the size of an area and the number of species it supports was a key generalization in the development of the theory of island biogeography.[18] I discussed this area-species relationship in chapters 4 and 7.

Rounded Boundaries

The shape of wilderness areas is important. More rounded boundaries protect against fragmentation and edge effects. For the same reasons that size is important, so are rounded boundaries. A long, narrow area has little interior habitat and is poorly buffered from road effects, poachers, and edge effects. An amoeba-shaped area with many lobes is weakened because of the relative narrowness of the lobes.

Cherrystems

Both agencies and conservation groups have proposed many wilderness areas that have long, narrow exclusions for roads up canyon bottoms or along ridges. These "cherrystems" compromise the protection of an area and effectively reduce its size, with all of the consequences discussed above. Cherrystems provide entry into the heart of wilderness areas for poachers, exotic species, off-road-vehicles, timber thieves, and other threats to wild nature. In those cases where vehicle routes provide access to stock tanks, windmills, or other facilities currently used by a grazing permittee and where it is politically impossible to close them, it is best to include such routes in a proposed wilderness area with locked gates open only to vehicle use by the permittee. This was done in the 1986 legislation designating wilderness areas in the El Malpais National Conservation Area in New Mexico. The New Mexico Wilderness Alliance has proposed this in some of its recent proposals.[19]

Landscape Context

Agencies (and sometimes conservation groups) have treated wilderness areas, national parks, and other protected areas as stand-alone units (islands), without regard to their landscape context. For protection of ecological values, context is highly important. Are other potential wilderness areas nearby? If so, boundary proposals should narrow the gap between wilderness areas so as to reduce fragmentation. Even if past human intrusions such as logging or roads separate the areas, wilderness boundaries should be brought as close together as possible. If feasible, conservationists should propose closing a dirt road to join two formerly separated wilderness areas. Landscape permeability between wilderness areas for large carnivores and other wide-ranging species and along streams for aquatic and riparian-dependent species is essential.

Habitat

In many cases, existing wilderness areas or roadless areas are limited to rugged mountains or other less-productive habitats. Habitat that is richer ecologically, despite the fact that it has dirt roads, jeep trails, or other intrusions, or has been logged, may lie outside the boundary. Such areas should be considered for wilderness recommendation from the standpoint of the ecological requirements of focal species. In the Sky Islands and New Mexico Highlands Wildlands Networks, proposed wilderness boundaries would close some dirt roads and ways up canyon bottoms because such areas are important habitat for the jaguar and riparian-dependent birds, mammals, fish, and reptiles that are vulnerable to road-borne poaching or harassment. Similarly, prime wolf habitat that may have dirt roads or other intrusions, such as high montane grasslands in the Gila National Forest or rolling Madrean woodland in the Coronado National Forest, are proposed for inclusion in wilderness areas. Montane forests that have had some logging are proposed as wilderness areas because of their value as habitat for species such as Mexican spotted owl and thick-billed parrot.[20]

In general, areas that are lower in elevation and less rugged should be given special consideration for inclusion in wilderness areas.

Riparian

In arid landscapes, riparian areas and available water are critical to many species. Researchers recommend that all Southwest riparian areas, no matter how small, be protected for migrating birds.[21] Wherever possible, then, the Sky Islands and New Mexico Highlands Wildlands Networks include riparian areas in proposed wilderness areas, wild and scenic rivers, linkages, and other protected areas, even if they have suffered from some human impact. As we've seen earlier, freshwater ecosystems and species are the most wounded in North America. Even in better-watered areas, wherever possible, streams, ponds, and lakes need to be protected in wilderness areas.

Wilderness Recovery Areas

Areas identified as important ecologically for designation as a wilderness area or for addition to a wilderness area but that are in need of major rehabilitation with motorized equipment, should be proposed as wilderness recovery areas. After such work is done and there is no longer a need for vehicles or power tools, the area becomes wilderness.

Now, I can hear some wilderness campaigners snorting at these guidelines, saying that if passing wilderness bills is hard now, it will be impossible with this pie-in-the-sky approach. Well, I wasn't born yesterday. What I do know is that if you don't ask for what you really want, you sure as hell aren't going to get it. If you compromise before you enter the battle, you only weaken yourself. As I think the history of the conservation movement as laid out in chapters 9 and 10 shows, success in protecting wilderness comes from having a vision of what is right. Besides, by basing our wilderness area proposals in solid science, we add robust new arguments and attract an additional constituency to the fight.

So much for protected area and wildlands network design. What about on-the-ground changes in the way wildlands are cared for? In chapter 14, I propose sensible reforms for land protection and management that would do much for creating de facto wildlands networks.

CHAPTER 14

Land Management Reforms for Implementing the North American Wildlands Network

It is one thing to craft a grand conservation vision into a detailed proposal. It is quite another to make the proposal a reality on the ground. So it is with regional wildlands networks, and so it is with the North American Wildlands Network. Early in the planning process for the regional Sky Islands Wildlands Network, for example, we realized that a detailed implementation plan that fit hand-in-glove with the wildlands network design was needed. To achieve this, the Wildlands Project hosted a workshop, led by David Johns and Rod Mondt, for over two dozen conservation leaders from the United States, Canada, and Mexico to tackle the theory and practice of implementing a wildlands network. At that workshop, I proposed that we use the metaphor of a jigsaw puzzle: The wildlands network represents the picture on the cover of the jigsaw puzzle box, and inside are the pieces (implementation- or conservation-action steps, or "actions") needed to create the cover picture. In such a scenario, some pieces of the wildlands network are already fitted together; others may not be fitted for years. Certain pieces are clearly matched with certain organizations or individuals, who have been working for weeks, months, or years to complete a portion of the puzzle; other pieces still wait to be worked on. But, despite these seemingly uncoordinated, individual efforts, we in fact have a picture of the whole puzzle and an understanding of what must be accomplished to complete it.

All Spine of the Continent wildlands networks, which are regional, rely on conservation-action steps (organized under each healing-the-wound goal described in chapter 7) to achieve the vision. Such detail is invaluable to regional wildlands networks.[1] Because of the vast sweep of the North American Wildlands Network, however, I'll approach its implementation by answering the following questions: Which management reforms and restoration actions would most practically and quickly help to establish the Four Continental MegaLinkages in the United States? What reforms would best protect and restore roadless habitat as well as protect and restore landscape permeability?

To answer these questions, I suggest using the following criteria:

- Good scientific backing
- Existing citizen conservationist support
- Fiscally responsible in long run
- Quick, observable effects
- Effectiveness in achieving rewilding goals

The specific actions I offer below generally meet these criteria. Some of these actions are already the focus of major campaigns by conservation groups; others have been largely ignored. Some are established methods requiring only a slight shift in emphasis; others are new approaches. Specific actions that best meet my criteria for continental-scale conservation are the following:

- Reintroduce carnivores wherever possible
- Reintroduce beavers and other highly interactive species
- Establish species recovery goals for ecologically effective populations
- Generally halt predator and "pest" control
- Reform wildlife management to adopt a more ecological approach
- Select and design new wilderness areas based on ecological principles
- Protect all large roadless areas on public lands
- Protect all small roadless areas on public lands
- Create larger roadless areas in the East
- Remove livestock from much of the public lands
- Reform livestock grazing where it continues
- Prioritize simple soil and gully erosion control
- Prohibit big-tree logging
- Develop standards for ecological restoration in wilderness areas
- Develop protection, restoration, and management standards for public lands wildlife linkages and compatible-use areas
- Remove abandoned and unnecessary livestock fencing
- Restrict all motorized vehicles to designated routes

- Reduce the miles of public lands roads
- Stop bogus R.S. 2477 (highway right-of-way) claims
- Establish landscape permeability as a public land management goal
- Identify and remove or mitigate barriers to wildlife movement
- Encourage ecological management of private, corporate, and tribal lands important for linkages
- Identify private lands that should be acquired on a willing-seller basis
- Restore a natural fire ecology
- Remove destructive, unnecessary dams
- Restore or mimic natural over-the-bank flooding, where possible
- Establish in-stream flow as a beneficial water use
- Prioritize removal of exotic species that threaten native species and wildlands
- Design networks for climate change

Although at this time a conservation-hostile administration and Congress may block reforms, conservationists and responsible land managers should work to develop solid strategies and reforms in anticipation of a future conservation-friendly administration or Congress that might pass them.[2] Of course, building support now for such policies is essential. Some actions can still be implemented, even while politicians beholden to extractive industries are in power.

Reintroduce Carnivores Wherever Possible

By now it's clear that many of the ecological problems in wildlands are due to the extermination of wolves, big cats, and other carnivores. Their recovery is essential where adequate, secure habitat can be protected or restored. Until now, carnivore recovery efforts have been localized and scattered. Conservation groups and scientists need to endorse the wolf and mountain lion recovery visions presented in chapter 8 and begin to campaign for significant recovery.

Reintroduction of large carnivores is difficult, and several attempts have failed. However, each year wildlife managers are gaining more experience and achieving greater success. For example, critics ranging from ranchers to animal rights activists damned the Colorado Division of Wildlife project to restore lynx in the San Juan Mountains. They charged that the program was a failure because lynx were failing to reproduce. Such charges were refuted by the lynx themselves in the early summer of 2003 when at least fourteen kittens from five different females were found.[3] Carnivore recovery requires patience. Often a reintroduction does not take off until wild-born animals produce wild-born young themselves. Brian Miller and his colleagues recently reviewed carnivore reintroductions and offered guidelines for future efforts in *Animal Conservation*.[4] The 2001 book, *Large Mammal Restoration*, is an excellent overview with case studies and recommendations.[5] Conservationists should study these publications to better understand the biological, social, and political aspects of wildlife reintroductions.

Let me just touch on two of the many lessons wildlife biologists have recently learned about restoration of extirpated carnivores. The first is that wolves can be reintroduced to an area with little or no loss to livestock. Predation by reintroduced wolves on livestock is the leading cause of opposition to their recovery. Wendy Brown and Dave Parsons, who coordinated the reintroduction of the Mexican wolf in Arizona and New Mexico for the U.S. Fish and Wildlife Service, write, "Wolves released into areas where livestock were not present for at least two months after release, and where elk were abundant, did not kill livestock."[6] The second is that natural recolonization of some species is not always possible. David Onorato and Eric Hellgren, in a study of how black bears repopulated the Big Bend country of Texas from Mexico, write, "In contiguous habitat, black bear and probably many other solitary carnivores spread by incremental range expansion by related females." They also point out that "large carnivores with limited female dispersal will be slow to recolonize disjunct portions of the their range from which they have been extirpated."[7] This work shows that we cannot expect natural recolonization by such species and that direct reintroduction of females is necessary.

Some conservationists have shied away from proposing carnivore reintroduction because of the fear of outspoken opposition from entrenched interests. Michael Soulé warns against such timidity, saying, "In the long run, without restoration of top predators, we'll never be able to protect most biodiversity."[8]

Reintroduce Beavers and Other Highly Interactive Species

Similar efforts for widespread recovery of beavers, prairie dogs, and other "ecosystem engineers" need to be advocated by the whole conservation community. Both the U.S. Forest Service and the Bureau of Land Management (BLM) have had stream restoration successes by reintroducing beavers. A key to successful beaver restoration is keeping cattle out of riparian areas.[9]

Establish Species Recovery Goals for Ecologically Effective Populations

As we saw in chapter 8, Michael Soulé, Jim Estes, Joel Berger, and Carlos Martinez del Rio argue that U.S. Fish and Wildlife Service Endangered Species Act "recovery objectives are becoming indefensible in light of increasing knowledge from community ecology." They recommend that "conservation plans should call for recovery or repatriation of such interactive species at ecologically effective densities in as many places as are currently realistic." A highly interactive species is one whose "virtual or effective absence leads to significant changes in some feature of its ecosystem(s)." Surveying those endangered and threatened species with published recovery plans, they find that "a substantial proportion of [threatened and endangered] species are strong interactors" and that "ecological function is simply unknown for the majority of listed species." This clearly demonstrates that the current approach to endangered and threatened species recovery, which strives only to preserve a minimum viable population that will stave off extinction of the species, must instead work to restore highly interactive species in all available habitat in their former ranges and at population densities where they can prevent or repair ecological wounds.[10]

Conservationists should embrace Soulé and company's call for a new approach to species recovery as detailed in their ecologically effective populations paper. We need to popularize it until its wisdom is widely accepted among conservationists, biologists, and land managers, just as the need for connectivity and the role of top-down regulation are widely accepted in the conservation community today.

Generally Halt Predator and "Pest" Control

The United States and Canada think of themselves as the most civilized, advanced societies in the history of the planet. Yet in the twenty-first century, both are practicing frontier-style wildlife management that was proven unsound over eighty years ago. The bloody slaughter of "problem" animals, be they wolves, big cats, seals, prairie dogs, bison, or elk, continues almost unabated from the gory, glory years of the gopher chokers. We cannot reasonably call ourselves civilized until the slaughter stops. Canada is highly sensitive to its international reputation; European attention to and criticism of its barbaric and prescientific wildlife management policies would be effective in changing them. Even though the United States seems not to give a fig for what other countries think of it, if African, Latin American, and Asian wildlife-rich countries were to unfavorably compare the United States' management of bison, wolves, and other flagship wildlife with their own efforts to manage tigers, elephants, rhinos, and jaguars, the desired effect might be achieved. I'd love to see protests in India, Zambia, and Mexico demanding that the United States protect the Yellowstone bison and restore wolves to Colorado.

Reform Wildlife Management to Adopt a More Ecological Approach

Many university wildlife management departments are housed in agricultural schools. Odd though it might seem, it was a logical choice, since for most of the past century wildlife management has been little more than "game farming": federal, state, and provincial wildlife agencies manipulate habitat to increase game to unnaturally high populations, hatchery-rear fish for put-and-take fishing, encourage trapping of "furbearers"—which are essential carnivores—without regard for what their ecologically effective populations may be, in addition to killing predators. Nonetheless, many outstanding wildlife biologists and ethical hunters and anglers have worked to make wildlife agencies more ecologically aware throughout the twentieth century. Further transformation of wildlife management agencies from an agricultural to an ecological mindset and practices needs to be a high priority for all conservationists.

Select and Design New Wilderness Areas Based on Ecological Principles

As I've stressed throughout *Rewilding North America*, wilderness areas are the heart of a wildlands network and are the best tool we have to protect wild things. To make wilderness areas even more effective as nature reserves, all wilderness conservation groups need to embrace ecological criteria for the selection and boundary design of proposed wilderness areas (chapter 13). Ecological characteristics and placement in the landscape should be adopted as key factors for deciding which proposed wilderness areas should be priorities for enactment. Using ecological values would also add a stronger set of arguments for protection and would help to bring in biologists as advocates. Wilderness groups should encourage biologists in their regions to help develop specific recommendations for how to select and design wilderness areas.

For example, the Committee for Biological Commentary on Utah Wilderness Issues proposed eleven ecological guidelines in 1995.[11]

Protect All Large Roadless Areas on Public Lands

A variety of research is showing that protecting roadless areas on the public lands would be a big step for protecting biodiversity and for putting together a wildlands network. Scientists with The Wilderness Society analyzed the ecological importance of roadless areas in the northern Rockies (i.e., Montana, Wyoming, and Idaho) and found that, in comparison to designated wilderness areas, roadless areas contain "rare, species-rich, and often-declining vegetation communities," more lower-elevation lands, and provide connectivity between existing wilderness areas. The report states, "Roadless areas on national forests . . . may become the missing link in a conservation reserve system for the United States."[12] This study follows in the steps of those done by Reed Noss, Jim Strittholt, and others for the Klamath-Siskiyou region in northwestern California and southwestern Oregon. I discussed their research in chapter 11, where I quoted Noss: "Somewhat to our surprise, roadless areas on public lands turned out to function well as the basic 'building blocks' of our reserve design."[13]

Wilderness designation, of course, is the best way to protect roadless areas, and conservationists should seek to protect most roadless areas through wilderness designation, but that is a difficult quest. In the meantime, roadless areas should be protected through whatever means are available. The roadless area protection rule that, for all its flaws, was adopted by the Clinton administration in January 2001, ranks with the passage of the Wilderness Act as a landmark conservation victory—had it been successfully implemented. Unfortunately, from its beginning, the Bush administration did everything possible to overturn roadless area protection for these 58.5 million acres of national forest. The Bush administration's statement in June 2003 that it would implement the roadless area protection policy was a whopper—even by Beltway standards. Soon after the widespread favorable media coverage, the roadless areas on the Tongass and Chugach National Forests in Alaska were dropped from the rule, and a provision to allow state governors to ask for "waivers of the roadless rule" was proposed by Mark Rey, the timber industry lobbyist who was appointed by Bush to oversee the Forest Service as Undersecretary for Natural Resources and Environment in the Department of Agriculture.[14] Very little media attention was given to how these changes gutted the rule.

The Bush administration also sapped protection of BLM roadless areas any way it could. For example, in a 2003 back-room legal settlement with the state of Utah, Secretary of the Interior Gale Norton yanked long-standing policy and procedures for identifying additional qualifying wilderness study areas.

Conservationists have long made protection of roadless areas a priority. The ecological importance of roadless areas adds strong additional arguments for their protection.

Protect All Small Roadless Areas on Public Lands

To qualify as a roadless area on the public lands, the agencies have generally set the bottom line at 5,000 contiguous acres. This acreage has a basis in the Wilderness Act: "An area of wilderness is further defined to mean in this Act an area of undeveloped Federal land . . . and which . . . has at least five thousand acres of land or is of sufficient size as to make practicable its preservation and use in an unimpaired condition."[15]

Nonetheless, 5,000 acres has never been an unbreakable rule for wilderness areas or roadless areas. Congress has established a number of wilderness areas smaller than 5,000 acres because it has recognized important values in certain small areas and has determined that they are practical for management. On their own, the federal land-managing agencies have studied and recommended areas smaller than 5,000 acres for wilderness area designation.

During the public comment period for the Roadless Area Conservation Rule in 2000, conservationists urged the Clinton administration to protect national forest roadless areas of 1,000 acres or more, but to no avail. Some criticized this effort as simply grabbing for every acre. However, a landmark scientific study published in *Conservation Biology* makes it clear that protecting these smaller roadless areas will achieve much that protecting larger roadless areas alone cannot. Jim Strittholt of the Conservation Biology Institute and Dominick DellaSala of the World Wildlife Fund studied roadless areas of 1,000 acres or more in the Klamath-Siskiyou ecoregion. They found that roadless areas between 1,000 and 5,000 acres in size contained "substantially more plant, vertebrate, and invertebrate occurrences" of heritage elements than did existing wilderness areas and larger roadless areas, provided "additional representation of low and medium elevations," "were particularly important in contributing to 54 different habitat types," and "would contribute to the protection of the overall landscape connectivity." They argue that protection of small roadless areas is "even more important in regions where the majority of roadless areas are small, such as the southern Appalachians."[16] Conservationists need to incorporate the Stritholt-DellaSala paper in their tool box and continue to press for protection of all roadless areas of 1,000 acres or more. Of course, the bigger the road-less area, the better; but in today's fragmented wildlands, much of the best remaining habitat and landscape permeability is in smaller roadless blocks.

Create Larger Roadless Areas in the East

East of the Rocky Mountains and south of the boreal forest in Canada and the United States, there are very few large roadless areas. In *The Big Outside*, Howie Wolke and I identified 311 roadless areas larger than 100,000 acres in the western United States, but only thirty-nine east of the Rockies.[17] At least ten of those eastern big roadless areas are questionable because of poor maps and lack of field study. The Forest Service should close many dirt roads in national forests and national grasslands east of the Rockies to create larger core wild areas. Conservationists should prod the Forest Service to do so during the forest planning process.

Remove Livestock from Much of the Public Lands

The damage domestic livestock have inflicted on the arid lands of North America is incontrovertible, despite what apologists for the livestock industry claim. The damage continues today. Moreover, the entrenched livestock associations in the western states and provinces are the primary source of opposition to protecting and restoring large carnivores. On the other hand, some private and public lands ranchers support wolf recovery and have restored streams, among other good practices. Despite promising innovations by these conservationist ranchers, much commercial livestock grazing on western public lands is clearly incompatible with maintaining and restoring a healthy landscape and with the recovery of native species—and especially with rewilding. Practical, fair approaches to the grazing issue should be based on the following principles:

- Livestock grazing is not appropriate on many (maybe most) public lands in the West.
- In the right context, excellent livestock management can be compatible with ecological restoration and recovery of native species, including large carnivores.

- Grazing by domestic livestock on public lands is a privilege, not a right.
- Grazing by domestic livestock on public lands must be managed to allow healing the wounds of degraded ecosystems.
- Recovery of the wolf and other carnivores must be accepted in public lands livestock management.
- Recovery and maintenance of healthy populations of elk, bighorn, pronghorn, beaver, prairie dogs, and other native species must be accepted in public lands livestock management.
- Where livestock grazing is incompatible with ecosystem recovery and the protection and recovery of native species, including large carnivores, fair solutions for the grazing permittee and taxpayer should be worked out.

Unfortunately, many public lands ranchers have made it clear that they will not reform their practices to welcome wolves or restore riparian areas. In the Sky Islands and New Mexico Highlands Wildlands Network Visions, I identified several approaches to getting cattle and sheep off the public lands:

Voluntary Retirement Option. Andy Kerr proposed this legislative approach in 1998. It would allow a grazing permittee to not run livestock on his or her allotment (under current rules, if a permittee does not graze, the allotment can be given to another rancher). A permittee could donate or sell his or her AUMs[18] to the government and the allotment would be permanently retired. Kerr proposes $175 an AUM, a generous price. It would in fact be cheaper in the long run for the government to buy out permits under this program because it costs the Forest Service and BLM much more to operate their grazing programs than they receive in fees. Annual deficits run several hundred million dollars. Alternatively, a rancher could sell his or her permit to a hunting or conservation group, who could then ask the agency to retire it.[19] A pilot bill to authorize buyouts in Arizona was introduced in Congress in 2003 with the support of many federal grazing permittees (one poll in Arizona found that two-thirds of permittees support the buyout).[20] All conservation organizations need to get behind this approach. Those who quail at the $175 per AUM price are being penny-wise and pound-foolish. Removing cattle and sheep from much of the public lands offers untold possibilities for conservation.

Grazing-Permit Reform. A progressive group of ranchers and conservationists convened by economist Karl Hess Jr. proposed a free-market approach that would allow anyone to bid on a federal grazing permit (now only ranchers may do so), would allow a permittee to not graze livestock, and would allow a permittee to sublease the permit to others, such as a conservation group that could choose not to run livestock.

Third-Party Buyout. Several wealthier conservation groups, including the Grand Canyon Trust, have bought out ranchers with federal grazing permits and then worked with the managing agency to retire the allotment.

State Lease Bidding. The southwestern conservation group Forest Guardians has successfully outbid ranchers for state trust lands grazing leases in New Mexico and Arizona. They've removed the livestock and undertaken riparian restoration. If other states would allow open bidding on trust lands, and the federal government would do so on BLM and Forest Service lands, we could remove livestock from many sensitive areas and return higher fees to the public.[21]

By taking on the public lands grazing problem with free-market approaches, conservationists can undercut the chest-thumping rhetoric of the cattlegrower and sheepgrower associations. Conservationists need to identify the federal grazing allotments that are the biggest problems for recovery of wolves and other species, and then prioritize them for buyout and retirement of some kind.

Grazing apologists and some researchers have argued that grasslands converted to shrublands from past overgrazing may not ever be able to recover, even if livestock are removed, because the ecosystem has shifted to a new "stable state." Recent research published in *Conservation Biology*, however, shows that while there may be little improvement after even twenty years of rest from livestock, from twenty years on there is remarkable recovery. This may be due to the "rare, episodic nature" of summer rainfall sufficient for "abundant seed production and establishment [that] may occur only once or twice per decade."[22] In a recent study of the removal of cattle from Arizona's San Pedro River Riparian National Conservation Area, David Krueper and his colleagues write, "Our results suggest that removing cattle from riparian areas in the southwestern United States can have profound benefits for breeding birds."[23] Conservationists working on livestock grazing issues should familiarize themselves with this research and use it to rebut grazing apologists.

Reform Livestock Grazing Where It Continues

In his recent book, *Farming with the Wild*, Dan Imhoff spotlights promising efforts to farm and ranch in harmony with wild nature. In the Sky Islands and New Mexico Highlands, large ranches owned or operated by Ted Turner, Jim Winder, Joe and Valer Austin, Mac Donaldson, the Hadley family, the Animas Foundation, Rocky Mountain Elk Foundation, and others are critical parts of the wildlands networks, as are smaller ranches owned by members of the Malpai Borderlands Group, the Holder family, and others. These ranchers are helping to restore imperiled species, including the Mexican wolf, jaguar, black-footed ferret, black-tailed prairie dog, desert bighorn sheep, aplomado falcon, California condor, Rio Grande chub, and Chiricahua leopard frog. They are restoring streams and riparian forests and putting wildfire back into the ecosystem. Jim Winder and Will and Jan Holder are strong supporters of restoring the Mexican wolf. They undertake no predator control and market "wolf-friendly" beef. Becky Weed and Dave Tyler ranch sheep outside of Bozeman, Montana, where they've learned to live with predators. They market predator-friendly, organic lamb and wool products.[24] These ranchers show that it is possible to do a much better job, minimizing the impacts their livestock have on wildlife. However, even the best ranchers, as Jim Winder has told me, probably cannot do a good job of livestock management in many areas of the public lands, such as rugged areas of the Gila National Forest. In these places, removal of livestock, as discussed above, should be the goal.

Farming with the Wild, has helped a promising new effort. The Wild Farm Alliance is bringing together farmers, ranchers, conservationists, and scientists to plan a new agriculture that goes well beyond sustainability and organic production to living with wild animals and wilderness, and protecting and restoring biodiversity.

Prioritize Simple Soil and Gully Erosion Control

Seventy years ago, during the dust bowl, soil conservation and erosion control were national priorities. Such efforts have slackened over the years, and erosion still eats away at millions of acres of national forests and BLM lands and degrades thousands of miles of stream with deadly impacts on native fish and other aquatic species. The agencies seem not to see much of this ongoing gully cutting and sheet erosion. Combating erosion does not have to be expensive or complex, though it requires a little sweat. Josiah and Valer Austin have shown on their El Coronado Ranch in Arizona's Chiricahua Mountains that by building gabions in eroded watercourses and gullies and on steep hillsides, most erosion can be effectively halted.[25] Gabions are simple gully plugs or low dams hand built with nearby rocks, two to twelve courses high. Because they are loose rock with no mortar, water flows through, but silt and other debris is captured. The results are quick and amazing. I propose a national program on the public lands to build gabions where needed. As part of this, I suggest that all Forest Service and BLM desk jockeys, particularly forest supervisors, BLM district managers, and the like, be required to spend one day a month in the field building gabions or removing old fence.

Prohibit Big-Tree Logging

Throughout North America, we have ravaged the land for big trees. We continue. Big tree logging here should be compared to that in the Amazon, central Africa, and Southeast Asia. Conservationists can show that the United States and Canada are as bad as the third-world timber beasts in our looting of forests and blithe disregard of wildlife. Although former Forest Service Chief Mike Dombeck instituted a prohibition on old-growth logging at the close of the Clinton administration, it has been overturned by the incoming Bush administration. Canada, too, should be an international pariah for its logging practices. Conservationists have campaigned valiantly since the early 1980s to stop logging of old-growth forests in North America. Millions of acres of ancient forests have been protected in Canada and the United States as a result. Such efforts are all the more important now in the United States, as the logging industry dishonestly uses the threat of forest fires to open more public forests to big-tree cutting.

Develop Standards for Ecological Restoration in Wilderness Areas

When the Wilderness Act was passed, it was believed that halting destructive uses would allow areas to naturally restore themselves. Now we know that some wounds will continue to worsen without healing intervention. There is no current consensus, nor are there guidelines for ecological restoration in wilderness areas. Conservationists, scientists, recreationists, and land managers need to continue to discuss the issue and work to establish guidelines that respect the special character of wilderness areas.

Develop Protection, Restoration, and Management Standards for Public Lands Wildlife Linkages and Compatible-Use Lands

Currently, agencies have no policies or directives on how to manage public lands to serve as compatible-use lands and linkages or how to protect and restore landscape permeability. Conservation groups also have little to guide their advocacy other than the guidelines offered in chapter 13 and in the Spine of the Continent Wildlands Network documents. The larger conservation community needs to publish such policies. This chapter is a starting point.

Remove Abandoned and Unnecessary Livestock Fencing

Across the public lands, including in wilderness areas, are tens of thousands of miles of barbed-wire and net-wire fence strung for livestock grazing. Much of this fencing has been abandoned or is no longer needed. Nonetheless, it remains, creating a barrier to wildlife movement, particularly for pronghorn, who can't jump fences. Other wildlife are also entangled and killed. Conservationists and hunting groups should push the agencies to remove such fences. Citizens could offer their services to take out fences, much as they do for trail maintenance. Fences that, for conservation reasons, remain in pronghorn country must be modified with "pronghorn passes," which replace the bottom strand of barbed wire with a barbless wire at least 16 inches above the ground, so that pronghorn can go under the fence.

Restrict All Motorized Vehicles to Designated Routes

Despite executive orders by Presidents Nixon and Carter, federal land-managing agencies have refused to control the scourge of off-road vehicles. Tens of millions of acres of the public's land are wide-open to cross-country travel by ATVs (all-terrain vehicles), dirt bikes, four-wheel drives, and snowmobiles; much of the land protected on paper from reckless off-road vehicle use is regularly invaded by outlaw recreationists. We conservationists need to redouble our efforts to restrict vehicles to designated roads only. I think there would be great public support for this. Who do you know who likes off-road vehicles except those who use them or those who sell them? We should not let this vocal and industry-funded minority intimidate us. Complaints about off-road vehicles, particularly ATVs, is rising even from unexpected quarters, including national forest supervisors, rural county governments, and businesspeople in outdoor recreation resorts.

Reduce the Miles of Public Lands Roads

Well over half a million miles of roads lace the public lands. Many of these roads are unneeded for any legitimate purpose. Based on a wealth of scientific research on the effects roads have on many wildlife species, a maximum should be set of 1 mile of road for every square mile of land and considerably less than that where possible. Reducing road mileage is one of the most effective ways to protect habitat and sensitive species. Mike Dombeck recognized this at the end of the Clinton administration and tried to establish a program that would evaluate what the optimum road network for each national forest was and then close unnecessary roads. Under the Bush administration the roads initiative was canned.

Stop Bogus R.S. 2477 (Highway Right-of-way) Claims

Revised Statute 2477 was a Civil War–era law to encourage road construction in the western states and territories by giving states and counties rights-of-way across public lands. This forgotten frontier relic was largely repealed by the Federal Lands Policy and Management Act in 1976. But, for over a decade, unscrupulous politicians, motorheads, and extractive industries have seized on a loophole to now argue that cow paths, foot trails, arroyo bottoms, and even less-visible routes are actually highways that should have their rights-of-way handed over to the locals. This provision is being consciously used in Alaska, Utah, and other benighted states to slice and dice national parks and wilderness areas with roads and to prevent future protection of public lands. A 1993 National Park Service memo warned that 17 million acres of parklands could suffer from these phony right-of-way claims.[26] In 2003, Interior Secretary Gale Norton cut a back-room deal with Utah Governor Mike Leavitt to allow wholesale approval of R.S. 2477 claims. Conservation groups, such as the Southern Utah Wilderness Alliance, have done their best to fight this rip-off.[27] However, many more groups must be alerted to the threat. Traveling road shows and editorial board visits have brought wilderness campaigns in Utah's redrock wilderness, Alaska's Tongass rainforest, and the Arctic National Wildlife Refuge to national attention. The time is now ripe for such an outreach campaign on R.S. 2477.

Establish Landscape Permeability as a Public Land Management Goal

Conservation groups and federal and state wildlife and land managing agencies should establish landscape permeability (i.e., wildlife movement connectivity) as an overarching goal for management of public lands. Forest Service researchers in the northern Rockies and Pacific Northwest have conducted solid research on landscape permeability, and citizens and wildlife managers are working together on landscape permeability campaigns in California, Washington, New Mexico, and other states. Highway departments need to be brought in, as they have been in California and New Mexico.

Identify and Remove or Mitigate Barriers to Wildlife Movement

Few people were thinking about wildlife-crossing structures over or under roads before the 1990s. That has changed. European countries have taken the lead on designing, building, and evaluating wildlife-crossing structures for animals ranging from toads to ibex. By experimenting with different structures in various locations and evaluating their use—what species use them, at what times of day, how often, and how "accessories" (fencing and vegetation) encourage use—biologists and engineers in North America have quickly advanced our state of knowledge about them. Maureen Hartmann at the University of Montana recently conducted a literature review of papers analyzing the effectiveness of wildlife-crossing structures. Based on that study, she offered these recommendations:

- Take a multispecies approach rather than a single-species focus, remembering that species do not function in isolation but are components of ecological systems;
- Know the biology of the species in the area, their distribution, abundance, and ecological and behavioral needs;
- Place the structures at known migration routes, away from human disturbance. This can be determined by roadkill data, infrared cameras, GIS [geographic information system] modeling, and track-count surveys;
- Make the passages wide to accommodate a larger number of species;
- Try to build structures that allow for natural lighting and low noise levels;
- Have a clear view to the other side;

- Use fencing designed to reduce wildlife intrusions;
- Conduct intensive monitoring before and after constructing the wildlife passages via track count surveys, radio-collaring, mark-recapture studies, etc.; and
- Share the results![28]

Encourage Ecological Management of Private, Corporate, and Tribal Lands Important for Linkages

Many of the areas needed for landscape permeability are in private ownership. Often these lands are being managed in ways incompatible with wildlife movement. Intensive agricultural operations, suburban and exurban sprawl, ski areas, and various other developments on private lands create difficult or impenetrable barriers for many species. Conservation groups, land trusts, and wildlife managers need to work with private landowners, corporations, and tribes to mitigate barriers.

Identify Private Lands That Should Be Acquired on a Willing-Seller Basis

Although conservation has traditionally focused on the public lands, we now realize that private lands also must play a major role in wildlands networks if permeability is to be restored across the landscape and if all ecosystems and biological hot spots are to be represented in protected area networks. Since the 1950s, The Nature Conservancy has worked to acquire private lands of high ecological value. Now the Foundation for Deep Ecology, the Wildlands Project, and other groups are encouraging *wildlands philanthropy*—the acquisition of large areas by conservation-minded people who will protect such lands for their ecological integrity.[29]

Often, only acquisition of private lands by land trusts, wildlands philanthropists, or government will safeguard such lands. Such conservation acquisitions can also restore or mitigate barriers to wildlife movement. Land trusts, including The Nature Conservancy, Trust for Public Land, and the Conservation Fund, as well as local and regional conservancies, should identify and prioritize properties important for landscape permeability for acquisition or easement.

Brian Czech analyzed conservation land acquisition from economic and ecological perspectives in *Conservation Biology* and suggested these priorities: "(1) relatively inexpensive lands in relatively intact ecosystems should be made a priority for acquisition; (2) fee-title acquisition should be heavily favored over easement acquisition, and (3) low-lying coastal properties should be given less priority [because of rising sea levels from global warming]."[30]

Restore a Natural Fire Ecology

After the news media overhyped forest fires in the West, everyone seemed to suddenly know what biologists and conservationists have known for years—that our forests are dangerously unhealthy because of fire suppression. Now politicians, demagogues, and timber industry representatives want to solve the problem with the same practices that created it. Conservationists are on solid footing with the scientific facts and proposals for reform, but we seem to have lost the advertising war, partly because the other side spins better and has more money to get their spin out, partly because they twist the truth, but partly because we haven't been very good at telling our story.

Natural fire regimes in the West are out of kilter because of

- Deliberate overgrazing in the early twentieth-century to remove the grass that carried natural, cool, ground fires, and continued overgrazing that has prevented ground cover from recovering so it can carry cool fires.
- Maniacal fire suppression, not only in economically valuable timberlands and near towns and habitations, but also in the most remote wilderness areas and in areas with no timber at all, such as sagebrush steppes.
- Targeting of big trees in logging because they are most valuable. Much of the national forests are now doghair thickets of little trees. Big trees withstand natural fire well, but doghair is fuel that carries the fire to the crown.
- Hundreds of thousands of miles of roads in fire-prone habitats that give access to careless people.
- The spread of summer homes, mansions, and suburbs into fire-prone forests.

Conservationists should make it clear that we are the original and strongest advocates of forest thinning projects that are designed to effectively reduce fire danger in unnaturally dense stands, not to give timber companies valuable trees. We need to sit down and craft our message, work with top advertisers, and talk sense to the American people and policy makers.

In his plenary talk to the 2003 Society of Conservation Biology conference, Mike Dombeck explained why it is so difficult to talk sense to the public about forest fires. The 2002 Biscuit Fire in Oregon received great interest from the news media when it was burning. News reports screamed that 499,000 acres had been "devastated." But, Dombeck said that a cool-headed analysis by the Forest Service after the fire was out revealed that only 16 percent of that half a million acres was severely burned, 23 percent moderately burned, and 61 percent lightly burned or not burned at all.

However, even some of the best-intentioned proposals for dealing with the fire "crisis" are doomed to failure because they ignore fire ecology. Andy Stahl, publisher of *Forest* magazine, editorializes, "It's time to face reality. Not only have we lost the war against forest fires, it is a war we cannot win. We must learn to live with fire."[31]

Remove Destructive, Unnecessary Dams

Dams have come down; more will come down, as we saw in chapter 10. Conservationists need to conduct nationwide surveys in the United States and Canada to identify and rank dams that are ecologically destructive, unnecessary, unsafe, and economically questionable, and then go after them in a coordinated way.

Restore or Mimic Natural over-the-Bank Flooding, Where Possible

In the Southwest and other areas, riparian forest ecosystems need regular over-the-bank flooding at appropriate seasons so that native trees and shrubs can reproduce. Such natural flooding also helps native fish and other organisms to spawn. The University of New Mexico (UNM) Biology Department prepared an in-depth report for the U.S. Fish and Wildlife Service from its research on the degradation of the Middle Rio Grande riparian forest (*bosque*) and how to heal it. They "predict that flooding previously isolated riparian forest will initiate reorganization of the ecosystem and that this process of reorganization will eventually return the riparian forest to a position similar to its historic state."[32] More recently, other UNM biologists, researching the invasion of the exotic salt cedar (*tamarisk*) on the Rio Grande, write, "Our results suggest that even in the presence of an invader [salt cedar] that positively responds to disturbance, reestablishment of historical flooding regimes and post-flood hydrology can restore this ecosystem by promoting its dominant plant species [cottonwood, willow]."[33] Restoring or mimicking natural hydrological cycles would do wonders for the health of rivers and the imperiled species living in them and their riparian forests.

Establish In-Stream Flow as a Beneficial Water Use

Most western states have bizarre and irrational water laws dating from nineteenth-century mining rushes. In the West, water rights are often separate from land ownership. Those who hold water rights must put them to "beneficial" use or they can be taken away by the state. In-stream flow is not considered a beneficial use of water rights in many western states. In other words, water for wildlife is not a beneficial use. Changing such benighted policies is critical, as is purchasing or leasing water rights by conservationists and government agencies for in-stream flow and other wildlife uses. Until this is done, more and more species could become endangered or extinct because they have no "rights" to water.

Prioritize Removal of Exotic Species That Threaten Native Species and Wildlands

Serious efforts to control exotic species are in place around the United States. For example, aquatic biologist Roland Knapp and his volunteers have physically removed fish from some naturally fishless lakes in Yosemite and Sequoia-Kings Canyon National Parks to protect the imperiled mountain yellow-legged frog, with considerable success.[34] The Federal Interagency Committee for Management of Noxious and Exotic Weeds has pulled together a remarkable collection of organizations, including federal and state agencies, Indian tribes, extractive industries, and conservation groups, to endorse the National Strategy for Invasive Plant Management.[35] The National Park Service has established Exotic Plant Management Teams, based on firefighting teams, to aggressively attack exotic plants in national parks.[36]

Conservation biologists should try to identify those exotic plants, animals, and pathogens that most seriously threaten highly interactive species, natural processes, and wildlands, and encourage federal and state agencies to put a priority on controlling them. A good beginning for developing such guidelines, the article "Directing Research to Reduce the Impacts of Nonindigenous Species," recently appeared in *Conservation Biology*.[37]

Design Networks for Climate Change

Reed Noss and some other biologists have begun to develop standards for managing lands to reduce greenhouse gas emissions and sequester carbon, and to design networks that will allow plants and animals to shift their ranges north or to higher elevations as temperatures rise. Noss presents his recommendations in the *New Mexico Highlands Wildlands Network Vision*.[38] An international group of biologists has recently recognized the vital role of wildlands networks for countering the negative effects of climate change. They write, "To be fully effective, regional reserve networks and landscape connectivity must be wed with effective modeling of future climate change and managed specifically for climate change." They warn, "Landscape connectivity and management of the matrix for biodiversity will be required on an unprecedented scale to avoid large numbers of extinctions due to climate change."[39]

I do not believe any of these proposed actions are radical or excessive. They are *conservative* in the true sense of that word. They are prudent, they are fiscally responsible, they are examples of people behaving responsibly and taking responsibility for their actions, they are pious before the majesty and mystery of nature, and they have a deep respect for posterity.

Each of these actions would help protect and restore an enduring resource of wilderness in the United States. Similar actions would help do so elsewhere in North America. We know how to undertake all of them. Nearly all would save taxpayers money. In a rational society, we would be doing them now. But human society is not rational. Nor are individual humans. In the first chapter, I discussed how most Americans are blissfully unaware of the mass extinction we are causing. The most important step conservationists and conservation biologists can take is to develop a strategy on how to take the story of ecological crisis to the public in a convincing way and to give them hope that we can do something about it. In the final chapter, I briefly tussle with how we can move from words and ideas to action.

CHAPTER 15

Hope for the Future

Can vision become reality? Some examples of continental-conservation successes on the ground have surprised even me since 2000.

At the Wilderness 2000 Conference in Denver, the Wildlands Project released the recently published *Sky Islands Wildlands Network Conservation Plan*, a joint effort with the Sky Island Alliance, New Mexico Wilderness Alliance, Naturalia (a Mexican conservation group), and others.[1] About this region, Aldo Leopold wrote: "To my mind these live oak-dotted hills fat with side oats grama, these pine-clad mesas spangled with flowers, these lazy trout streams burbling along under great sycamores and cottonwoods, come near to being the cream of creation."[2]

The landscape that gripped Leopold was where the Sierra Madre and the Rocky Mountains overlap, where the plants and animals of the Neotropics mingle with those of the Nearctic, where jaguar and grizzly hunted the same canyons, and northern goshawks took thick-billed parrots on the wing. This landscape of southwestern New Mexico, southeastern Arizona, northwestern Chihuahua, and northeastern Sonora is mind-boggling in the variety of life it holds; its wild, rugged beauty sings of times long ago. It is the center of my universe.

The United States portion of the Sky Islands region includes the Gila Wilderness, famous birding meccas such as the Chiricahua Mountains and the San Pedro River, the Mexican wolf recovery area, large private ranches managed by their owners to protect and restore nature, and innovative efforts between conservationists and ranchers to work together for the health of the land and of the human community. In Mexico, it includes threatened wild mountains, river canyons, and grasslands that provide breeding habitat for thick-billed parrots and jaguars; the largest prairie dog town left in North America (where black-footed ferrets have been reintroduced); and farsighted agreements between conservationists and local people to protect wildlands and wildlife while increasing family incomes.

Some thought the *Sky Islands Wildlands Network Conservation Plan* radical and impossible when it was published. But, only two years later, in the fall of 2002, some three hundred conservationists, recreationists, ranchers, land owners, government agency professionals, academics, and just regular folks from the United States and Mexico gathered in Tucson to celebrate the Sky Islands vision and explore how to make it happen. I told the crowd that the conference was the high point of my thirty years in conservation. It was a stunning example of how, if you build a bold, hopeful vision, the people will come.[3]

Elsewhere in the United States, conservationists, wildlife biologists, and road engineers are working together to solve barrier and fragmentation problems. The Missing Linkages campaign in Southern California, sparked by the South Coast Wildlands Project, has brought biologists, citizens, and government agencies together to identify the most important barriers to movement by mountain lions and other species in the Los Angeles–San Diego megacity. One of the key linkages identified was Coal Canyon, which contained on- and off-ramps for a busy freeway between the cities of Anaheim and Riverside. Private lands on both sides were slated for subdivision and industrial-park development. North of the freeway is Puente–Chino Hills State Park and south are the Santa Ana Mountains and Cleveland National Forest; the ten- to twelve-lane freeway splits important mountain lion and bobcat habitat. Encouraged by conservationists, the California State Parks agency purchased the nearly 700 acres threatened by development for $53.5 million. Caltrans (the California Department of Transportation) then closed and tore up the ramps and converted the underpass to a wildlife linkage. The importance of this project is summed up by Reed Noss, Paul Beier, and W. Shaw: "Restoring a natural linkage in what is now a roaded underpass would set a global precedent. We are aware of no other restored biological corridor of this type and scale."[4] Coal Canyon, however, is only the most spectacular success of the South Coast Wildlands Project and its partners.

The major fracture zone in Washington's Cascade Mountains for wolf, lynx, wolverine, and grizzly bear is Interstate 90 and associated development through Snoqualmie Pass. A significant complication is the large amount of private land checkerboarded in a 20-mile-wide swath along the interstate. These railroad grant lands from the 1800s have generally been heavily logged, although 15,000 acres of old-growth forest remain. But much of the remaining ancient forest is slated for cutting in the next few years. The Cascades Conservation Partnership is pursuing an unprecedented deal to acquire 75,000 acres of private land here to link Mount Rainier National Park with the Alpine Lakes Wilderness by raising $25 million from private contributions and working with Congress to appropriate $100 million in federal funds. The specific linkages being acquired are those identified by Peter Singleton and associates in their research on landscape permeability in Washington.[5] I contributed to this effort by giving a talk in May 2003 at Microsoft Corporation, whose employees have contributed several million dollars. Like the South Coast Wildlands Project, the Cascades Partnership is an outstanding effort by wonderful people who, as a result of their hard work, have enjoyed considerable success.[6]

In 2003, the Wildlands Project undertook a critical-linkages campaign, "Room to Roam," for the four Spine of the Continent Wildlands Networks and the Yellowstone to Yukon Conservation Initiative. For each network, a particularly important wildlife linkage was highlighted, and key barriers needing mitigation and a focal species for each were identified. See table 15.1 and figure 15.1.

This effort is already bearing fruit in New Mexico where state and federal wildlife biologists organized the Critical Mass workshop in June of 2003 to bring together agency managers, biologists, conservationists, and the New Mexico State Highway Department to identify the most troublesome stretches of road from the standpoint of wildlife permeability. The workshop accepted the Wildlands Project's New Mexico Highlands Wildlands Network map as the connectivity layer. Interstate 40 through Tijeras Canyon east of Albuquerque was rated the area of highest priority, and several other highway stretches were also deemed priorities. The interstate highway and its associated development in Tijeras Canyon present an almost impassable barrier to black bear, mountain lion, and other species. Without a wildlife crossing of some kind, the

TABLE 15.1. Endangered Linkages

Sky Islands	Mexican border	Jaguar
New Mexico Highlands	Tijeras Canyon on I-40	Black bear
Southern Rockies	Vail Pass on I-70	Lynx
Heart of the West	Powder Rim	Greater sage grouse
Yellowstone to Yukon	Crowsnest Pass	Grizzly bear

Source: Room to Roam, The Wildlands Project, 2003.

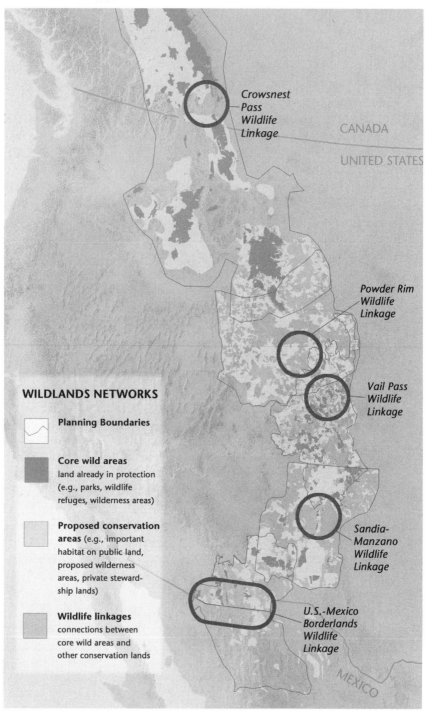

WILDLANDS NETWORKS

Planning Boundaries

Core wild areas
land already in protection
(e.g., parks, wildlife
refuges, wilderness areas)

Proposed conservation
areas (e.g., important
habitat on public land,
proposed wilderness
areas, private steward-
ship lands)

Wildlife linkages
connections between
core wild areas and
other conservation lands

Crowsnest
Pass
Wildlife
Linkage

CANADA

UNITED STATES

Powder Rim
Wildlife
Linkage

Vail Pass
Wildlife
Linkage

Sandia-
Manzano
Wildlife
Linkage

U.S.-Mexico
Borderlands
Wildlife
Linkage

MEXICO

FIGURE 15.1. Endangered linkages identified by the Wildlands Project in the Spine of the Continent MegaLinkage wildlands networks. (Adapted by Todd Cummings from "Room to Roam" brochure, the Wildlands Project.)

Sandia Mountains Wilderness to the north of Tijeras Canyon could become an isolated habitat for bears and cats. The most exciting aspect of this workshop was the enthusiasm of the New Mexico State Highway Department staffers and their desire to participate.

These efforts show that visionary campaigns to identify and fix barriers to large carnivore movement not only capture strong public support and dedicated participation by state and federal agencies, but also can get the job done on the ground. State by state, county by county, and town by town, conservationists and transportation officials, particularly roads departments, should meet and work together to overcome barriers to wildlife movement and to restore landscape permeability.

But—are these isolated examples proof that continental-scale conservation is becoming a success? Is a North American Wildlands Network possible? I don't know. But we have no other choice than to try.

Michael Soulé and Reed Noss write, "Rewilding with extirpated carnivores and other keystone species is a means as well as an end. The 'end' is the moral obligation to protect wilderness and to sustain the remnants of the Pleistocene—animals and plants—not only for our human enjoyment, but because of their intrinsic value."[7]

The point of religion, society, ethics, and good manners is to check those parts of human behavior that harm the community. Aldo Leopold believed that history could be seen as a progressive extension of ethics to include more and more people in the community.[8] He wrote:

> All ethics so far evolved rest upon a single premise: that the individual is a member of a community of interdependent parts. . . . The land ethic simply enlarges the boundaries of the community to include soils, waters, plants, and animals, or collectively: the land. . . . In short, a land ethic changes the role of *Homo sapiens* from conqueror of the land-community to plain member and citizen of it. It implies respect for his fellow-members, and also respect for the community as such.[9]

David Ehrenfeld built on Leopold's land ethic with his Noah Principle: "[Species and ecological communities] should be conserved because they exist and because this existence is itself but the present expression of a continuing historical process of immense antiquity and majesty."[10] Unfortunately, there is a great gulf between high-sounding ethical ideals and human behavior. Witness the violent barbarism done over the ages in the name of religion. Hominid paleontologist Ian Tattersall warns that "our elimination of the competition [other hominid species] should make us think hard about the kind of creature we are."[11]

Moreover, much of the damage we do to Earth comes from our seemingly inherent inability to plan more than a couple of decades into the future and our inability to fully understand the consequences of our actions. Perhaps our shortsightedness can be explained in evolutionary terms. Thinking is a function of our brain. Like any other organ, the brain is a product of evolution. Given short individual life spans and slow ecological change for most of our evolutionary history, we should not assume that our intelligence is adapted to long-term thinking and prediction of the effects of our actions. In 1992, J. T. Heinen and R. S. Low proposed that "humans have evolved to be concerned primarily with short-term costs and benefits on a restricted temporal and spatial scale."[12]

How then do we act according to our ethics? How then do we begin to behave in keeping with the recognition that our actions have long-term consequences? How do we become responsible?

I think that the best way to act according to our ethics is to *consciously* act according to our ethics. For example, I am finding that my memory fails me more and more as I grow older. Therefore, I compensate for my weakening memory by consciously helping it with reminders and by making notes for myself, or by doing things as soon as I think of them instead of thinking I'll remember to do them later. Consciously, deliberately, physically acting to heal ecological wounds may be a way to overcome the gulf between a land ethic and land caring. Assuming that we have to thoughtfully work to practice our ethics toward nature may lead to better behavior. We might be able to practice our land ethic only by consciously *practicing* it. Physically restoring streams, pulling exotic weeds, helping with native species reintroductions, closing harmful roads—such actions may be how we become consciously responsible. We need to create a hopeful vision for the future and *consciously* work to gain it, not naively assume that humans will unconsciously move in the right direction.

One of the highlights of my life happened a couple of years ago when I was privileged to help with the release of black-footed ferrets in the sprawling Janos prairie-dog town in northern Chihuahua. The release site was on a private ranch whose owner was willing to let the prairie dogs and ferrets live and play out their evolutionary dance. The other participants included biologists, wildlife managers, conservationists, and ranchers from both sides of the border.[13] The ferrets did not arrive from the United States until after dark. In the full moon, cages with individual ferrets were distributed. I took mine to a previously selected prairie-dog hole. It took a while for the ferret to decide to come out of her cage. When she did, she immediately began to explore her new world, going from prairie-dog hole to prairie-dog hole within a small area. I sat, watching, alone with her for half an hour. I don't think I've ever known such boundless and hopeful joy. For her and her kind—and for us. We are capable of greathearted acts for nature; we are capable of halting the mass extinction.

The joy and hope the ferret gave me yet lingers. But that one priceless moment is too rare, because most of the time we humans continue to domesticate, simplify, and kill the wild pulse of evolution.

I am not optimistic. I think that the exuberant optimism that drives modern society is irrational. But I do have *hope*. Tom Butler, editor of *Wild Earth*, writes that "hope is natural. To early hominids . . . who constantly faced an inconsistent ability to exploit food resources, hope would have been a powerful advantage. It might have been a key factor in getting through the hungry times. Hope is wild."[14] Conservationists can rewild nature only if they are lifted up by wild hope.

Since around 1990, conservation biology has wrought a revolution. The goal for nature reserves has moved beyond protecting scenery to protecting all nature—the diversity of genes, species, ecosystems, and natural processes. No longer are conservationists fulfilled with protecting remnant and isolated roadless areas; more and more we have come to agree with Reed Noss, who says, "Wilderness recovery, I firmly believe, is the most important task of our generation."[15]

Wilderness and wildlife, both as natural realities and as philosophical ideas, are fundamentally about human humility and restraint. Remember that in Old English *wil-der-ness* means self-willed land and *wildeor* means self-willed beast. Our war on nature comes from trying to impose our will over the whole Earth. To develop and practice a land ethic, we must hold dear both wil-der-ness and the wildeor. Only by making the moral leap to embrace, celebrate, love, and *restore* self-willed nature can we stop the war on nature and save ourselves. Recycling, living more simply, and protecting human health through pollution control are all important. But it is only by rewilding and healing the ecological wounds of the land that we can learn humility and respect; that we can come home, at last. And that the grand dance of life will sashay on in all its beauty, integrity, and evolutionary potential.

For More Information

Although I have only briefly mentioned The Rewilding Institute in *Rewilding North America*, the book is about the vision and work of The Rewilding Institute. The Institute is a 501(c)3 conservation think tank dedicated to the development and promotion of ideas and strategies to advance continental-scale conservation in North America, particularly the need for large carnivores and a permeable landscape for their movement, and promoting a bold, scientifically credible, practically achievable, and hopeful vision for the future of wild nature and human civilization in North America. The Wildlands Project board of directors and I established The Rewilding Institute as a separate organization in the summer of 2003.

The Wildlands Project publishes *Wild Earth* journal and works on the design and implementation of regional wildlands networks as I've described in various parts of *Rewilding North America*. The Rewilding Institute and the Wildlands Project work together closely to create a North American Wildlands Network. *Wild Earth* is the essential source for discussion and updates on continental-scale conservation.

Rewilding North America is a call to action. Only through the bold and thoughtful action of those who love nature, can nature, in any semblance of wholeness, diversity, integrity, and beauty, long endure. If you are not already involved in conservation, I encourage you to get active to protect wild nature. Many groups are carrying out the general vision and strategy I offer in *Rewilding North America*. However, The Rewilding Institute and the Wildlands Project can provide information on how to become part of continental-scale conservation. Web sites and mailing addresses for these organizations are listed below. Both organizations can refer you to other groups involved in all aspects of envisioning and creating a North American Wildlands Network.

In writing *Rewilding North America*, I found I could not avoid discussing issues in terms of what was happening at the time or what might happen in the near future. No doubt some of this information will be out of date by the time you read this. Thus, two appendixes providing pertinent updates can be found on the Island Press Web site at www.islandpress.org/appendix/rewilding/index.html. Appendix A lists core wilderness complexes in the Pacific, Spine of the Continent, and Atlantic Megalinkages. Appendix B provides details about the cores, linkages, and compatible-use areas that make up wildlands networks.

In the next edition of *Rewilding North America* in five years or so, I hope we can celebrate wild wolves in Oregon and wild cougars in the Appalachians. Readers may contact me with additional information or corrections for the next edition through The Rewilding Institute.

The Rewilding Institute
P.O. Box 13768, Albuquerque, NM 87192
http://TheRewildingInstitute.org
The Wildlands Project
P.O. Box 455, Richmond, VT 05477
www.wildlandsproject.org

Notes

Introduction

1. Aldo Leopold, *A Sand County Almanac* (Oxford University Press, New York, 1987), vii.
2. Douglas W. Scott, *A Wilderness-Forever Future: A Short History of the National Wilderness Preservation System* (Pew Wilderness Center, Washington, D.C., 2001).
3. Scott, *Wilderness-Forever Future*.
4. Public Law 88-577 (16 U.S. C. 1131-1136), 88th Cong., 2d Sess., September 3, 1964, in *The Wilderness Act Handbook* (The Wilderness Society, Washington, D.C., August 2000).
5. Jared Diamond, *The Third Chimpanzee: The Evolution and Future of the Human Animal* (HarperCollins, New York, 1992); Richard Leakey and Roger Lewin, *The Sixth Extinction* (Doubleday, New York, 1995); Stuart L. Pimm, *The World According to Pimm* (McGraw-Hill, New York, 2001); Edward O. Wilson, *The Future of Life* (Alfred A. Knopf, New York, 2002).
6. Paul S. Martin and Richard G. Klein, eds., *Quaternary Extinctions* (University of Arizona Press, Tucson, 1984); Diamond, *Third Chimpanzee*; Peter D. Ward, *The Call of Distant Mammoths* (Springer-Verlag, New York, 1997); Richard G. Klein and Blake Edgar, *The Dawn of Human Culture* (John Wiley, New York, 2002).
7. Michael E. Soulé, "What Do We Really Know about Extinction?" in *Genetics and Conservation*, ed. Christine M. Schonewald-Cox et al. (Benjamin-Cummings, Menlo Park, Calif., 1983), 116; Ernst Mayr, *What Evolution Is* (Basic Books, New York, 2001).
8. D. S. Wilcove, D. Rothstein, J. Dubow, A. Philips, and E. Losos, "Quantifying Threats to Imperiled Species in the United States," *BioScience* 48, no. 8 (August 1, 1998): 607–615.
9. Michael E. Soulé and Bruce A. Wilcox, "Conservation Biology: Its Scope and Challenge," in *Conservation Biology: An Evolutionary-Ecological Perspec-*

tive, ed. Michael E. Soulé and Bruce A. Wilcox (Sinauer Associates, Sunderland, Mass., 1980), 4.

10. Roderick Frazier Nash, *Wilderness and the American Mind*, 4th ed. (Yale University Press, New Haven, Conn., 2001); J. C. Hendee, G. H. Stankey, and R. C. Lucas, eds., *Wilderness Management* 2nd ed., rev. (Fulcrum Publishing, Golden, Colo., 1990); Dave Foreman and Howie Wolke, *The Big Outside* (Crown, New York, 1992); Dave Foreman, "The Wildlands Project and the Rewilding of North America," *Denver University Law Review* 76, no. 2 (1999): 535–553.

11. Scott, *Wilderness-Forever Future*; Michael Soulé, personal correspondence.

12. Aldo Leopold, "The Round River—A Parable," in *Round River: From the Journals of Aldo Leopold* (Oxford University Press, New York, 1972), 165.

13. Michael E. Soulé and John Terborgh, eds., *Continental Conservation: Scientific Foundations of Regional Reserve Networks* (Island Press, Washington, D.C., 1999).

14. Michael E. Soulé and Reed Noss, "Rewilding and Biodiversity: Complementary Goals for Continental Conservation," *Wild Earth* Fall 1998, 18–28.

15. J. Terborgh, L. Lopez, P. Nunez, V. M. Rao, G. Shahabuddin, G. Orihuela, M. Riveros, R. Ascanio, G. H. Adler, T. D. Lambert, and L. Balbas, "Ecological Meltdown in Predator-free Forest Fragments," *Science* 294 (2001): 1923–1926; Brian Miller, Barbara Dugelby, Dave Foreman, Carlos Martinez del Rio, Reed F. Noss, Michael Phillips, Richard Reading, Michael E. Soulé, John Terborgh, and Louisa Willcox, "The Importance of Large Carnivores to Healthy Ecosystems," *Endangered Species Update* 18, no. 5 (2001): 202–210.

16. Soulé and Noss, "Rewilding and Biodiversity"; Soulé and Terborgh, *Continental Conservation*.

17. Victor E. Shelford, ed., *Naturalist's Guide to the Americas* (Williams and Wilkins, Baltimore, Md., 1926); Victor E. Shelford, "Ecological Society of America: A Nature Sanctuary Plan Unanimously Adopted by the Society, December 28, 1932," *Ecology* 14 (1933): 240–245.

18. Paul S. Sutter,, *Driven Wild* (University of Washington Press, Seattle, 2002).

19. Scott, *Wilderness-Forever Future*.

20. Nash, *Wilderness and the American Mind*.

21. Jim D. Fish, ed., *Wildlands: Statewide Proposal* (New Mexico BLM Wilderness Coalition, 1987); Arizona Wilderness Coalition, *Arizona Wilderness* (Arizona Wilderness Coalition, 1987); Utah Wilderness Coalition, *Wilderness at the Edge* (Utah Wilderness Coalition, 1990); Tom Price, Kevin Walker, and Jim Catlin, "Utah Wilderness Inventory," *Wild Earth*, Winter 1998–1999, 74–77; *California Wild Heritage Campaign*, 2002; Michael Scialdone and Greg Magee, eds., *New Mexico Wilderness Alliance BLM Wilderness Inventory*, 2003.

22. Reed F. Noss, "Protecting Natural Areas in Fragmented Landscapes," *Natural Areas Journal* 7, no. 1 (1987): 2–13.

23. James Cox, Randy Kautz, Maureen MacLaughlin, and Terry Gilbert, *Closing the Gaps in Florida's Wildlife Habitat Conservation System* (Florida Game and Fresh Water Fish Commission, Tallahassee, 1994).

24. Dave Foreman, Kathy Daly, Barbara Dugelby, Rosanne Hanson, Robert E. Howard, Jack Humphrey, Leanne Klyza Linck, Rurik List, and Kim Vacariu, *Sky Islands Wildlands Network Conservation Plan* (The Wildlands Project, Tucson, Ariz., 2000).

25. *Wild Earth* Special Issue 1992; "Great Dreams: 10th Anniversary Publication," (The Wildlands Project, Richmond, Vt., 2001).

26. David Johns, "The Wildlands Project outside North America," in *Seventh World Wilderness Congress Symposium: Science and Stewardship to Protect and Sustain Wilderness Values*, comp. Alan Watson and Janet Sproull, November 2–8, 2001. Port Elizabeth, South Africa, Proceedings RMRS-P-000, Ogden, Utah, U.S. Department of Agriculture, Forest Service, Rocky Mountain Research Station, 2001.

Part I. Bad News

Epigraph: Michael E. Soulé, "The End of Evolution?" *IUCN World Conservation* January 1996.

I. The Extinction Crisis

1. E. O. Wilson, *The Diversity of Life*, (Harvard University Press, Cambridge, Mass., 1992), 280. For the calculations on how this rate is estimated, see Edward O. Wilson, *The Future of Life* (Alfred A. Knopf, New York, 2002), 99–101. *The Future of Life* is a superb overview of the extinction crisis and what we can do about it.

2. Wilson, *Diversity of Life*, 278.

3. M. E. Soulé, "Thresholds for Survival: Criteria for Maintenance of Fitness and Evolutionary Potential," in *Conservation Biology: An Evolutionary-Ecological Perspective*, ed. M. E. Soulé and B. A. Wilcox (Sinauer Associates, Sunderland, Mass., 1980), 168.

4. Michael E. Soulé, "The End of Evolution?" *IUCN World Conservation* January 1996.

5. Joby Warrick, *Washington Post*, April 21, 1998.

6. Warrick, *Washington Post*.

7. *Sierra Club Action Daily* 2, no. 203 (April 17, 2000).

8. Thanks to Brian Miller of the Denver Zoo for sharing some of these reasons.

9. Jared Diamond, "New Guineans and Their Natural World," in *The Biophilia Hypothesis*, ed. Stephen R. Kellert and Edward O. Wilson (Island Press, Washington, D.C., 1993), 255–257.

10. Michael E. Soulé, "The Social Siege of Nature," in *Reinventing Nature? Responses to Postmodern Deconstruction*, ed. Michael E. Soulé and Gary Lease (Island Press, Washington, D.C., 1995), 151–152.

11. Michael E. Soulé, "The Real Work of Systematics," *Annals of the Missouri Botanical Garden* 77 (1990): 4–12; Terry L. Erwin, "Tropical Forests: Their Richness in Coleoptera and Other Arthropod Species," *Coleoptera Bulletin* 36 (1982): 74–75; Terry L. Erwin, "Tropical Forest Canopies, the Last Biotic Frontier," *Bulletin Entomological Society of America* 29 (1983): 14–19.

12. Remember the old cartoon cats, Felix and Sylvester? Their cartoonists knew binomial nomenclature.

13. Gretchen C. Daily and Paul R. Ehrlich, "Population Extinction and the Biodiversity Crisis," in *Biodiversity Conservation*, ed. C. A. Perrings et al., (Kluwer Academic Publishers, The Netherlands, 1995), 49.

14. Daily and Ehrlich, "Population Extinction," 49.

15. Niles Eldredge, *Life in the Balance: Humanity and the Biodiversity Crisis* (Princeton University Press, Princeton, N.J., 1998), 156.

16. Alfonso Alonso, Francisco Dallmeier, Elise Granek, and Peter Raven, *Biodiversity: Connecting with the Tapestry of Life* (Smithsonian Institution / Monitoring and Assessment of Biodiversity Program and President's Committee of Advisors on Science and Technology, Washington, D.C., 2001), is an excellent overview of biodiversity and extinction. This thirty-one-page booklet with many color photographs is arresting and understandable.

17. Reed F. Noss and Allen Y. Cooperrider, *Saving Nature's Legacy: Protecting and Restoring Biodiversity* (Island Press, Washington, D.C., 1994), 5.

18. Noss and Cooperrider, *Saving Nature's Legacy*, 5.

19. Stuart L. Pimm, Gareth J. Russell, John L. Gittleman, and Thomas M. Brooks, "The Future of Biodiversity," *Science* 269 (July 21, 1995): 347.

20. Pimm et al., "The Future of Biodiversity," 347.

21. Soulé, "Real Work of Systematics," 4. Recent field work in remote areas and DNA analysis of species may lead to identifying more new vertebrate species than once believed. See Wilson, *Future of Life*, 17–19.

22. Richard B. Primack, *Essentials of Conservation Biology* (Sinauer Associates, Sunderland, Mass., 1993), 78.

23. David Macdonald, ed., *The Encyclopedia of Mammals* (Facts on File Publications, New York, 1985), 3.

24. Donald K. Grayson, "Nineteenth-Century Explanations of Pleistocene Extinctions: A Review and Analysis," in *Quaternary Extinctions: A Prehistoric Revolution*, ed. Paul S. Martin and Richard G. Klein (University of Arizona Press, Tucson, 1984), 6. Grayson's chapter (pp. 5–39) is an excellent summary of how scientists came to accept the reality of past extinction.

25. Stephen E. Ambrose, *Undaunted Courage: Meriwether Lewis, Thomas Jefferson, and the Opening of the American West* (Simon & Schuster, New York, 1997), 55, 91.

26. Grayson, "Pleistocene Extinctions," 6–12.
27. Grayson, "Pleistocene Extinctions," 13.
28. Grayson, "Pleistocene Extinctions," 27.
29. Grayson, "Pleistocene Extinctions," 28.
30. Grayson, "Pleistocene Extinctions," 21. Lyell, of course, used "unoccupied" in the sense of "unoccupied by civilized societies."
31. Erik Eckholm, "Wild Species Versus Man: The Losing Struggle for Survival," *The Living Wilderness*, July–September 1978, 12.
32. William T. Hornaday, *Wild Life Conservation* (Yale University Press, New Haven, Conn., 1914), 12. The spelling of the species is Hornaday's. At the time of Hornaday's writing, the Eskimo curlew was believed to be extinct. However, it survived at that time in tiny numbers. A handful may still exist. Chapter 5 provides more information on the curlew.
33. Aldo Leopold, "Naturschutz in Germany," *Bird-Lore* 38.2 (1936): 102.
34. Colin Bertram, "Man Pressure," in *The Subversive Science: Essays Toward an Ecology of Man*, ed. Paul Shepard and Daniel McKinley (Houghton Mifflin, Boston, 1969), 210–215.
35. The talk was later reprinted in Hugh H. Iltis, "Technology Versus Wild Nature: What Are Man's Biological Needs?" *Northwest Conifer* (Pacific Northwest Chapter of the Sierra Club newsletter), May 22, 1971. Among his many accomplishments, Iltis discovered the wild ancestor of corn in Mexico.
36. Norman Myers, *The Sinking Ark: A New Look at the Problem of Disappearing Species* (Pergamon Press, New York, 1979).
37. Eckholm, "Wild Species Versus Man," 11.
38. Michael E. Soulé and Bruce A. Wilcox, eds., *Conservation Biology: An Evolutionary-Ecological Perspective* (Sinauer Associates, Sunderland, Mass., 1980).
39. Thomas E. Lovejoy, "Foreword," Soulé and Wilcox, *Conservation Biology*, ix.
40. Michael E. Soulé and Bruce A. Wilcox, "Conservation Biology: Its Scope and Its Challenge," Soulé and Wilcox, *Conservation Biology*, 7–8.
41. Peter D. Ward, *The Call of Distant Mammoths* (Copernicus, New York, 1997), 62.
42. Tim Flannery, *The Eternal Frontier: An Ecological History of North America and Its Peoples* (Atlantic Monthly Press, New York, 2001).
43. Ward, *Call of Distant Mammoths*, 35–37.
44. Soulé, "Future of Biodiversity," 347.
45. Michael E. Soulé, "What Do We Really Know about Extinction?" in *Genetics and Conservation*, ed. Christine M. Schonewald-Cox et al. (Benjamin-Cummings, Menlo Park, Calif., 1983), 116.
46. David Quammen, *The Song of the Dodo: Island Biogeography in an Age of Extinctions* (Scribner, New York, 1996), 294–296, 515–519.
47. Soulé, "Extinction?" 112.
48. David S. Wilcove, D. Rothstein, J. Dubow, A. Phillips, and E. Losos, "Quantifying Threats to Imperiled Species in the United States," *BioScience* 48 (August 1, 1998): 607–615. Another categorization uses the

acronym HIPPO, which stands for habitat destruction, invasive species, pollution, population (human), and overharvesting. See Wilson, *Future of Life*, 50.

49. Richard P. Reading and Brian Miller, eds., *Endangered Animals: A Reference Guide to Conflicting Issues* (Greenwood Press, Westport, Conn., 2000). This is an essential reference on the extinction crisis.

50. Alison M. Rosser and Sue A. Mainka, "Overexploitation and Species Extinctions," *Conservation Biology* 16, no. 3 (June 2002): 584–586.

51. Alfred W. Crosby, *Ecological Imperialism: The Biological Expansion of Europe, 900–1900* (Cambridge University Press, New York, 1986).

52. Ernst Mayr, *What Evolution Is* (Basic Books, New York, 2001), 203. This, Mayr's latest book, is probably the best overview of evolution. All conservationists should read it for a solid grounding in biology.

2. The Pleistocene-Holocene Event

1. William Stolzenburg, "Extinction for the Record," *Nature Conservancy* May–June 1996, 6.

2. Stuart L. Pimm, Gareth J. Russell, John L. Gittleman, and Thomas M. Brooks, "The Future of Biodiversity," *Science* 269 (July 21, 1995): 348.

3. Lyanda Haupt, "Feathers and Fossils: Hawaiian Extinctions and Modern Conservation," *Wild Earth*, Spring 1996, 44–49; Storrs L. Olson and Helen F. James, "The Role of Polynesians in the Extinction of the Avifauna of the Hawaiian Islands," in *Quaternary Extinctions: A Prehistoric Revolution*, eds. Paul S. Martin and Richard G. Klein (University of Arizona Press, Tucson, 1984), 768–780.

4. Edward O. Wilson, *The Future of Life* (Alfred A. Knopf, New York, 2002), 46.

5. John Terborgh, "Top-down or Bottom-up, What Does It Matter?" unpublished draft in author's files. Australia has four species of large kangaroos that fill the ecological role of ungulates.

6. Chris Stuart and Tilde Stuart, *Field Guide to the Mammals of Southern Africa* (Struik Publishers, Cape Town, South Africa, 1995). However, I saw wildlife only in protected areas in Africa. Outside such places, the land is more barren of wild animals than is the United States. With exploding human populations, African wildlife is crowded into ever smaller and more isolated reserves.

7. Mule deer, white-tailed deer, elk, moose, pronghorn, bighorn sheep, bison, mountain goat, and woodland caribou.

8. Paul S. Martin and David A. Burney, "Bring Back the Elephants!" *Wild Earth*, Spring 1999, 58.

9. Quoted in Peter D. Ward, *The Call of Distant Mammoths* (Copernicus, New York, 1997), 138.

10. Paul Martin, "Prehistoric Overkill," in *Pleistocene Extinctions: The Search*

for a Cause, ed. Paul S. Martin and H. E. Wright Jr. (Yale University Press, New Haven, Conn., 1967), 75–120.

11. Paul S. Martin, "Prehistoric Overkill: The Global Model," in *Quaternary Extinctions: A Prehistoric Revolution*, 354–403.

12. Donald K. Grayson, "Nineteenth-Century Explanations of Pleistocene Extinctions: A Review and Analysis," in *Quaternary Extinctions: A Prehistoric Revolution*, 28.

13. I first proposed these three waves in October 1999. Richard Cincotta and Robert Engelman independently described four waves of extinction in 2000, although they defined the waves differently than I do. Richard P. Cincotta and Robert Engelman, *Nature's Place: Human Population and the Future of Biological Diversity* (Population Action International, Washington, D.C., 2000), 24–31.

14. Niles Eldredge, *The Miner's Canary: Unraveling the Mysteries of Extinction* (Prentice Hall Press, New York, 1991), 207.

15. Ian Tattersall, *Becoming Human: Evolution and Human Uniqueness* (Harcourt, Brace, New York, 1998), 217.

16. *BP* means "before present," so 3000 BP is 3,000 years before present, or 1000 BC.

3. The First Wave

1. Ian Tattersall and Jeffrey Schwartz, *Extinct Humans* (Westview Press, Boulder, Colo., 2000), 31–34. Also see Richard G. Klein, *The Human Career: Human Biological and Cultural Origins* 2nd ed. (University of Chicago Press, Chicago, 1999), xxiii–xxiv, 255–257.

2. Tattersall and Schwartz, *Extinct Humans*. In his most recent book, Ernst Mayr embraces this "bushy" view of human evolution.

3. Ian Tattersall, "Once We Were Not Alone," *Scientific American*, January 2000, 56–62.

4. Ian Tattersall, "A Hundred Years of Missing Links," *Natural History*, December 2000–January 2001, 65.

5. Christopher Stringer and Robin McKie, *African Exodus: The Origins of Modern Humanity* (Henry Holt, New York, 1996) makes the case for the "Out of Africa" model.

6. Donald Johanson and Blake Edgar, *From Lucy to Language* (Simon & Schuster, New York, 1996), 32.

7. Klein, *Human Career*, 227–228.

8. Robert Lee Hotz, *Los Angeles Times*, "Fossils May Mark African Migration," *Albuquerque Journal*, May 13, 2000.

9. Klein, *Human Career*, xxiv, 255–279; Tattersall and Schwartz, *Extinct Humans*, 148, 160.

10. Klein, *Human Career*, xxiii–xxiv, 255–257.

11. Klein, *Human Career*, 286, 395, 489–490.

12. Tattersall and Schwartz, *Extinct Humans*, 227.

13. In my recent novel (written 1991–1993), one of my characters expresses this now-outdated view. Dave Foreman, *The Lobo Outback Funeral Home* (University Press of Colorado, Boulder, 2000), 36–37. A paperback edition was just published by Johnson Books, Boulder, Colo., 2004.

14. Ian Tattersall, *The Last Neanderthal: The Rise, Success, and Mysterious Extinction of our Closest Human Relatives*, rev. ed. (Westview Press, Boulder, Colo., 1999), 115–116.

15. Klein, *Human Career*, 587. Tattersall gives 690–555 million years ago for the split into Neanderthal and *Homo sapiens* lineages, Tattersall, *Last Neanderthal*, 115.

16. Jared Diamond, *The Third Chimpanzee: The Evolution and Future of the Human Animal* (HarperCollins, New York, 1992), 38.

17. Diamond, *Third Chimpanzee*, 39.

18. Diamond, *Third Chimpanzee*, 364.

19. Klein, *Human Career*, 588. "Ky" is an abbreviation for "thousand years."

20. Recent discoveries in South Africa may push this estimate back a few thousand years.

21. Diamond, *Third Chimpanzee*, 47.

22. Diamond, *Third Chimpanzee*, 54–56.

23. Ian Tattersall, *Becoming Human: Evolution and Human Uniqueness* (Harcourt, Brace, New York, 1998), 166–173; Tattersall, *Last Neanderthal*, 170–173; Tattersall and Schwartz, *Extinct Humans*, 242–247; Klein, *Human Career*, 514–517, 590–591.

24. Richard G. Klein with Blake Edgar, *The Dawn of Human Culture: A Bold New Theory on What Sparked the "Big Bang" of Human Consciousness* (John Wiley, New York, 2002), 24.

25. Tattersall, *Becoming Human*, 188.

26. Tattersall, *Last Neanderthal*, 183.

27. Tattersall and Schwartz, *Extinct Humans*, 241.

28. Klein, *Human Career*, 264. Klein's recent popular treatment of human evolution is the most authoritative and accessible source for nontechnical readers. I highly recommend it: Klein, *The Dawn of Human Culture*.

29. Stringer and McKie, *African Exodus*, 115–117. Populations of apes from Richard P. Cincotta and Robert Engelman, *Nature's Place: Human Population and the Future of Biological Diversity* (Population Action International, Washington, D.C., 2000), 13.

30. Stringer and McKie, *African Exodus*, 156–160.

31. Tattersall and Schwartz, *Extinct Humans*, 220; Klein, *Human Career*, 273.

32. John L. Gittleman and Matthew E. Gompper, "The Risk of Extinction— What You Don't Know Will Hurt You," *Science* 291 (February 9, 2001): 997–999.

33. Richard Leakey and Roger Lewin, *The Sixth Extinction: Patterns of Life and the Future of Humankind* (Doubleday, New York, 1995), 174.

34. Tattersall and Schwartz, *Extinct Humans*, 176.

35. Tattersall, *Becoming Human*, 156–157.

36. Klein, *Human Career*, 459.

37. Diamond, *Third Chimpanzee*, 51–52.
38. Paul S. Martin, "Prehistoric Overkill: The Global Model," in *Quaternary Extinctions: A Prehistoric Revolution*, ed. Paul S. Martin and Richard G. Klein (University of Arizona Press, Tucson, 1984), 386.
39. Peter D. Ward, *The Call of Distant Mammoths* (Copernicus, New York, 1997), 113; Stringer and McKie, *African Exodus*, 163; Klein, *Human Career*, 273, 395; Tattersall and Schwartz, *Extinct Humans*, 165. An overview of *Homo erectus* can be found in Carl C. Swisher, III, Garniss H. Curtis, and Roger Lewin, *Java Man* (Scribner, New York, 2000).
40. Klein, *Human Career*, 491, 566–571.
41. Martin, "Prehistoric Overkill," 376–378. See also Peter Murray, "Extinctions Downunder: A Bestiary of Extinct Australian Late Pleistocene Monotremes and Marsupials," in Martin and Klein, *Quaternary Extinctions*, 600–628.
42. Brian M. Fagan, *The Great Journey: The Peopling of Ancient America* (Thames and Hudson, London, 1987), 92; Klein, *Human Career*, 490.
43. Klein, *Human Career*, 559–564.
44. Martin, "Prehistoric Overkill," 360–367.
45. Martin, "Prehistoric Overkill," 370–375.
46. Ross MacPhee, "Digging Cuba: The Lesson of the Bones," *Natural History*, December 1997–January 1998.
47. Martin, "Prehistoric Overkill," 389–391.
48. Ward, *Call of Distant Mammoths*, 194–196.
49. Stuart L. Pimm, Gareth J. Russell, John L. Gittleman, and Thomas M. Brooks, "The Future of Biodiversity," *Science* 269 (July 21, 1995): 348.
50. Michael M. Trotter and Beverley McCulloch, "Moas, Men, and Middens," in Martin and Klein, *Quaternary Extinctions*, 708.
51. Diamond, *Third Chimpanzee*, 319–320.
52. In comparison, a bald eagle only weighs nine and a half pounds.
53. Diamond, *Third Chimpanzee*, 319–323.
54. Diamond, *Third Chimpanzee*, 326–328.
55. Ward, *Call of Distant Mammoths*, 51–52.
56. Ward, *Call of Distant Mammoths*, 152.
57. Leakey and Lewin, *Sixth Extinction*, 178–179.
58. Ward, *Call of Distant Mammoths*, 141.
59. Ward, *Call of Distant Mammoths*, 186.
60. Ward, *Call of Distant Mammoths*, 190.
61. Diamond, *Third Chimpanzee*, 321.
62. Niles Eldredge, *Life in the Balance: Humanity and the Biodiversity Crisis* (Princeton University Press, Princeton, N.J., 1998), 34–35.
63. Curt Meine, *Humans and Other Catastrophes: Perspectives on Extinction* (Center for Biodiversity and Conservation at the American Museum of Natural History, New York, 1999), 7.
64. Ward, *Call of Distant Mammoths*, 216–220.
65. Richard A. Kerr, "Megafauna Died from Big Kill, not Big Chill," *Science* 300 (May 9, 2003): 885.

66. Sasha Nemecek, "Who Were the First Americans?" *Scientific American*, September 2000, 80–87.

67. Jared Diamond, *Guns, Germs, and Steel: The Fates of Human Societies* (W. W. Norton, New York, 1997), 47–49; see also Diamond, *Third Chimpanzee*, 343–345.

68. Johanson and Edgar, *From Lucy to Language*, 49.

69. Anna Curtenius Roosevelt, "Who's on First?" *Natural History*, July–August 2000, 76–79.

70. C. Vance Haynes, "Stratigraphy and Late Pleistocene Extinction in the United States," in Martin and Klein, *Quaternary Extinctions*, 350–351; Ward, *Call of Distant Mammoths*, 121.

71. Brian Miller, personal communication, 2000.

72. Thomas D. Dillehay, *The Settlement of the Americas: A New Prehistory* (Basic Books, New York, 2000), 74.

73. John Mulvaney and Johan Kamminga, *The Prehistory of Australia* (Smithsonian Institution Press, Washington, D.C., 1999), 130–147.

74. Nicholas Wade, "Dating of Australian Remains Backs Theory of Early Migration of Humans," *New York Times*, February 19, 2003.

75. Klein, *Human Career*, 568.

76. Johanson and Edgar, *From Lucy to Language*, 247–249.

77. Klein, *Human Career*, 569.

78. Klein, *Human Career*, 572.

79. Ross D. E. MacPhee and Preston A. Marx, "The 40,000-Year Plague: Humans, Hyperdisease, and First-Contact Extinctions," in *Natural Change and Human Impact in Madagascar*, ed. S. M. Goodman and B. D. Patterson (Smithsonian Institution Press, Washington, D.C., 1997), 191. I thank Ross MacPhee for kindly sending me a copy of this interesting paper.

80. Ward, *Call of Distant Mammoths*, 182.

81. Ward, *Call of Distant Mammoths*, 183.

82. MacPhee and Marx, "The 40,000-Year Plague," 191.

83. Swisher et al., *Java Man*, 235.

84. Edward O. Wilson, *The Future of Life* (Alfred A. Knopf, New York, 2002), 102.

85. Klein and Edgar, *Dawn of Human Culture*, 252.

4. The Second and Third Waves

1. Clive Ponting, *A Green History of the World* (St. Martin's Press, New York, 1991), 161.

2. Ponting, *Green History*, 187.

3. Ponting, *Green History*, 162–163.

4. Ponting, *Green History*, 185.

5. Reed Noss and Allen Y. Cooperrider, *Saving Nature's Legacy: Protecting and Restoring Biodiversity* (Island Press, Washington, D.C., 1994), 63.

6. Ross MacPhee and Clare Flemming, "Losing Mammals since AD 1500," *Natural History*, April 1997, 84–88.

7. MacPhee and Flemming, "Losing Mammals," 84–88.

8. Stuart L. Pimm, Gareth J. Russell, John L. Gittleman, and Thomas M. Brooks, "The Future of Biodiversity," *Science* 269 (July 21, 1995): 348.

9. William Stolzenburg, "Hot Waters," *Nature Conservancy*, March–April 1998, 8.

10. David S. Wilcove, *The Condor's Shadow: The Loss and Recovery of Wildlife in America* (W. H. Freeman, New York, 1999), 106–107. *The Condor's Shadow* has an excellent chapter detailing the extinction and endangerment of freshwater species.

11. Pimm et al., "Future of Biodiversity," 348.

12. Anthony Ricciardi and Joseph B. Rasmussen, "Extinction Rates of North American Freshwater Fauna," *Conservation Biology* 13, no. 5 (October 1999): 1220–1222.

13. David L. Propst, "Sustainable Natural Resource Use and Endangered Species," *¡Bravo!* (Newsletter of Amigos Bravos) 1994, 26–27.

14. "Two N.M. Fish Extinct, State Agency Announces," *Albuquerque Journal*, March 19, 1998.

15. Donald K. Grayson, "Nineteenth-Century Explanations of Pleistocene Extinctions: A Review and Analysis," in *Quaternary Extinctions: A Prehistoric Revolution*, ed. Paul S. Martin and Richard G. Klein (University of Arizona Press, Tucson, 1984), 21.

16. Michael Soulé, "An Unflinching Vision: Networks of People Defending Networks of Land," in *Nature Conservation 4: The Role of Networks*, ed. D. A. Saunders et al. (Surrey Beatty, 1995), 1–8, reprinted in *Wild Earth*, Winter 1999–2000, 38–46.

17. John Terborgh and Blair Winter, "Some Causes of Extinction," in *Conservation Biology: An Evolutionary-Ecological Perspective*, ed. Michael E. Soulé and Bruce A. Wilcox (Sinauer Associates, Sunderland, Mass., 1980), 120.

18. Bruce A. Wilcox, "Insular Ecology and Conservation," in Soulé and Wilcox, *Conservation Biology*, 114–115. This is perhaps the most thorough discussion of the species-area relationship and how it applies to conservation.

19. Edward O. Wilson, *The Diversity of Life* (Harvard University Press, Cambridge, Mass., 1992), 277. Wilson describes how to estimate extinction rates in *The Future of Life*, ed. Edward O. Wilson, (Alfred A. Knopf, New York, 2002), 98–102.

20. Associated Press, "New Study Doubles Estimate of Rain Forest Destruction," *Albuquerque Tribune*, April 8, 1999.

21. Stuart L. Pimm, *The World According to Pimm: A Scientist Audits the Earth* (McGraw-Hill, New York, 2001), 64.

22. Pimm, *World According to Pimm*, 73.

23. Peter H. Raven, "Our Diminishing Tropical Forests," in *Biodiversity*, ed. E. O. Wilson, (National Academy Press, Washington, D.C., 1988), 119–122.

24. Critics of science typically attack on an embarrassingly superficial and ignorant level.

25. For example, many Eastern songbirds also nest in the boreal forests of Quebec, Ontario, and Labrador, which have not as yet been cleared.

26. Pimm et al., "Future of Biodiversity," 349; see also *World According to Pimm*, 229–230.

27. Peter D. Ward, *The Call of Distant Mammoths* (Copernicus, New York, 1997), 174–175.

28. Thomas M. Brooks, Stuart L. Pimm, and Joseph O. Oyugi, "Time Lag between Deforestation and Bird Extinction in Tropical Forest Fragments," *Conservation Biology* 13, no. 5 (October 1999): 1140.

29. Brooks et al., "Time Lag," 1146–1147.

30. Guy Cowlishaw, "Predicting the Pattern of Decline of African Primate Diversity: An Extinction Debt from Historical Deforestation," *Conservation Biology* 13, no. 5 (October 1999): 1183–1193.

31. Niles Eldredge, *Life in the Balance* (Princeton University Press, Princeton, N.J., 1998), 174.

32. Jared Diamond, *The Third Chimpanzee: The Evolution and Future of the Human Animal* (HarperCollins, New York, 1992), 351.

33. Diamond, *Third Chimpanzee*, 353.

34. Diamond, *Third Chimpanzee*, 354.

35. Stuart Pimm, "Interview," *Wild Earth*, Winter 1997–1998, 30–31.

36. Pimm, "Interview," 31.

37. "Patterns of Species Collapse," Interview with Mark Lomolino, *Environmental Review* 4, no. 1 (January 1997), 1–4.

38. *GREENlines*, a daily electronic news digest published by the Grassroots Environmental Effectiveness Network, March 26, 1998. http://www.defenders. org/grnhome.html.

39. E. O. Wilson, "The Little Things That Run the World (The Importance and Conservation of Invertebrates)," *Conservation Biology* 1, no. 4 (December 1987), 345.

40. William Weber and Alan Rabinowitz, "A Global Perspective on Large Carnivore Conservation," *Conservation Biology* 10, no. 1 (August 1996): 1046. Weber and Rabinowitz cite T. K. Fuller, "An International Review of Large Carnivore Conservation Status," in *Integrating People and Wildlife for a Sustainable Future*, ed. J. A. Bissonette and P. R. Krausman (The Wildlife Society, Bethesda, Md., 1995), 410–412.

41. Weber and Rabinowitz, "A Global Perspective," 1051.

42. "Indian Elephants Almost Extinct," *GREENlines*, a daily electronic news digest published by the Endangered Species Coalition, no. 1159. June 26, 2000. http://www.stopextinction.org.

43. Joseph B. Verrengia, Associated Press, "Ten Percent of Primates Imperiled," *Albuquerque Journal*, May 9, 2000.

44. Kenneth R. Weiss, "Leatherback Turtles Lose Out to Fishermen's Nets," *Los Angeles Times*, May 26, 2003.

45. George B. Rabb, "Global Extinction Threat," *Defenders* Winter 1996–1997, 34.

46. Andrew Kitchener, *The Natural History of the Wild Cats* (Comstock/Cornell University Press, Ithaca, N.Y., 1991), 228.

47. Kitchener, *Wild Cats*, 221–230.

48. Weber and Rabinowitz, "Global Perspective," 1047.

49. BBC News, September 18, 2003, reported in "Extinction Stalks Lions," *GREENlines*, a daily electronic news digest published by the Endangered Species Coalition, no. 1956, September 24, 2003. http://www.stopextinction.org.

50. David Macdonald, ed., *The Encyclopedia of Mammals* (Facts on File Publications, New York, 1985), 226–230.

51. Macdonald, *Encyclopedia of Mammals*, 490–492.

52. U.S. World Wildlife Fund, *Focus*, November–December 2000.

53. Wilson, *Future of Life*, 85–86.

54. Sue Pleming, "Illegal Loggers Threaten Orangutans in Borneo," *Reuters*, Environmental News Network, October 1, 2003.

55. Richard P. Cincotta and Robert Engelman, *Nature's Place: Human Population and the Future of Biological Diversity* (Population Action International, Washington, D.C., 2000), 12.

56. Jocelyn Kaiser, "Ebola, Hunting Push Ape Populations to the Brink," *Science* 300 (April 11, 2003): 232.

57. John F. Oates, *Myth and Reality in the Rain Forest: How Conservation Strategies Are Failing in West Africa* (University of California Press, Berkeley, 1999).

58. N. J. Collar and A. T. Juniper, "Dimensions and Causes of the Parrot Conservation Crisis," in *New World Parrots in Crisis: Solutions from Conservation Biology*, ed. Steven R. Beissinger and Noel F. R. Snyder (Smithsonian Institution Press, Washington, 1992), 1–3.

59. Collar and Juniper, "Parrot Conservation Crisis," 1.

60. Andrea Dorfman, "On the Brink," *Time*, October 9, 2000.

61. Paul R. Ehrlich and Anne H. Ehrlich, *The Population Explosion* (Simon and Schuster, New York, 1990), 58.

62. P. M. Vitousek, P. R. Ehrlich, A. H. Ehrlich, and P. A. Matson, "Human Appropriation of the Products of Photosynthesis," *BioScience* 36 (June 1986): 368–373.

63. Ehrlich and Ehrlich, *Population Explosion*, 36–37.

64. Stuart L. Pimm, *The World According to Pimm: A Scientist Audits the Earth* (McGraw-Hill, New York, 2001), 10.

65. Pimm, *World According to Pimm*, 23.

66. Pimm, *World According to Pimm*, 11.

67. Pimm, *World According to Pimm*, 105.

68. Pimm, *World According to Pimm*, 163.

69. Pimm, *World According to Pimm*, 112–116.

70. Pimm, *World According to Pimm*, 6.

71. J. R. Weeks, *Population: An Introduction to Concepts and Issues*, 5th ed. (Wadsworth Publishing, Belmont, Calif., 1992), 29.

72. Warren M. Hern, "How Many Times Has the Human Population Dou-

bled? Comparisons with Cancer," *Population and Environment: A Journal of Interdisciplinary Studies* 21, no. 1 (September 1999): 59–80.

73. J. Kenneth Smail, "Confronting the 21st Century's Hidden Crisis: Reducing Human Numbers by 80 %," *The NPG Forum*, August 1995.

74. Warren M. Hern, "Is Human Culture Carcinogenic for Uncontrolled Population Growth and Ecological Destruction?" *BioScience* 43, no. 11 (December 1993): 769.

75. William R. Catton Jr., *Overshoot: The Ecological Basis of Revolutionary Change* (University of Illinois Press, Urbana, 1982), 126–127.

76. Hugh H. Iltis, "Tropical Forests: What Will Be Their Fate?" *Environment* 25, no. 10 (December 1983): 55–60.

77. Michael E. Soulé, "Thresholds for Survival: Maintaining Fitness and Evolutionary Potential," in Soulé and Wilcox, *Conservation Biology*, 164–165.

78. Soulé, "Thresholds for Survival," 168.

79. Eldredge, *Life in the Balance*, 66.

80. Ian Tattersall and Jeffrey Schwartz, *Extinct Humans* (Westview Press, Boulder, Colo., 2000), 9.

81. Richard Wrangham and Dale Peterson, *Demonic Males: Apes and the Origins of Human Violence* (Houghton Mifflin, Boston, 1996), 257–258.

5. Ecological Wounds of North America I

1. Aldo Leopold, "The Round River—A Parable," in *Round River: From the Journals of Aldo Leopold* (Oxford University Press, New York, 1972), 165.

2. Aldo Leopold, "Conservationist in Mexico," *American Forests*, March 1937, reprinted in David E. Brown and Neil B. Carmony, *Aldo Leopold's Southwest*, (University of New Mexico Press, Albuquerque, 1995), 201–208.

3. Charisse A. Sydoriak, Craig D. Allen, and Brian F. Jacobs, "Would Ecological Landscape Restoration Make the Bandelier Wilderness More or Less of a Wilderness?" *Wild Earth*, Winter 2000–2001, 83–90.

4. Leopold, "Conservationist in Mexico."

5. David S. Wilcove, D. Rothstein, J. Dubow, A. Philips, and E. Losos, "Quantifying Threats to Imperiled Species in the United States," *BioScience* 48, no. 8 (August 1, 1998): 607–615.

6. Thomas R. Vale, "The Myth of the Humanized Landscape: An Example from Yosemite National Park," *Natural Areas Journal* 18, no. 3 (1998), reprinted in *Wild Earth* Fall 1999, 34–40; Thomas R. Vale, ed., *Fire, Native Peoples, and the Natural Landscape* (Island Press, Washington, D.C., 2002). Vale's work solidly debunks the proponents of a domesticated North America before Europeans.

7. William M. Denevan, "The Pristine Myth: The Landscape of the Americas in 1492," *Annals of the Association of American Geographers*, 1992, 369–385.

8. Douglas H. Ubelaker, "North American Indian Population Size, AD 1500 to 1985," *American Journal of Physical Anthropology* 77 (1988): 291.

9. Denevan, "The Pristine Myth."

10. Peter S. White, Stephanie P. Wilds, and Gwendolyn A. Thunhorst, "Regional Trends of Biological Resources—Southeast," in *Status and Trends of the Nation's Biological Resources*, ed. M. J. Mac, P. A. Opler, C. E. Puckett Haecker, and P. D. Doran, 2 vols. (U.S. Department of the Interior, U.S. Geological Survey, Reston, Va., 1998), 258.

11. Joe Truett, "Bison and Elk in the American Southwest: In Search of the Pristine," *Environmental Management* 20, no. 2, 1996, 195–206; and Craig D. Allen, "Elk Reintroductions," in Mac et al., *Status and Trends*, 577.

12. David J. Mattson and Troy Merrill, "Extirpations of Grizzly Bears in the Contiguous United States, 1850–2000," *Conservation Biology* 16, no. 4 (August 2002): 1124.

13. Dan Scurlock and Deborah M. Finch, "A Historical Review," in *Songbird Ecology in Southwestern Ponderosa Pine Forests: A Literature Review*, ed. William M. Block and Deborah M. Finch, General Technical Report RM-GTR-292, U.S. Department of Agriculture, Forest Service, Rocky Mountain Forest and Range Experiment Station, Fort Collins, Colo., 1997, 44.

14. The extermination of the megafauna, however, had effects cascading down through many ecosystems. For a fascinating account of these effects, see Connie Barlow, *The Ghosts of Evolution: Nonsensical Fruit, Missing Partners, and Other Ecological Anachronisms* (Basic Books, New York, 2000); Connie Barlow, "Goodbye Eternal Frontier," *Wild Earth*, Summer 2002, 16–22; and David A. Burney, David W. Steadman, and Paul S. Martin, "Evolution's Second Chance," *Wild Earth*, Summer 2002, 12–14.

15. Peter Matthiessen, *Wildlife in America* (Viking, New York, 1987), 119.

16. Adrian Forsyth, *Mammals of the American North* (Camden House, Camden East, Ontario, 1985), 233.

17. Fred B. Samson, Fritz L. Knopf, and Wayne R. Ostlie, "Regional Trends of Biological Resources—Grasslands," in Mac et al., *Status and Trends*, 460.

18. M. J. Mac, P. A. Opler, C. E. Puckett Haecker, and P. D. Doran, eds., *Status and Trends of the Nation's Biological Resources*, 2 vols. (U.S. Department of the Interior, U.S. Geological Survey, Reston, Va., 1998); Matthiessen, *Wildlife in America*; David S. Wilcove, *The Condor's Shadow* (W. H. Freeman, New York, 1999). *Status and Trends* is also available on CD.

19. Dave Foreman, *Confessions of an Eco-Warrior* (Crown, New York, 1991), 69–86; Dave Foreman and Howie Wolke, *The Big Outside* (Crown, New York, 1992), 25–45.

20. "Game-hogging" is the classic term used by early wildlife advocates for those sporthunters who killed vast numbers of ducks, deer, and other animals.

21. Daniel Pauly, Villy Christensen, Sylvie Guénette, Tony J. Pitcher, U.

Rashid Sumaila, Carl J. Waters, R. Watson, and Dirk Zeller, "Towards Sustainability in World Fisheries," *Nature* 418 (August 8, 2002): 689–695.

22. Carl O. Sauer, *Northern Mists* (University of California Press, Berkeley, 1968), 41.

23. Farley Mowat, *Sea of Slaughter* (Bantam Books, New York, 1986), 166; Matthiessen, *Wildlife in America*, 19–21, 27–28.

24. Wilcove, *Condor's Shadow*, 142–143.

25. Loh-Lee Low, Allen M. Shimada, Steven L. Swartz, and Michael P. Sissenwine, "Regional Trends of Biological Resources—Marine Resources," in Mac et al., *Status and Trends*, 801–802. Note: In this and subsequent references to *Status and Trends*, only primary authors are listed. Contributing authors are listed in relevant sections of *Status and Trends*. Also, I do not list the citations used in articles in *Status and Trends*. Please consult it for full citations.

26. Wilcove, *Condor's Shadow*, 154–155.

27. Jeremy B. C. Jackson, Michael X. Kirby, Wolfgang H. Berger, Karen A. Bjorndal, Louis W. Botsford, Bruce J. Bourque, Roger H. Bradbury, Richard Cooke, Jon Erlandson, James A. Estes, Terence P. Hughes, Susan Kidwell, Carina B. Lange, Hunter S. Lenihan, John M. Pandolfi, Charles H. Peterson, Robert S. Steneck, Mia J. Tegner, and Robert R. Warner, "Historical Overfishing and the Recent Collapse of Coastal Ecosystems," *Science* 293 (July 27, 2001), 629.

28. Pauly et al., "Towards Sustainability in World Fisheries," 690.

29. Low et al., "Marine Resources," 782.

30. Low et al., "Marine Resources," 784.

31. Gerald Smith, "Distortion of World Fisheries by Capital," *Wild Earth*, Winter 2002–2003, 15.

32. Julia K. Baum, Ransom A. Myers, Daniel G. Kehler, Boris Worm, Shelton J. Harley, and Penny A. Doherty, "Collapse and Conservation of Shark Populations in the Northwest Atlantic," *Science* 299 (January 17, 2003): 389–392.

33. Hannah Gillelan, "Homeless Fish: Bottom Trawls Bulldoze Seafloor Habitat," *Wild Earth*, Winter 2002–2003, 34–37.

34. Brendan Cummings, "Unfulfilled Promise: Using the ESA to Protect Imperiled Marine Wildlife," *Wild Earth*, Winter 2002–2003, 62–67.

35. "Horseshoe Moratorium Lucky Break for Red Knot," *GREENlines*, a daily electronic news digest published by the Endangered Species Coalition, no. 1817, March 10, 2003. http://www.stopextinction.org.

36. Thomas A. Edsall, "Regional Trends of Biological Resources—Great Lakes," in Mac et al., *Status and Trends*, 222.

37. David R. Klein, David F. Murray, Robert H. Armstrong, and Betty A. Anderson, "Regional Trends of Biological Resources—Alaska," in Mac et al., *Status and Trends*, 718.

38. Klein et al., "Alaska," 737.

39. Stuart L. Pimm, *The World According to Pimm: A Scientist Audits the Earth* (McGraw-Hill, New York, 2001), 166.

40. James H. W. Hain, "North Atlantic Right Whale," in Mac et al., *Status and Trends*, 791–792.

41. James Estes, "From Killer Whales to Kelp: Food Web Complexity in Kelp Forest Ecosystems," *Wild Earth*, Winter 2002–2003, 27.

42. Low et al., "Marine Resources," 786.

43. Joe Roman and Stephen R. Palumbi, "Whales before Whaling in the North Atlantic," *Science* 301 (July 25, 2003): 508–510.

44. Wilcove, *Condor's Shadow*, 142–143.

45. Jackson et al., "Historical Overfishing," 630–631.

46. Jackson et al., "Historical Overfishing," 630–631.

47. Wilcove, *Condor's Shadow*, 144.

48. James A. Estes, "Ecological Chain Reactions in Kelp Forest Ecosystems," Plenary Address, Carnivores 2002 Conference, Monterey, Calif., November 18, 2002.

49. Matthiessen, *Wildlife in America*, 92–93.

50. Matthiessen, *Wildlife in America*, 101–105.

51. Wilcove, *Condor's Shadow*, 144.

52. Matthiessen, *Wildlife in America*, 106–108.

53. Matthiessen, *Wildlife in America*, 239.

54. Matthiessen, *Wildlife in America*, 65.

55. Wilcove, *Condor's Shadow*, 44.

56. White et al., "Southeast," 280.

57. Matthiessen, *Wildlife in America*, 82.

58. Edsall, "Great Lakes," 222.

59. Thomas J. Stohlgren, "Regional Trends of Biological Resources—Rocky Mountains," in Mac et al., *Status and Trends*, 494–495.

60. Stohlgren, "Rocky Mountains," 495.

61. Klein et al., "Alaska," 726.

62. John Crenshaw, "Making Tracks: A Century of Wildlife Management," *New Mexico Wildlife* 47, no. 4 (2002), 7–10.

63. David Day, *Vanished Species* (Gallery Books, New York, 1989), 36–37; Errol Fuller, *Extinct Birds* (Facts on File Publications, New York, 1988), 116.

64. Wilcove, *Condor's Shadow*, 147–148.

65. Wilcove, *Condor's Shadow*, 146–147.

66. Wilcove, *Condor's Shadow*, 148.

67. Matthiessen, *Wildlife in America*, 168.

68. Matthiessen, *Wildlife in America*, 115–116.

69. Matthiessen, *Wildlife in America*, 148–149.

70. Crenshaw, "Making Tracks."

71. Jon K. Fischer, "Future Bright for California Elk," *Outdoor California*, May–June 1994, 12–13.

72. Matthiessen, *Wildlife in America*, 144.

73. William T. Hornaday, *Wild Life Conservation in Theory and Practice* (Yale University Press, New Haven, Conn., 1914), 19.

74. Matthiessen, *Wildlife in America*, 55.

75. Matthiessen, *Wildlife in America*, 77–82.
76. Monica G. Turner, Stephen R. Carpenter, Eric J. Gustafson, Robert J. Naiman, and Scott M. Pearson, "Factors Affecting Biological Resources—Land Use," in Mac et al., *Status and Trends*, 48.
77. Lisa Mighetto, *Wild Animals and American Environmental Ethics* (University of Arizona Press, Tucson, 1991), 29.
78. Peter F. Brussard, David A. Charlet, and David S. Dobkin, "Regional Trends of Biological Resources—Great Basin," in Mac et al., *Status and Trends*, 525.
79. Klein et al., "Alaska," 720.
80. Matthiessen, *Wildlife in America*, 248.
81. Matthiessen, *Wildlife in America*, 57.
82. Wilcove, *Condor's Shadow*, 20–21.
83. Matthiessen, *Wildlife in America*, 58.
84. Matthiessen, *Wildlife in America*, 62.
85. Fuller, *Extinct Birds*, 150–152.
86. Matthiessen, *Wildlife in America*, 168–171.
87. Michael A. Bogan, Craig D. Allen, Esteban H. Muldavin, Steven P. Platania, James N. Stuart, Greg H. Farley, Patricia Mehlhop, and Jayne Belnap, "Regional Trends of Biological Resources—Southwest," in Mac et al., *Status and Trends*, 577.
88. Thomas R. Dunlap, *Saving America's Wildlife: Ecology and the American Mind, 1850–1990* (Princeton University Press, Princeton, N.J., 1988).
89. Richard West Sellars, *Preserving Nature in the National Parks: A History* (Yale University Press, New Haven, Conn., 1997).
90. William J. Ripple and Eric J. Larsen, "Historic Aspen Recruitment, Elk, and Wolves in Northern Yellowstone National Park, USA," *Biological Conservation* 95 (2000): 367.
91. David E. Brown, *The Wolf in the Southwest: The Making of an Endangered Species* (University of Arizona Press, Tucson, 1984); David E. Brown, *The Grizzly in the Southwest* (University of Oklahoma Press, Norman, 1985); Sutter, *Preserving Nature in the National Parks*; Dunlap, *Saving America's Wildlife*.
92. David F. Pelly, *Thelon: A River Sanctuary* (Canadian Recreational Canoeing Association, Merrickville, Ontario, 1996), 106–107.
93. David E. Brown and Carlos A. Lopez Gonzalez, *Borderland Jaguars* (University of Utah Press, Salt Lake City, 2001).
94. Predator Conservation Alliance, February 2002.
95. Stohlgren, "Rocky Mountains," 493.
96. Brian Miller, Richard P. Reading, and Steve Forrest, *Prairie Night: Black-Footed Ferrets and the Recovery of Endangered Species* (Smithsonian Institution Press, Washington, D.C., 1996), 24.
97. Miller et al., *Prairie Night*.
98. Raymond Herrmann, Robert Stottlemyer, and Laura Schebarth, "Factors Affecting Biological Resources—Water Use," in Mac et al., *Status and Trends*, 78.
99. Klein et al., "Alaska," 737.

100. Brussard et al., "Great Basin," 521.

101. Brussard et al., "Great Basin," 521.

102. Bogan et al., "Southwest," 571–572.

103. Turner et al., "Land Use," 38.

104. Reed F. Noss, Edward T. LaRoe III, and J. Michael Scott, *Endangered Ecosystems of the United States: A Preliminary Assessment of Loss and Degradation* Biological Report 28 (U.S. Department of the Interior, National Biological Service, Washington, D.C., February 1995); Reed F. Noss and Robert L. Peters, *Endangered Ecosystems: A Status Report on America's Vanishing Habitat and Wildlife* (Defenders of Wildlife, Washington, D.C., December 1995).

105. Noss et al., *Endangered Ecosystems of the United States*, 2.

106. Noss and Peters, *Endangered Ecosystems*, 2.

107. Noss and Peters, *Endangered Ecosystems*, 9.

108. William Cronon, *Changes in the Land: Indians, Colonists, and the Ecology of New England* (Hill and Wang, New York, 1983), 108–126.

109. Stephen C. Trombulak and Christopher McGrory Klyza, "The New Natural History," *Natural Areas Journal* 20, no. 3 (2000): 267.

110. Samson et al., "Grasslands," 439.

111. Noss et al., *Endangered Ecosystems of the United States*, 43.

112. Noss and Peters, *Endangered Ecosystems*, xiii.

113. M. Van Cleave, "Vegetation Change in the Middle Rio Grande Conservancy District" (M.S. thesis, University of New Mexico, Albuquerque, 1935); Greg H. Farley, Lisa M. Ellis, James N. Stuart, and Norman J. Scott Jr., "Avian Species Richness in Different-Aged Stands of Riparian Forest along the Middle Rio Grande, New Mexico," *Conservation Biology* 8, no. 4, (December 1994): 1098–1108.

114. Stephen D. Veirs Jr. and Paul A. Opler, "Regional Trends of Biological Resources—California," in Mac et al., *Status and Trends*, 597.

115. Noss et al., *Endangered Ecosystems of the United States*, 47.

116. Jeff P. Smith and Michael W. Collopy, "Regional Trends of Biological Resources—Pacific Northwest," in Mac et al., *Status and Trends*, 649.

117. Duane C. Chapman, Diana M. Papoulias, and Chris P. Onuf, "Environmental Change in South Texas," in Mac et al., *Status and Trends*, 268.

118. Samson et al., "Grasslands," 444.

119. Paul B. Sears, *Deserts on the March* 3rd ed. (University of Oklahoma Press, Norman, 1959); Vernon Gill Carter and Tom Dale, *Topsoil and Civilization* rev. ed. (University of Oklahoma Press, Norman, 1974); Donald Worster, *Dust Bowl: The Southern Plains in the 1930s* (Oxford University Press, New York, 1979).

120. Noss et al., *Endangered Ecosystems of the United States*, 37.

121. David A. Clary, *Timber and the Forest Service* (University Press of Kansas, Lawrence, 1987).

122. Cronon, *Changes in the Land*, 110.

123. Michael Williams, *Americans and Their Forests: A Historical Geography* (Cambridge University Press, New York, 1989), 118.

124. Turner et al., "Land Use," 41.

125. Frederick Merk, *History of the Westward Movement* (Alfred A. Knopf, New York, 1980), 451.

126. Veirs and Opler, "California," 601.

127. Smith and Collopy, "Northwest," 646–647.

128. Smith and Collopy, "Northwest," 650–651.

129. Smith and Collopy, "Northwest," 660–665.

130. Smith and Collopy, "Northwest," 668.

131. Smith and Collopy, "Northwest," 682.

132. Klein et al., "Alaska," 737.

133. Turner et al., "Land Use," 43. Referencing P. H. Morrison, D. Kloepfer, D. A. Leversee, C. M. Socha, and D. L. Ferber, *Ancient Forests in the Pacific Northwest: Analysis and Maps of Twelve National Forests* (The Wilderness Society, Washington, D.C., 1991).

134. Smith and Collopy, "Northwest," 647.

135. Farley et al., "Avian Species Richness"; D. Scurlock, "The Rio Grande Bosque: Ever Changing," *New Mexico Historical Review* 63 (1988): 131–140; Van Cleave, "Vegetation Change in the Middle Rio Grande Conservancy District."

136. C. J. Bahre, "Late 19th Century Human Impacts on the Woodlands and Forests of Southeastern Arizona's Sky Islands," *Desert Plants*, University of Arizona at the Boyce Thompson Southwestern Arboretum, June 1998.

137. Scurlock and Finch, "A Historical Review," 48–49.

138. Scurlock and Finch, "A Historical Review," 62.

139. Kieran Suckling, *Forests Forever! A Plan to Restore Ecological and Economic Integrity to the Southwest's National Forests and Forest Dependent Communities* (Southwest Forest Alliance, 1996), 22.

140. Suckling, *Forests Forever!* , 28.

141. Bogan et al., "Southwest," 547.

142. Noss et al., *Endangered Ecosystems of the United States*, 48.

143. Dave Foreman, Kathy Daly, Barbara Dugelby, Rosanne Hanson, Robert E. Howard, Jack Humphrey, Leanne Klyza Linck, Rurik List, and Kim Vacariu, *Sky Islands Wildlands Network Conservation Plan* (The Wildlands Project, Tucson, Ariz., 2000), 81. Rurik List, a Wildlands Project board member and biologist from Mexico, wrote this paragraph for the *Sky Islands Wildlands Network Conservation Plan*.

144. A. J. Belsky, A. Matzke, and S. Uselman, "Survey of Livestock Influences on Stream and Riparian Ecosystems in the Western United States," *Journal of Soil and Water Conservation*, First Quarter 1999, 419–431.

145. Belsky et al., "Survey of Livestock Influences," 419.

146. Scurlock and Finch, "Historical Review," 45.

147. Veirs and Opler, "California," 603.

148. Denzel Ferguson and Nancy Ferguson, *Sacred Cows at the Public Trough* (Maverick Publications, Bend, Ore., 1983), 14–15.

149. Steve Johnson, "Learning to Miss What We Never Knew," *The Home Range* (Predator Project), Summer 1997.

150. Craig D. Allen, Julio L. Betancourt, and Thomas W. Swetnam, "Landscape Changes in the Southwestern United States: Techniques, Long-term Data Sets, and Trends," in Thomas D. Sisk, ed., *Perspectives on the Land Use History of North America: A Context for Understanding Our Changing Environment* (U.S. Geological Service, Biological Resources Division, Biological Science Report USGS/BRD/BSR-1998-0003, September 1998), 72.

151. Belsky et al., "Survey of Livestock Influences," 427.

152. Bogan et al., "Southwest," 546.

153. Bogan et al., "Southwest," 554.

154. Belsky et al., "Survey of Livestock Influences."

155. Belsky et al., "Survey of Livestock Influences."

156. Leopold, "Conservationist in Mexico."

157. Wilcove, *Condor's Shadow*, 196–197.

158. Belsky et al., "Survey of Livestock Influences."

159. Bogan et al., "Southwest," 555–559.

160. Brussard et al., "Great Basin," 508–509.

161. Brussard et al., "Great Basin," 522.

162. Brussard et al., "Great Basin,"511.

163. John Horning, *Grazing to Extinction: Endangered, Threatened, and Candidate Species Imperiled by Livestock Grazing on Western Public Lands* (National Wildlife Federation, Washington, D.C., June 1994); Debra L. Donahue, *The Western Range Revisited: Removing Livestock from Public Lands to Conserve Native Biodiversity* (University of Oklahoma Press, Norman, 1991); George Wuerthner and Mollie Matteson, *Welfare Ranching: The Subsidized Destruction of the American West* (Foundation for Deep Ecology / Island Press, Washington, D.C., 2002). After her book was published, Donahue was attacked by cowboy politicians in Wyoming, who demanded her firing and the closure of the Wyoming College of Law. *Welfare Ranching* features essays from various authorities and many photographs.

164. Jerome E. Freilich, John M. Emlen, Jeffrey J. Duda, D. Carl Freeman, and Philip J. Cafaro, "Ecological Effects of Ranching: A Six-Point Critique," *BioScience* 53, no. 8 (August 2003): 759–765.

165. Stohlgren et al., "Rocky Mountains," 487.

166. Miller et al., *Prairie Night.*

167. Jackson et al., "Historical Overfishing," 631.

168. Jackson et al., "Historical Overfishing," 634.

169. Jackson et al., "Historical Overfishing," 633–634.

170. Jackson et al., "Historical Overfishing," 635.

171. Michele A. McMillan and Douglas W. Larson, "Effects of Rock Climbing on the Vegetation of the Niagara Escarpment in Southern Ontario, Canada," *Conservation Biology* 16, no. 2 (April 2002): 389–398.

172. James R. Miller and Richard J. Hobbs, "Conservation Where People Live and Work," *Conservation Biology* 16, no. 2 (April 2002): 332.

173. Wilcove, *Condor's Shadow*, 38–41.

174. Low et al., "Marine Resources," 802.

175. Miller and Hobbs, "Conservation Where People Live and Work," 333.
176. Noss et al., *Endangered Ecosystems of the United States*, 46.
177. Michael E. Soulé, "Land Use Planning and Wildlife Maintenance: Guidelines for Conserving Wildlife in an Urban Landscape," *APA Journal* 57, no. 3 (Summer 1991): 313–323.
178. Hannah Gillelan, "Homeless Fish: Bottom Trawls Bulldoze Seafloor Habitat," *Wild Earth*, Winter 2002–2003, 34–38.
179. Pauly et al., "Towards Sustainability in World Fisheries," 691.
180. Turner et al., "Land Use," 49.
181. Samson et al., "Grasslands," 440–441.
182. Veirs and Opler, "California," 603.
183. Veirs and Opler, "California," 604.
184. Veirs and Opler, "California,"612.
185. Herrmann et al., "Water Use," 64.
186. Herrmann et al., "Water Use,"64.
187. Herrmann et al., "Water Use," 64.
188. Wilcove, *Condor's Shadow*, 108.
189. Herrmann et al., "Water Use," 65–66.
190. Turner et al., "Land Use," 51.
191. Noss et al., *Endangered Ecosystems of the United States*, 12.
192. Low et al., "Marine Resources," 783.
193. Turner et al., "Land Use," 51.
194. Herrmann et al., "Water Use," 67.
195. Herrmann et al., "Water Use," 68.
196. Clair Stalnaker, and Dale Crawford, "Impounded River Systems," in Mac et al., *Status and Trends*, 69.
197. Brussard et al., "Great Basin," 510.
198. Brussard et al., "Great Basin," 519–520.
199. Bogan et al., "Southwest," 566–567. This section is an excellent overview of native fish loss in the Southwest.
200. Bogan et al., "Southwest," 570.
201. Bogan et al., "Southwest," 575.
202. Bogan et al., "Southwest," 548.
203. Veirs and Opler, "California," 620–621.
204. White et al., "Southeast," 296–297.
205. White et al., "Southeast," 298.

6. Ecological Wounds of North America II

1. Michael E. Soulé and John Terborgh, "The Policy and Science of Regional Conservation," in *Continental Conservation: Scientific Foundations of Regional Reserve Networks*, ed. Michael E. Soulé and John Terborgh (Island Press, Washington, D.C., 1999), 12.
2. Dave Foreman, "The Big Outside," in *The Big Outside*, by Dave Foreman and Howie Wolke (Crown, New York, 1992), 10–11.
3. Stephen C. Trombulak and Christopher A. Frissell, "Review of Ecologi-

cal Effects of Roads on Terrestrial and Aquatic Communities," *Conservation Biology* 14, no. 1 (February 2000), 18–30.

4. Richard T. T. Forman, "Estimate of the Area Affected Ecologically by the Road System in the United States," *Conservation Biology* 14, no. 1 (February 2000), 31–35.

5. *Forest Service Roadless Area Conservation: Draft Environmental Impact Statement Summary and Proposed Rule* (USDA, Forest Service, Washington, D.C., May 2000), S-35.

6. Trombulak and Frissell, "Ecological Effects of Roads."

7. Dave Foreman, Kathy Daly, Robert E. Howard, Reed Noss, Matt Clark, Kurt Menke, and David R. Parsons, *New Mexico Highlands Wildlands Network Vision* (The Wildlands Project, Richmond, Vt., 2003); David R. Parsons, *Natural History Characteristics of Focal Species in the New Mexico Highlands Wildlands Network Vision*, available on CD (The Wildlands Project, Richmond, Vt., 2003).

8. Trombulak and Frissell, "Ecological Effects of Roads," 19.

9. Trombulak and Frissell, "Ecological Effects of Roads," 21.

10. Trombulak and Frissell, "Ecological Effects of Roads," 22.

11. Craig D. Allen, Julio L. Betancourt, and Thomas W. Swetnam, "Landscape Changes in the Southwestern United States: Techniques, Long-term Data Sets, and Trends," in *Perspectives on the Land Use History of North America: A Context for Understanding Our Changing Environment*, ed. Thomas D. Sisk (U.S. Geological Service, Biological Resources Division, Biological Science Report USGS/BRD/BSR-1998-0003, September 1998), 77.

12. Trombulak and Frissell, "Ecological Effects of Roads," 20.

13. Skidmarks #61, e-mail newsletter of the Wildlands Center for Preventing Roads, February 10, 2003.

14. Trombulak and Frissell, "Ecological Effects of Roads," 20.

15. David R. Klein, David F. Murray, Robert H. Armstrong, and Betty A. Anderson, "Regional Trends of Biological Resources—Alaska," in *Status and Trends of the Nation's Biological Resources*, ed. M. J. Mac, P. A. Opler, C. E. Puckett Haecker, and P. D. Doran, 2 vols. (U.S. Department of the Interior, U.S. Geological Survey, Reston, Va., 1998), 735.

16. Richard L. Bury, Robert C. Wendling, and Stephen F. McCool, *Off-Road Recreation Vehicles—A Research Summary, 1969–1975* (Texas Agricultural Experiment Station, College Station, July 1976).

17. David Sheridan, *Off-Road Vehicles on Public Lands: A Report to the Council on Environmental Quality*, draft, August 1978.

18. Sheridan, *Off-Road Vehicles*, 121.

19. Paul S. Sutter, *Driven Wild: How the Fight against Automobiles Launched the Modern Wilderness Movement* (University of Washington Press, Seattle, 2002).

20. Peter F. Brussard, David A. Charlet, and David S. Dobkin, "Regional Trends of Biological Resources—Great Basin," in Mac et al., *Status and Trends*, 529–530.

21. Jacob Smith, "Snowmobiles Stress Wildlife in Winter," *The Road RIPorter*, April–May 1996. This article has a good bibliography of snowmobile impacts.
22. Peter S. White, Stephanie P. Wilds, and Gwendolyn A. Thunhorst, "Regional Trends of Biological Resources—Southeast," in Mac et al., *Status and Trends*, 288.
23. Abby Powell, "Western Snowy Plovers and California Least Terns," in Mac et al., *Status and Trends*, 629.
24. Stephen D. Veirs Jr. and Paul A. Opler, "Regional Trends of Biological Resources—California," in Mac et al., *Status and Trends*, 616.
25. Brussard et al., "Great Basin," 521.
26. Brussard et al., "Great Basin," 516.
27. James A. Rodgers Jr. and Stephen T. Schwikert, "Buffer-Zone Distances to Protect Foraging and Loafing Waterbirds from Disturbance by Personal Watercraft and Outboard-Powered Boats," *Conservation Biology* 16, no. 1 (February 2002), 216–224.
28. Louisa Willcox, "Roads Kill: Grizzly Bears and the Effects of Human Access," *The Road-RIPporter*, May–June 1998.
29. Douglas Gantenbein, "Reckless Driving on the Beach," *Audubon*, September–October 1997, 16.
30. Michael A. Bogan, Craig D. Allen, Esteban H. Muldavin, Steven P. Platania, James N. Stuart, Greg H. Farley, Patricia Mehlhop, and Jayne Belnap, "Regional Trends of Biological Resources—Southwest," in Mac et al., *Status and Trends*, 548.
31. Bogan et al., "Southwest," 567–568.
32. Jeff P. Smith and Michael W. Collopy, "Regional Trends of Biological Resources—Pacific Northwest," in *Status and Trends*, 652.
33. Loh-Lee Low, Allen M. Shimada, Steven L. Swartz, and Michael P. Sissenwine, "Regional Trends of Biological Resources—Marine Resources," in Mac et al., *Status and Trends*, 822.
34. C. H. O'Leary and D. W. Nyberg, "Treelines between Fields Reduce the Diversity of Grassland Birds," *Natural Areas Journal* 20 (2000): 243–249.
35. Veirs and Opler, "California," 632.
36. David S. Wilcove, *The Condor's Shadow* (W. H. Freeman, New York, 1999), 41–42.
37. White et al., "Southeast," 288.
38. Daniel J. Simberloff, Dan Doak, Martha Groom, Steve Trombulak, Andy Dobson, Steve Gatewood, Michael E. Soulé, Michael Gilpin, Carlos Martinez del Rio, and Lisa Mills, "Regional and Continental Restoration," in Soulé and Terborgh, *Continental Conservation*, 88.
39. Reed F. Noss and Robert L. Peters, *Endangered Ecosystems: A Status Report on America's Vanishing Habitat and Wildlife* (Defenders of Wildlife, Washington, D.C., December 1995), 48.
40. White et al., "Southeast," 273.
41. White et al., "Southeast," 273.
42. Jeff S. Glitzenstein, Donna R. Streng, and Dale D. Wade, "Fire Fre-

quency Effects on Longleaf Pine (*Pinus palustris* P. Miller) Vegetation in South Carolina and Northeast Florida, USA," *Natural Areas Journal* 23, no. 1 (January 2003): 22–37.

43. White et al., "Southeast," 283.

44. Fred B. Samson, Fritz L. Knopf, and Wayne R. Ostlie, "Regional Trends of Biological Resources—Grasslands," in Mac et al., *Status and Trends*, 444–445.

45. Thomas W. Swetnam and Julio L. Betancourt, "Fire–Southern Oscillation Relations in the Southwestern United States," *Science* 249 (1990): 1017–1020; Thomas W. Swetnam and Julio L. Betancourt, "Mesoscale Disturbance and Ecological Response to Decadal Climatic Variability in the American Southwest," *Journal of Climate* 11 (1998): 3128–3147; Thomas W. Swetnam and C. H. Baisan, "Fire Histories of Montane Forests in the Madrean Borderlands," in *Effects of Fire on Madrean Province Ecosystems: A Symposium Proceedings*, coordinated by P. F. Ffolliott, L. F. DeBano, M. B. Baker, G. J. Gottfried, G. Solis-Garza, C. B. Edminster, D. G. Neary, L. S. Allen, and R. H. Hamre, U.S. Department of Agriculture, Forest Service, General Technical Report, RM-GTR-289, 1996, pp. 15–36.

46. Bogan et al., "Southwest," 547, 551–553; Dan Scurlock and Deborah M. Finch, "A Historical Review," in *Songbird Ecology in Southwestern Ponderosa Pine Forests: A Literature Review*, ed. William M. Block and Deborah M. Finch, General Technical Report RM-GTR-292, U.S. Department of Agriculture, Forest Service, Rocky Mountain Forest and Range Experiment Station, Fort Collins, Colo., 1997, p. 47.

47. Bogan et al., "Southwest," 547.

48. R. R. Humphrey, *The Desert Grassland* (University of Arizona Press, Tucson, 1958); C. J. Bahre, "Late 19th Century Human Impacts on the Woodlands and Forests of Southeastern Arizona's Sky Islands," *Desert Plants*, Boyce Thompson Southwestern Arboretum, June 1998; M. M. Pollock and Kieran Suckling, *Presettlement Conditions of Ponderosa Pine Forests in the American Southwest* (Southwest Forest Alliance and Southwest Center for Biological Diversity, May 27, 1997); Kieran Suckling, *Fire and Forest Ecosystem Health in the American Southwest* (Southwest Forest Alliance, 1996); Dennis Morgan and Kieran Suckling, *Grazing Is the Major Cause of Forest Health Problems in Southwestern Forests* (The Southwest Forest Alliance, 1995); P. Z. Fule and W. W. Covington, "Comparisons of Fire Regimes and Stand Structures in Unharvested Petran and Madrean Pine Forests," in *Biodiversity and Management of the Madrean Archipelago*, 408–415.

49. R. F. Fisher, M. J. Jenkins, and W. F. Fisher, "Fire and the Prairie Forest Mosaic of Devils Tower National Monument," *American Midland Naturalist* 117 (1987): 250–257.

50. Allen et al., "Landscape Changes."

51. Thomas R. Vale, "The Myth of the Humanized Landscape: An Example from Yosemite National Park," *Natural Areas Journal* 18, no. 3 (1998), reprinted in *Wild Earth*, Fall 1999.

52. Allen et al., "Landscape Changes."
53. Bogan et al., "Southwest," 550.
54. Smith and Collopy, "Northwest," 647–648.
55. Bogan et al., "Southwest," 560.
56. Bogan et al., "Southwest," 560–563.
57. Samson et al., "Grasslands," 463.
58. Thomas J. Stohlgren, "Regional Trends of Biological Resources—Rocky Mountains," in Mac et al., *Status and Trends*, 492.
59. Smith and Collopy, "Northwest," 652.
60. Simberloff et al., "Regional and Continental Restoration," 88–90.
61. Greg H. Farley, Lisa M. Ellis, James N. Stuart, and Norman J. Scott Jr., "Avian Species Richness in Different-Aged Stands of Riparian Forest along the Middle Rio Grande, New Mexico," *Conservation Biology* 8, no. 4 (December 1994), 1098–1108.
62. Farley et al., "Avian Species Richness," 1106.
63. Wilcove, *Condor's Shadow*, 173–179.
64. White et al., "Southeast," 291.
65. John Terborgh, James A. Estes, Paul Paquet, Katherine Ralls, Diane Boyd-Heger, Brian J. Miller, and Reed F. Noss, "The Role of Top Carnivores in Regulating Terrestrial Ecosystems," in Soulé and Terborgh, *Continental Conservation*; Michael E. Soulé and Reed F. Noss, "Rewilding and Biodiversity: Complementary Goals for Continental Conservation," *Wild Earth* Fall 1998, 18–28.
66. Bogan et al., "Southwest," 550.
67. David S. Wilcove, D. Rothstein, J. Dubow, A. Philips, and E. Losos, "Quantifying Threats to Imperiled Species in the United States," *Bio-Science* 48, no. 8 (August 1, 1998), 607–615.
68. James D. Williams and Gary K. Meffe, "Factors Affecting Biological Resources—Nonindigenous Species," in Mac et al., *Status and Trends*, 118.
69. Williams and Meffe, "Nonindigenous Species," 118.
70. Williams and Meffe, "Nonindigenous Species," 120.
71. Williams and Meffe, "Nonindigenous Species," 121.
72. Williams and Meffe, "Nonindigenous Species," 123.
73. Williams and Meffe, "Nonindigenous Species," 121–122.
74. Jonathan L. Gelbard and Jayne Belnap, "Roads as Conduits for Exotic Plant Invasions in a Semiarid Landscape," *Conservation Biology* 17, no. 2 (April 2003): 420–432.
75. William F. Porter and Jennifer A. Hill, "Regional Trends of Biological Resources—Northeast," in Mac et al., *Status and Trends*, 196.
76. Stohlgren, "Rocky Mountains," 497.
77. Williams and Meffe, "Nonindigenous Species," 122.
78. Brussard et al., "Great Basin," 528.
79. Williams and Meffe, "Nonindigenous Species," 122.
80. Noss and Peters, *Endangered Ecosystems*, 26.
81. Samson et al., "Grasslands," 463–464.

82. Stohlgren, "Rocky Mountains," 497.
83. Brussard et al., "Great Basin," 511–512.
84. Brussard et al., "Great Basin," 529, 531.
85. Smith and Collopy, "Northwest," 649.
86. Bogan et al., "Southwest," 549.
87. Farley et al., "Avian Species Richness"; Anna A. Sher, Diane L. Marshall, and Steven A. Gilbert, "Competition between Native *Populus deltoides* and Invasive *Tamarix ramosissima* and the Implications for Reestablishing Flooding Disturbance," *Conservation Biology* 14, no. 6 (December 2000): 1744–1754.
88. Brussard et al., "Great Basin," 509.
89. Veirs and Opler, "California," 616.
90. James D. Williams and Gary K. Meffe, "American Chestnut Blight," in Mac et al., *Status and Trends*, 121.
91. Wilcove, *Condor's Shadow*, 47.
92. Wilcove, *Condor's Shadow*, 47.
93. Wilcove, *Condor's Shadow*, 47.
94. White et al., "Southeast," 276.
95. Porter and Hill, "Northeast," 184.
96. Jonathan M. Adams, Gianluca Piovesan, Steve Strauss, and Sandra Brown, "The Case for Genetic Engineering of Native and Landscape Trees against Introduced Pests and Diseases," *Conservation Biology* 16, no. 4 (August 2002): 875.
97. James R. Strittholt and Dominick A. DellaSala, "Importance of Roadless Areas in Biodiversity Conservation in Forested Ecosystems: Case Study of the Klamath-Siskiyou Ecoregion of the United States," *Conservation Biology* 15, no. 6 (December 2001): 1742–1754.
98. Katherine C. Kendall, "Whitebark Pine," in *Status and Trends*, 483–485.
99. David J. Mattson and Troy Merrill, "Extirpations of Grizzly Bears in the Contiguous United States, 1850–2000," *Conservation Biology* 16, no. 4 (August 2002): 1123–1136.
100. Katherine C. Kindle, "Limber Pine," in Mac et al., *Status and Trends*, 486.
101. Ben Shouse, "Plant Pathologists at the Center of a Circus," *Science* 300 (April 18, 2003): 418–419. See also Adams et al., "Case for Genetic Engineering," 875.
102. Peter Fimrite, "Breakthrough for Treatment of Oak Death," *San Francisco Chronicle*, October 3, 2003.
103. Kevin D. Lafferty and Leah R. Gerber, "Good Medicine for Conservation Biology: The Intersection of Epidemiology and Conservation Theory," *Conservation Biology* 16, no. 3 (June 2002): 593–604.
104. Miller et al., *Prairie Night*, 21–22.
105. Miller et al., *Prairie Night*.
106. Milton Friend, "Duck Plague: Emergence of a New Cause of Waterfowl Mortality," in Mac et al., *Status and Trends*, 458–460.
107. David Malakoff, "Researchers Scramble to Track Virus's Impact on Wildlife," *Science* 299 (February 21, 2003): 1176.

108. Stohlgren, "Rocky Mountains," 489.

109. Williams and Meffe, "Nonindigenous Species," 125.

110. Thomas A. Edsall, "Regional Trends of Biological Resources—Great Lakes," in Mac et al., *Status and Trends*, 235.

111. William L. Perry, Jeffrey L. Feder, and David M. Lodge, "Implications of Hybridization between Introduced and Resident *Orconectes* Crayfishes," *Conservation Biology* 15, no. 6 (December 2001): 1656–1666.

112. Low et al., "Marine Resources," 821.

113. Low et al., "Marine Resources," 849.

114. Williams and Meffe, "Nonindigenous Species," 125.

115. Williams and Meffe, "Nonindigenous Species," 126.

116. Williams and Meffe, "Nonindigenous Species," 124.

117. Edsall, "Great Lakes," 239.

118. Low et al., "Marine Resources," 849.

119. Stohlgren, "Rocky Mountains," 492.

120. James D. Williams and Gary K. Meffe, "Eastern and Western Mosquitofishes," in Mac et al., *Status and Trends*, 124.

121. Wilcove, *Condor's Shadow*, 118.

122. Bogan et al., "Southwest," 570.

123. Stohlgren, "Rocky Mountains," 487.

124. Michael P. Murray, "Natural Processes: Wilderness Management Unrealized," *Natural Areas Journal* 16 (1996): 55–61.

125. William J. Liss and Gary L. Larson, "Complex Interactions of Introduced Trout and Native Biota in High-Elevation Lakes," in Mac et al., *Status and Trends*, 659–660.

126. Veirs and Opler, "California," 621–622.

127. Martin Forstenzer, "When the Trout Arrive, the Amphibian Exodus Begins," *New York Times*, November 29, 2000.

128. Bogan et al., "Southwest," 575.

129. Veirs and Opler, "California," 621–622.

130. Kelly R. McAllister, "Spotted Frogs in the Western Pacific Northwest," in Mac et al., *Status and Trends*, 669.

131. Veirs and Opler, "California," 634.

132. Noss, Reed, personal communication.

133. Klein et al., "Alaska," 728, 739–740.

134. White et al., "Southeast," 288.

135. Christopher J. Schmitt, "Factors Affecting Biological Resources—Environmental Contaminants," in Mac et al., *Status and Trends*, 142–143.

136. Schmitt, "Environmental Contaminants," 150.

137. Dusheck, Jennie, "The Interpretation of Genes," *Natural History*, October 2002, 56.

138. Bogan et al., "Southwest," 548.

139. Schmitt, "Environmental Contaminants," 144–146.

140. Schmitt, "Environmental Contaminants," 132.

141. Schmitt, "Environmental Contaminants," 132–133.

142. Schmitt, "Environmental Contaminants," 134.
143. Bogan et al., "Southwest," 571.
144. Schmitt, "Environmental Contaminants," 135.
145. Wilcove, *Condor's Shadow*, 166.
146. Schmitt, "Environmental Contaminants," 135–138.
147. Noss and Peters, *Endangered Ecosystems*, 35.
148. Schmitt, "Environmental Contaminants," 138.
149. Wilcove, *Condor's Shadow*, 129.
150. Klein et al., "Alaska," 732.
151. Low et al., "Marine Resources," 851.
152. Stephen H. Schneider, and Terry L. Root, "Factors Affecting Biological Resources—Climate Change," in Mac et al., *Status and Trends*, 98.
153. Schneider and Root, "Climate Change," 101–102.
154. Schneider and Root, "Climate Change," 102.
155. Schneider and Root, "Climate Change," 102.
156. Schneider and Root, "Climate Change," 110.
157. Schneider and Root, "Climate Change," 112.
158. Klein et al., "Alaska," 732.

Part II. Good News

Epigraph: John Terborgh, James A. Estes, Paul Paquet, Katherine Ralls, Diane Boyd-Heger, Brian J. Miller, and Reed F. Noss, "The Role of Top Carnivores in Regulating Terrestrial Ecosystems," in Soulé and Terborgh, *Continental Conservation*, p. 58.

7. Conservation Biology

1. Lucy Rosenau, *Wilderness Record: Proceedings of the California Wilderness Coalition* November 1994, Davis, Calif. This issue describes each of the seventy new wilderness areas and four enlarged wilderness areas, totaling 7.6 million acres, established by the California Desert Protection Act.
2. William K. Stevens, "Latest Endangered Species: Natural Habitats of America," *New York Times*, February 14, 1995.
3. Reed F. Noss, Edward T. LaRoe III, and J. Michael Scott, *Endangered Ecosystems of the United States: A Preliminary Assessment of Loss and Degradation* (USDI, National Biological Service, Washington, D.C., Biological Report 28, February 1995).
4. Victor E. Shelford, "Ecological Society of America: A Nature Sanctuary Plan Unanimously Adopted by the Society, December 28, 1932," *Ecology* 14, no. 2 (April 1933): 240–245.
5. William Schwarz, ed., *Voices for the Wilderness* (Ballantine Books, New York, 1969).
6. Aldo Leopold, *A Sand County Almanac and Sketches Here and There*, special commemorative edition (Oxford University Press, New York, 1989), 196.

7. Leopold, *A Sand County Almanac*, 188–201. The section "Wilderness" is eye opening, showing how Leopold anticipated much of modern conservation biology.

8. It is common nowadays to use the terms "NGO" (nongovernmental organization) and "environmental activist" to describe conservationists or conservation groups not associated with governments. In the 1970s, however, The Wilderness Society used "citizen conservationist." I think the latter term is more accurate and should be resurrected.

9. Dave Foreman, "The Wildlands Project and the Rewilding of North America," *Denver University Law Review* 76, no. 2 (1999): 535–553.

10. Michael Scialdone and Greg Magee, eds., *New Mexico Wilderness Alliance BLM Wilderness Inventory*, draft, February 2003.

11. Michael E. Soulé and John Terborgh, eds., *Continental Conservation: Scientific Foundations of Regional Reserve Networks* (Island Press, Washington, D.C., 1999). This is the comprehensive resource for understanding and practicing science-informed conservation. Contributors include many of the leading ecological scientists in North America: Hector Arita, Diane Boyd-Heger, Eric Dinerstein, Rudolfo Dirzo, Dan Doak, Andy Dobson, Jim Estes, Mercedes Foster, Steve Gatewood, Barrie Gilbert, Michael Gilpin, Martha Groom, Deborah Jensen, David Johns, Richard L. Knight, Carlos Martinez del Rio, Dave Mattson, Brian Miller, L. Scott Mills, Lisa Mills, Elliott Norse, Reed Noss, Paul Paquet, Katherine Ralls, Sadie Ryan, J. Michael Scott, Daniel Simberloff, Michael Soulé, John Terborgh, and Steve Trombulak.

12. Leopold called wilderness the "theater" of the "pageant of evolution." Leopold, *Sand County Almanac*, 199.

13. Michael Soulé, "What Is Conservation Biology?" *BioScience* December 1985, 727–734.

14. Michael E. Soulé and Bruce A. Wilcox, "Conservation Biology: Its Scope and Its Challenge," in *Conservation Biology: An Evolutionary-Ecological Perspective*, ed. Michael E. Soulé and Bruce A. Wilcox (Sinauer Associates, Sunderland, Mass., 1980), 4.

15. Michael E. Soulé, ed., *Conservation Biology: The Science of Scarcity and Diversity* (Sinauer Associates, Sunderland, Mass., 1986).

16. Robert H. MacArthur and Edward O. Wilson, *The Theory of Island Biogeography* (Princeton University Press, Princeton, N.J., 1967). David Quammen's outstanding book, *The Song of the Dodo: Island Biogeography in an Age of Extinctions* (Scribner, New York, 1996), looks at island biogeography and extinction in fascinating detail.

17. Jared Diamond, "The Island Dilemma: Lessons of Modern Biogeographic Studies for the Design of Natural Reserves," *Biological Conservation* 7 (1975): 129–146; John Terborgh, "Preservation of Natural Diversity: The Problem of Extinction Prone Species," *BioScience* 24 (1974): 715–722; M. E. Soulé and A. J. Sloan, "Biogeography and Distribution of the Reptiles and Amphibians on Islands in the Gulf of California, Mexico," *Transactions of the San Diego Society of Natural History*, 14, no. 11 (1966): 2137–2156.

18. Jared Diamond, "Dammed Experiments!" *Science* 294 (November 30, 2001): 1847–1848.

19. M. E. Soulé, B. A. Wilcox, and C. Holtby, "Benign Neglect: A Model of Faunal Collapse in the Game Reserves of East Africa," *Biological Conservation* 15 (1979): 259–272. Their predictions were later confirmed. See William D. Newmark, "Insularization of Tanzanian Parks and the Local Extinction of Large Mammals," *Conservation Biology*, December 1996, 1549–1556.

20. David S. Wilcove, Charles H. McLellan, and Andrew P. Dobson, "Habitat Fragmentation in the Temperate Zone," in *Conservation Biology: The Science of Scarcity and Diversity* ed. Michael E. Soulé (Sinauer Associates, Sunderland, Mass., 1986), 237–256.

21. Martha Groom and Nathan Schumaker, "Patterns of Worldwide Deforestation and Fragmentation," in *Biotic Interactions and Global Change*, ed. P. M. Kareiva, J. G. Kingsolver, and R. B. Huey (Sinauer, Sunderland, Mass., 1993), 37.

22. William D. Newmark, "A Land-Bridge Island Perspective on Mammalian Extinctions in Western North American Parks," *Nature* 325 (January 29, 1987): 430–432.

23. Andy Dobson, "Metalife!" *Science* 301 (September 12, 2003): 1488–1490.

24. Soulé, "What Is Conservation Biology?" 730.

25. Par K. Ingvarsson, "Lone Wolf to the Rescue," *Nature* 420 (December 2002): 472.

26. Bruce A. Wilcox and Dennis D. Murphy, "Conservation Strategy: The Effects of Fragmentation on Extinction," *American Naturalist* 125 (1985): 879–887.

27. Reed F. Noss, "Protecting Natural Areas in Fragmented Landscapes," *Natural Areas Journal* 7 no. 1 (1987): 2–13.

28. James Cox, Randy Kautz, Maureen MacLaughlin, and Terry Gilbert, *Closing the Gaps in Florida's Wildlife Habitat Conservation System: Recommendations to Meet Minimum Conservation Goals for Declining Wildlife Species and Rare Plant and Animal Communities* (Florida Game and Fresh Water Fish Commission, Tallahassee, 1994).

29. Reed Noss, personal correspondence.

30. S. T. A. Pickett and J. N. Thompson, "Patch Dynamics and the Design of Nature Reserves," *Biological Conservation* 13 (1978): 27–37.

31. Leopold, *Sand County Almanac*, 132.

32. Michael Soulé and Reed Noss, "Rewilding and Biodiversity as Complementary Goals for Continental Conservation," *Wild Earth*, Fall 1998, 22; John Terborgh, Lawrence Lopez, Percy Nuñez V., Madhu Rao, Ghazala Shahbuddin, Gabriela Orihuela, Mailen Riveros, Rafael Ascanio, Greg H. Adler, Thomas D. Lambert, and Luis Balbas, "Ecological Meltdown in Predator-Free Forest Fragments," *Science* 294 (November 30, 2001): 1923–1926.

33. John Terborgh, James A. Estes, Paul Paquet, Katherine Ralls, Diane Boyd-Heger, Brian J. Miller, and Reed F. Noss, "The Role of Top Carni-

vores in Regulating Terrestrial Ecosystems," in Soulé and Terborgh, *Continental Conservation*, 41.

34. Brian Miller, Barbara Dugelby, Dave Foreman, Carlos Martinez del Rio, Reed Noss, Mike Phillips, Rich Reading, Michael E. Soulé, John Terborgh, and Louisa Willcox, "The Importance of Large Carnivores to Healthy Ecosystems," *Endangered Species Update* 18, no. 5 (September–October 2001): 203.

35. Miller et al., "Importance of Large Carnivores," 203.

36. Terborgh et al., "Role of Top Carnivores," 39–64.

37. Terborgh et al., "Ecological Meltdown."

38. Miller et al., "Importance of Large Carnivores."

39. Terborgh et al., "Role of Top Carnivores," 42.

40. Miller et al., "Importance of Large Carnivores," 204.

41. Terborgh et al., "Role of Top Carnivores," 42.

42. Terborgh et al., "Role of Top Carnivores," 48; Douglas W. Smith, Rolf O. Peterson, and Douglas B. Houston, "Yellowstone after Wolves," *BioScience* 53, no. 4 (April 2003): 330–340.

43. Michael Soulé, personal communication.

44. S. E. Henke and F. C. Bryant, "Effects of Coyote Removal on the Faunal Community in Western Texas," *Journal of Wildlife Management* 63 (1999): 1066–1081; Miller et al., "Importance of Large Carnivores," 205.

45. Miller et al., "Importance of Large Carnivores," 204; J. A. Estes, N. S. Smith, and J. F. Palmisano, "Sea Otter Predation and Community Organization in the Western Aleutian Islands, Alaska," *Ecology* 59 (1978): 822–833; J. A. Estes, D. O. Duggins, and G. B. Rathbun, "The Ecology of Extinctions in Kelp Forest Communities," *Conservation Biology* 3, no. 3 (September 1989): 252–264.

46. James Estes, "From Killer Whales to Kelp: Food Web Complexity in Kelp Forest Ecosystems," *Wild Earth*, Winter 2002–2003, 24–28; see also Michael E. Soulé, James A. Estes, Joel Berger, and Carlos Martinez del Rio, "Ecological Effectiveness: Conservation Goals for Interactive Species," *Conservation Biology* 17, no. 5 (October 2003): 1238–1250.

47. William S. Alverson, Donald M. Waller, and Steve L. Solheim, "Forests too Deer: Edge Effects in Northern Wisconsin," *Conservation Biology* 2, no. 4 (December 1988): 348–358; William S. Alverson, Walter Kuhlmann, and Donald M. Waller, *Wild Forests: Conservation Biology and Public Policy* (Island Press, Washington, D.C., 1994), 30–32. A more recent review is Tom Rooney, Don Waller, and Shannon Wiegmann, "Revisiting the Northwoods: A Lesson in Biotic Homogenization," *Wild Earth*, Spring 2001, 45–49.

48. Theo Stein, "Wolves Have Set Up Natural Smorgasbord Ecologist: Yellowstone Packs Key to Diversity," *Denver Post*, July 9, 2001, is an excellent summary of the positive impact wolves are having. See also Smith et al., "Yellowstone after Wolves," and Soulé et al., "Ecological Effectiveness."

49. William J. Ripple and Eric J. Larsen, "Historic Aspen Recruitment, Elk, and Wolves in Northern Yellowstone National Park, USA," *Biological*

Conservation 95 (2000): 361–370. See also William J. Ripple and Robert L. Beschta, "Wolf Reintroduction, Predation Risk, and Cottonwood Recovery in Yellowstone National Park," *Forest Ecology and Management* 184 (2003): 299–313.

50. Joel Berger, P. B. Stacey, L. Belliss, and M. P. Johnson, "A Mammalian Predator-prey Imbalance: Grizzly Bear and Wolf Extinction Affects Avian Neotropical Migrants," *Ecological Applications* 11 (2001): 947–960.

51. Michael E. Soulé, Douglas T. Boulger, Allison C. Alberts, Raymond Sauvajot, John Wright, Marina Sorice, and Scott Hill, "Reconstructed Dynamics of Rapid Extinctions of Chaparral-Requiring Birds in Urban Habitat Islands," *Conservation Biology* 2, no. 1 (March 1988): 75–92; K. R. Crooks and M. E. Soulé, "Mesopredator Release and Avifaunal Extinction in a Fragmented System," *Nature* 400 (1999): 563–566.

52. Wilcove et al., "Habitat Fragmentation," 237–256.

53. Terborgh et al., "Role of Top Carnivores," 49–50; Terborgh et al., "Ecological Meltdown."

54. Terborgh et al., "Role of Top Carnivores," 55–56.

55. Terborgh et al., "Role of Top Carnivores," 41.

56. Terborgh et al., "Role of Top Carnivores," 58.

57. Miller et al., "Importance of Large Carnivores," 208.

58. Kevin D. Lafferty and Leah R. Gerber, "Good Medicine for Conservation Biology: The Intersection of Epidemiology and Conservation Theory," *Conservation Biology* 16, no. 3 (June 2002): 593–604.

59. Soulé et al., "Ecological Effectiveness," 1238–1250.

60. Michael E. Soulé, "Are Ecosystem Processes Enough?" *Wild Earth*, Spring 1996, 59–60.

61. Daniel Simberloff, Dan Doak, Martha Groom, Steve Trombulak, Andy Dobson, Steve Gatewood, Michael E. Soulé, Michael Gilpin, Carlos Martinez del Rio, and Lisa Mills, "Regional and Continental Restoration," in Soulé and Terborgh, *Continental Conservation*, 67. Chapter 4, "Regional and Continental Restoration," in *Continental Conservation* provides state-of-the-art guidance for wildlands restoration.

62. Simberloff et al., "Regional and Continental Restoration," 66.

63. E. C. Pielou, *After the Ice Age: The Return of Life to Glaciated North America* (University of Chicago Press, Chicago, 1991).

64. Simberloff et al., "Regional and Continental Restoration," 69.

65. Simberloff et al., "Regional and Continental Restoration," 71.

66. Dave Foreman, Kathy Daly, Reed Noss, Matt Clark, Kurt Menke, David R. Parsons, and Robert E. Howard, *New Mexico Highlands Wildlands Network Vision* (The Wildlands Project, Richmond, Vt., 2003), 56–58.

8. Rewilding North America

1. Michael Soulé and Reed Noss, "Rewilding and Biodiversity as Complementary Goals for Continental Conservation," *Wild Earth*, Fall 1998, 22.

2. Lois Crisler, *Arctic Wild* (Ballantine Books, New York, 1958).

3. Soulé and Noss, "Rewilding and Biodiversity," 22.

4. Soulé and Noss, "Rewilding and Biodiversity," 23–24.

5. Rewilding, of course, is only part of the process of comprehensive ecological protection and restoration, and is not a complete protected-areas strategy. To protect adequate samples of all plant communities and habitat for all native species and to heal all seven ecological wounds requires planning for more than the habitat needed by large carnivores; it requires focusing on *representation* of all plant communities and protection of *special elements* (rare species, threatened and endangered species, endemic species, "hot spots" of biodiversity, and so on). Such conservation planning is essential for halting the extinction crisis, and wherever possible it should be done in conjunction with planning based on rewilding.

6. In 1964, David Brower wrote that "*real* wilderness" was "big wilderness—country big enough to have a beyond to it and an inside." David Brower, "Wilderness—Conflict and Conscience," in *Voices for the Wilderness*, ed. William Schwartz (Ballantine Books, New York, 1969), 3.

7. These wolf and cougar vision statements (and others, such as for the grizzly bear) will be published and distributed by The Rewilding Institute.

8. Robert Burns, "To a Mouse."

9. Michael E. Soulé, James A. Estes, Joel Berger, and Carlos Martinez del Rio, "Ecological Effectiveness: Conservation Goals for Interactive Species," *Conservation Biology* 17, no. 5 (October 2003): 1238–1250.

10. Aldo Leopold, "Conservation," *Round River* (Oxford University Press, New York, 1953), 147.

11. Peter H. Singleton, William L. Gaines, and John F. Lehmkuhl, *Landscape Permeability for Large Carnivores in Washington: A Geographic Information System Weighted-Distance and Least-Cost Corridor Assessment* (U.S. Department of Agriculture, Forest Service, Pacific Northwest Research Station, Research Paper PNW-RP-549, December 2002), 1–2. It should be recognized that Lance Craighead has been using least-cost path analysis in the Greater Yellowstone Ecosystem for several years.

12. Singleton et al., *Landscape Permeability*, 2.

13. Peter H. Singleton, John F. Lehmkuhl, and Williams Gaines, "Using Weighted Distance and Least-Cost Corridor Analysis to Evaluate Regional-Scale Large Carnivore Habitat Connectivity in Washington," *A Time For Action: 2001 Proceedings ICOET* (International Conference on Ecology and Transportation, September 24–28, 2002, Keystone, Colo.), 583–594.

14. Reed Noss, "A Recipe for Reserve System Design and Management," special issue, *Wild Earth*, 1992, 24.

15. Singleton et al., *Landscape Permeability*, 2.

16. Singleton et al., *Landscape Permeability*, 2–3.

17. Singleton et al., *Landscape Permeability*, 14–56.

18. Singleton et al., *Landscape Permeability*, 14.

19. Singleton et al., *Landscape Permeability*, 40.

20. By "sensitive," I mean species not tolerant of human disturbance and species of which some humans are intolerant.

21. Kenneth A. Logan, and Linda L. Sweanor, *Desert Puma: Evolutionary Ecology and Conservation of an Enduring Carnivore* (Island Press, Washington, D.C., 2001).

22. Michael Soulé tells me that shades of landscape permeability are "probably 95 percent correlated with the wildness indices and maps that people have developed for the U.S. and Australia."

23. Douglas W. Scott, *A Wilderness-Forever Future: A Short History of the National Wilderness Preservation System* (Pew Wilderness Center, Washington, D.C., 2001).

24. Section 2(a), The Wilderness Act, Public Law 88-577 (16. U.S.C. 1131-1136), 88th Cong., 2d Sess., September 3, 1964, in *The Wilderness Act Handbook*, 4th ed., rev. ed., Jay Watson and Ben Beach (The Wilderness Society, Washington, D.C., 2000), 5.

25. Samuel Hays, "The Trouble with Bill Cronon's Wilderness," *Environmental History* 1, no. 1 (January 1996): 30.

26. Dave Foreman, John Davis, David Johns, Reed Noss, and Michael Soulé, "The Wildlands Project Mission Statement," special issue, *Wild Earth*, 1992, 3.

9. Selecting and Designing Protected Areas: The Early Days

1. Aldo Leopold, *A Sand County Almanac* (Oxford University Press, New York, 1949), 149.

2. Dave Foreman, "Around the Campfire: The River Wild," *Wild Earth*, Winter 1998–1999, inside front cover–4. A more detailed discussion of "River Wild" will appear in a future book.

3. Nonetheless, some national parks, including Yosemite and Crater Lake, were saved through campaigns by local citizens, who knew the proposed parks on the ground.

4. Samuel P. Hays, *Conservation and the Gospel of Efficiency: The Progressive Conservation Movement 1890–1920* (Atheneum, New York, 1979), 32, 41; Roderick Frazier Nash, *Wilderness and the American Mind*, 4th ed. (Yale University Press, New Haven, Conn., 2001), 135–138.

5. Richard West Sellars, *Preserving Nature in the National Parks: A History* (Yale University Press, New Haven, Conn., 1997), 17, 61.

6. Aldo Leopold, "Wilderness as a Form of Land Use," *The Journal of Land and Public Utility Economics* 1, no. 4 (October 1925): 398–404.

7. Susan L. Flader, "Aldo Leopold and the Wilderness Idea," *The Living Wilderness* 43, no. 147 (December 1979): 6.

8. Paul S. Sutter, *Driven Wild: How the Fight against Automobiles Launched the Modern Wilderness Movement* (University of Washington Press, Seattle, 2002), 81–84.

9. Sutter, *Driven Wild*, 84.

10. Sutter, *Driven Wild*, 153–160.

11. Sutter, *Driven Wild*, 167.
12. Flader, "Aldo Leopold and the Wilderness Idea," 7.
13. Sutter, *Driven Wild*, 169.
14. Sutter, *Driven Wild*, 174–175.
15. Robert Marshall, "The Problem of the Wilderness," *Scientific Monthly* 30, no. 2 (March 1930): 273–280; Sutter, *Driven Wild*, 215–217.
16. Sutter, *Driven Wild*, 73.
17. Sutter, *Driven Wild*, 74.
18. Sutter, *Driven Wild*, 224–225. This "senile" forest misunderstanding was used as an argument against wilderness areas by many Forest Service leaders until recently. It is still used by ecologically benighted corporate foresters to this day.
19. Aldo Leopold, "The Wilderness and Its Place in Forest Recreation Policy," *Journal of Forestry* 19, no. 7 (November 1921): 718–721, reprinted in Susan Flader and J. Baird Callicott, eds., *The River of the Mother of God and Other Essays by Aldo Leopold* (University of Wisconsin Press, Madison, 1991), 49–52.
20. Sutter, *Driven Wild*, 71.
21. Sutter, *Driven Wild*, 87.
22. Sutter, *Driven Wild*, 223.
23. Victor E. Shelford, "Ecological Society of America: A Nature Sanctuary Plan Unanimously Adopted by The Society, December 28, 1932," *Ecology* 14, no. 2 (April 1933): 242.
24. Sutter, *Driven Wild*, 123.
25. Sutter, *Driven Wild*, 113.
26. Sutter, *Driven Wild*, 130–135. Yard acknowledged that the astonishing abundance of waterbirds in the Everglades was a monumental display of evolutionary forces.
27. Hays, *Gospel of Efficiency*, 189–190.
28. William K. Wyant, *Westward in Eden: The Public Lands and the Conservation Movement* (University of California Press, Berkeley, 1982), 118.
29. Hays, *Gospel of Efficiency*, 189–190.
30. David S. Wilcove, *The Condor's Shadow* (W. H. Freeman, New York, 1999), 149; Wyant, *Westward in Eden*, 118.
31. Shelford, "Nature Sanctuary Plan," 240–245.
32. Sutter, *Driven Wild*, 246–247.
33. Sutter, *Driven Wild*, 248.
34. Robert Marshall, "The Universe of the Wilderness Is Vanishing," *Nature Magazine* 9, no. 4 (April 1937): 239.
35. Sutter, *Driven Wild*, 97, 249.
36. Aldo Leopold, "Why the Wilderness Society?" *The Living Wilderness*, September 1935.
37. Flader, "Aldo Leopold and the Wilderness Idea," 5.
38. Leopold, *Sand County Almanac*, 196.
39. The Nature Conservancy, *The Preservation of Natural Diversity: A Survey*

and Recommendations, Prepared for the U.S. Department of the Interior, 1975, 2–3.

40. David A. Clary, *Timber and the Forest Service* (University Press of Kansas, Lawrence, 1986); Paul W. Hirt, *A Conspiracy of Optimism: Management of the National Forests Since World War Two* (University of Nebraska Press, Lincoln, 1994).

41. Michael Frome, *Battle for the Wilderness*, rev. ed. (University of Utah Press, Salt Lake City, 1997 [1974]).

42. Dennis M. Roth, *The Wilderness Movement and the National Forests: 1964–1980* (Forest Service History Series FS 391, Washington, D.C., December 1984).

43. These studies were not required by the Wilderness Act; they came about from administrative decisions.

44. See James Morton Turner, "Wilderness East: Reclaiming History," *Wild Earth*, Spring 2001, 19–27, for an excellent historical study of the Eastern Wilderness Areas Act.

45. The 1976 Federal Lands Policy and Management Act (FLPMA) ordered the Bureau of Land Management to inventory and study its roadless areas. The late Harry Crandell of The Wilderness Society was largely responsible for the wilderness review sections in FLPMA. Other Wilderness Society field reps and I worked under Harry's direction to encourage citizens to testify in favor of the wilderness sections at field hearings on FLPMA.

46. Draft Action Plan and Instructions for Ecosystem Representation Data Collection RARE II (Forest Service, August 31, 1977); Assignment of Regional Targets (Ecosystem Representation, Landform Representation, Wilderness Associated Wildlife Representation) for NWPS (Forest Service, January 16, 1978).

47. In 1971 and 1972, the Forest Service proposed to declassify large sections of the Black Range and Gila Primitive Areas in New Mexico thereby separating its proposed Aldo Leopold and Gila Wilderness Areas by up to 10 miles. Before construction of the North Star Road in the 1930s, both areas had been part of the original Gila Wilderness. I led conservationists in opposing the Forest Service's proposal on the basis of keeping the two wildernesses contiguous to allow wildlife to move freely between them. We succeeded with the passage of the 1980 New Mexico Wilderness Act. Only a half mile on either side of the dirt road separates the two wilderness areas today. Similar efforts were made in other states.

48. Clif Merritt has not received the recognition he deserves as a leader and visionary of the wilderness movement.

49. The best reference for the National Wild and Scenic Rivers System is Tim Palmer, *The Wild and Scenic Rivers of America* (Island Press, Washington, D.C., 1993).

50. I recognize that some highly significant protected areas have since been formally designated in other nations. Only time will tell if they have the permanence of protection that the Alaska areas do—though, to be honest,

the same must now be said about the Alaska areas after we've witnessed the "stewardship" of Secretary of the Interior Gale Norton and President George W. Bush. For sobering and realistic discussions of protected-area management elsewhere in the world, see John Terborgh, *Requiem for Nature* (Island Press, Washington, D.C., 1999) and John Terborgh, Carel van Schaik, Lisa Davenport, and Madhu Rao, eds., *Making Parks Work: Strategies for Preserving Tropical Nature* (Island Press, Washington, D.C., 2002).

10. Selecting and Designing Protected Areas: The Past Two Decades

1. John Terborgh, "Preservation of Natural Diversity: The Problem of Extinction Prone Species," *BioScience* 24 (1974): 715–722; Jared M. Diamond, "The Island Dilemma: Lessons of Modern Biogeographic Studies for the Design of Natural Preserves," *Biological Conservation* 7 (1975): 1027–1029; E. O. Wilson and E. O. Willis, "Applied Biogeography," in *Ecology and Evolution of Communities*, ed. M. L. Cody, and J. M. Diamond (Harvard University Press, Belknap Press, Cambridge, Mass., 1975), 522–534; J. M. Diamond and R. M. May, "Island Biogeography and the Design of Natural Reserves," in *Theoretical Ecology: Principles and Applications*, ed. R. M. May (W. B. Saunders, Philadelphia, 1976), 163–186.
2. International Union for the Conservation of Nature and Natural Resources (IUCN), *World Conservation Strategy* (Gland, Switzerland, 1980).
3. Reed F. Noss and Allen Y. Cooperrider, *Saving Nature's Legacy* (Island Press, Washington, D.C., 1994), 138–139.
4. Whereupon it continued through *Wild Earth* and the Wildlands Project.
5. Earth First did not have an exclamation mark as part of its name in 1980.
6. Unfortunately, the Bush administration has done everything possible to overturn the Roadless Area Rule.
7. Susan Whaley, "An Idaho Daily Breaches the Northwest's Silence over Tearing Down Dams," *High Country News*, September 1, 1997.
8. Editorial, "APS's Powerful Project," *Arizona Republic*, November 30, 1999; Sandy Bahr, personal communication.
9. Carey Goldberg, "Fish Are Victorious over Dam as U.S. Agency Orders Shutdown," *New York Times*, November 26, 1997; David A. Malakoff, "Agency Says Dam Should Come Down," *Science* 277 (August 8, 1997): 762.
10. Associated Press, "Demolition Begins on Maine Dam," *Albuquerque Tribune*, July 1, 1999.
11. Patrick Joseph, "The Battle of the Dams," *Smithsonian*, November 1998, 49–61.
12. Dave Foreman, Howie Wolke, and Bart Koehler, "The Earth First! Wilderness Preserve System," *Earth First! Journal*, June 1983, reprinted in *Wild Earth*, Spring 1991.

13. Dave Foreman and Howie Wolke, *The Big Outside*, rev. ed. (Harmony Books/Crown, New York, 1992); Howie Wolke, *Wilderness on the Rocks* (Ned Ludd Books, Tucson, Ariz., 1991).

14. Reed F. Noss, "Protecting Natural Areas in Fragmented Landscapes," *Natural Areas Journal* 7, no. 1 (1987): 2–13; Reed F. Noss, "Wilderness Recovery and Ecological Restoration: An Example for Florida," *Earth First! Journal*, September 22, 1985, 18–19.

15. Michael E. Soulé, "Land Use Planning and Wildlife Maintenance: Guidelines for Conserving Wildlife in an Urban Landscape," *Journal of the American Planning Association* 57 (1991): 313–323. See also M. E. Soulé, D. T. Bolger, A. C. Alberts, R. Sauvajot, J. Wright, M. Sorice, and S. Hill, "Reconstructed Dynamics of Rapid Extinctions of Chaparral-Requiring Birds in Urban Habitat Islands," *Conservation Biology* 2, no. 1 (March 1988), 75–92.

16. Mike Bader, "A Northern Rockies Proposal for Congress," special issue, *Wild Earth*, 1992, 61–64; Dave Foreman, "The Northern Rockies Ecosystem Protection Act and the Evolving Wilderness Area Model," *Wild Earth*, Winter 1993–1994, 57–62.

17. Harvey Locke, "Yellowstone to Yukon: A Strategy for Preserving the Wild Heart of North America," *Wild Earth* Winter 1993–1994, 68–72.

18. Susan Marynowski, "Paseo Pantera: The Great American Biotic Interchange," special issue, *Wild Earth*, 1992, 71–74.

19. J. W. Thomas, E. D. Forsman, J. B. Lint, E. C. Meslow, B. R. Noon, and J. Verner, *A Conservation Strategy for the Northern Spotted Owl* (USDA Forest Service, USDI Bureau of Land Management, USDI Fish and Wildlife Service, and USDI National Park Service, Portland, Ore., 1990).

20. Reed F. Noss, "The Wildlands Project Land Conservation Strategy," special issue, *Wild Earth*, 1992, 12.

21. Maxine McCloskey, "Protected Areas on the High Seas and the Case for Marine Wilderness," *Wild Earth*, Spring 1997, 87–92.

22. Bradley Barr and James Lindholm, "Conserving the Sea Using Lessons from the Land," *Wild Earth*, Winter 2002–2003, 54–61. This issue of *Wild Earth* is devoted to ocean conservation.

23. "Marine Reserves: Thinking out of the Box," *Conservation in Practice* 4, no. 3 (Summer 2003): 6–7. This article is a report on M. H. Carr et al., "Comparing Marine and Terrestrial Ecosystems: Implications for the Design of Coastal Marine Reserves," *Ecological Applications* 13, no. 1, supplement (2003): S90–S107.

24. Sabine Jessen and Natalie Ban, "Baja California to the Bering Sea," *Wild Earth*, Winter 2002–2003, 76–79.

25. The Wildlands Project was originally called "North American Wilderness Recovery." Rod Mondt organized its first meeting. Attendees were John Davis, Bill Devall, Jim Eaton, Dave Foreman, Mitch Friedman, Monte Hummel, David Johns, Jerry Mander, Roz McClellan, Rod Mondt, Reed Noss, Jamie Sayen, Michael Soulé, Doug Tompkins, and George Wuerthner.

26. Conservative, in the true sense of the word and not reckless in the sense "conservative" has been applied to land management by resource extraction industries and many politicians.

27. Reed F. Noss, "Wildlands Project," 24.

28. Reed F. Noss and Allen Y. Cooperrider, *Saving Nature's Legacy* (Island Press, Washington, D.C., 1994).

29. Michael Soulé and John Terborgh, eds., *Continental Conservation: Scientific Foundations of Regional Reserve Networks* (Island Press, Washington, D.C., 1999).

30. We first used the name "Sky Islands–Greater Gila Nature Reserve Network" before switching to the simpler Sky Islands Wildlands Network. Deciding on a name was one of the more challenging parts of the whole planning process.

II. The Importance of Wilderness Areas

1. Michael E. Soulé and Bruce A. Wilcox, "Conservation Biology: Its Scope and Its Challenge," in *Conservation Biology: An Evolutionary-Ecological Perspective*, ed. Michael E. Soulé and Bruce A. Wilcox (Sinauer Associates, Sunderland, Mass., 1980), 4.

2. J. Baird Callicott and Michael P. Nelson, eds., *The Great New Wilderness Debate* (University of Georgia Press, Athens, 1998); William Cronon, ed., *Uncommon Ground: Rethinking the Human Place in Nature* (W. W. Norton, New York, 1996). These two books pretty much cover the gamut of the criticism. *The Great New Wilderness Debate* also includes defenses of wilderness areas by several conservationists, including me.

3. John Terborgh, Carel van Schaik, Lisa Davenport, and Madhu Rao, eds., *Making Parks Work: Strategies for Preserving Tropical Nature* (Island Press, Washington, D.C., 2002); John Terborgh, *Requiem for Nature* (Island Press, Washington, D.C., 1999); John F. Oates, *Myth and Reality in the Rain Forest: How Conservation Strategies Are Failing in West Africa* (University of California Press, Berkeley, 1999).

4. Dave Foreman, "Wilderness Areas for Real," in Callicott and Nelson, *The Great New Wilderness Debate*, 395–407. *Wild Earth*, Winter 1996–1997, has a number of responses to the postmodern-deconstructionist critique of wilderness, including one by Gary Snyder, "Nature as Seen from Kitkitdizze Is No 'Social Construction,'" 8–9. The most powerful response to the deconstruction of nature is Michael E. Soulé and Gary Lease, eds., *Reinventing Nature? Responses To Postmodern Deconstruction* (Island Press, Washington, D.C., 1995). Contributors include the editors, Paul Shepard, Donald Worster, Stephen Kellert, and others.

5. Reed Noss, Eric Dinerstein, Barrie Gilbert, Michael Gilpin, Brian Miller, John Terborgh, and Steve Trombulak, "Core Areas: Where Nature Reigns," in Soulé and Terborgh, *Continental Conservation*, 99.

6. I consider the National Wilderness Preservation System, the National Park System, and the National Wildlife Refuge System, though different

in management, as the protected areas system for the United States. In this sense, wilderness areas on federal national forests, national parks, national wildlife refuges, and Bureau of Land Management (BLM) lands; national parks and national wildlife refuges not yet designated as wilderness; and wilderness areas on state lands like New York's Adirondack Forest Preserve and California's Anza-Borrego State Park make up the basic protected areas system in the United States.

7. Aldo Leopold, "Pioneers and Gullies," *Sunset Magazine*, May 1924, reprinted in David E. Brown and Neil B. Carmony, eds., *Aldo Leopold's Southwest* (University of New Mexico Press, Albuquerque, 1995), 164–174.

8. Aldo Leopold, "Wilderness as a Land Laboratory," *The Living Wilderness*, July 1941.

9. Postmodern-deconstructionist critics of the wilderness idea seem unable to understand this important point. See, for example, J. Baird Callicott and Michael P. Nelson, "Introduction," in Callicott and Nelson, *The Great New Wilderness Debate*, 12–13.

10. Michael McCloskey, "Conservation Biologists Challenge Traditional Nature Protection Organizations," *Wild Earth*, Winter 1996–1997, 67–70.

11. Brock Evans personal communication, January 21, 1994.

12. I include many sportfishers and hunters here.

13. Reed Noss, "A Reserve Design for the Klamath-Siskiyou Ecoregion," *Wild Earth* Winter 1999–2000, 72.

14. Reed F. Noss, James R. Strittholt, Kenneth Vance-Borland, Carlos Carroll, and Pamela Frost, "A Conservation Plan for the Klamath-Siskiyou Ecoregion," *Natural Areas Journal* 19, no. 4 (October 1999): 403.

15. Noss et al., "Core Areas," 105.

Part III. Taking Action

Epigraph: Reed F. Noss, "The Wildlands Project Land Conservation Strategy," special issue, *Wild Earth* 1992, 10.

12. Putting the Pieces Together: Building a North American Wildlands Network

1. The George Wright Society is a professional organization for biologists and other scientists in the National Park Service, U.S. Geological Survey, and other agencies. George Wright was an early (and visionary) biologist for the Park Service, who died in a tragic accident.

2. Reed F. Noss, "Appendix: A Recipe for Reserve System Design and Management," special issue, *Wild Earth*, 1992, 24–25.

3. For a more detailed description of the units, see Dave Foreman, Kathy Daly, Reed Noss, Matt Clark, Kurt Menke, David R. Parsons, and Robert

E. Howard, *New Mexico Highlands Wildlands Network Vision* (The Wildlands Project, Richmond, Vt., 2003), 146–148.

4. Brian Miller, Richard Reading, Jim Strittholt, Carlos Carroll, Reed Noss, Michael Soulé, Oscar Sanchez, John Terborgh, Donald Brightsmith, Ted Cheeseman, and Dave Foreman, "Focal Species in the Design of Nature Reserve Networks," *Wild Earth*, Winter 1998–1999, 82.

5. Each of the published Spine of the Continent wildlands network documents describes its particular approach to focal species and selection of focal species. The wildlands networks have shifted to using fewer focal species over time.

6. Miller et al., "Focal Species," 82.

7. Michael E. Soulé, James A. Estes, Joel Berger, and Carlos Martinez del Rio, "Ecological Effectiveness: Conservation Goals for Interactive Species," *Conservation Biology* 17, no. 5 (October 2003): 1238–1250.

8. David S. Maehr, Thomas S. Hoctor, and Larry D. Harris, "Remedies for a Denatured Biota: Restoring Landscapes for Native Carnivores," in *Wildlife, Land, and People: Priorities for the 21st Century*, ed. Rebecca Field, Robert J. Warren, Henryk Okarma, and Paul R. Sievert (The Wildlife Society, Bethesda, Maryland, 2001), 123–127.

9. Thomas Stauffer, "Gray Wolf Shot, Killed; Reward for Info Is $10K," *Arizona Daily Star*, April 18, 2003; Tania Soussan, "Endangered Wolves Killed," *Albuquerque Journal*, September 26, 2003; Thomas Stauffer, "Public Help Is Sought to Solve Deaths of 7 Wolves," *Arizona Daily Star*, October 4, 2003.

10. David S. Maehr, "Restoring the Large Mammal Fauna in the East: What Follows the Elk?" *Wild Earth*, Spring 2001, 50–53. The theme of this issue of *Wild Earth* is rewilding the East.

11. Foreman et al., *New Mexico Highlands*, 88–114. The full focal species accounts are on CD: David R. Parsons, *Natural History Characteristics of Focal Species in the New Mexico Highlands Wildlands Network*, available from the Wildlands Project, P.O. Box 455, Richmond, Vt., 05477, (802) 434-4077.

12. Peter H. Singleton, William L. Gaines, and John F. Lehmkuhl, *Landscape Permeability for Large Carnivores in Washington: A Geographic Information System Weighted-Distance and Least-Cost Corridor Assessment* (U.S. Department of Agriculture, Forest Service, Pacific Northwest Research Station, Research Paper PNW-RP-549, Portland, Ore., 2002), 6.

13. Reed F. Noss, Carlos Carroll, Ken Vance-Borland, and George Wuerthner, "A Multicriteria Assessment of the Irreplaceability and Vulnerability of Sites in the Greater Yellowstone Ecosystem," *Conservation Biology* 16, no. 4 (August 2002): 895–908. See also Foreman et al., *New Mexico Highlands*, 117–144.

14. Foreman et al., *New Mexico Highlands*, 152.

15. James R. Strittholt and Dominick A. DellaSala, "Importance of Roadless Areas in Biodiversity Conservation in Forested Ecosystems: Case Study of the Klamath-Siskiyou Ecoregion of the United States," *Conservation Biology* 15, no. 6 (December 2001): 1742–1754.

16. Singleton et al., *Landscape Permeability*, 3.
17. Foreman et al., *New Mexico Highlands*, 70–72.
18. See the South Coast Wildlands Project Web site at www.scwildlands.org.
19. Rurik List, Oscar Moctezuma, and Carlos Martinez del Rio, "Cooperative Conservation: Wildlands Project Efforts in the Sierra Madre Occidental," *Wild Earth*, Spring 2000, 51–54; Allan McDonell and Kim Vacariu, "Ejido Cebadillas, Imperiled Parrots, and an Historic Conservation Partnership," *Wild Earth*, Spring 2000, 55–56.

13. An Ecological Approach to Wilderness Area Selection and Design

1. Michael Scialdone and Greg Magee, eds., *New Mexico Wilderness Alliance BLM Wilderness Inventory*, draft, February 2003.
2. Jay Hansford Vest, "Will of the Land," *Environmental Review*, Winter 1985, 321–329.
3. Roderick Frazier Nash, *Wilderness and the American Mind*, 4th ed. (Yale University Press, New Haven, Conn., 2001), 1–2.
4. Aldo Leopold, "Wilderness as a Land Laboratory," *The Living Wilderness*, July 1941.
5. Douglas W. Scott, "Congress's Practical Criteria for Designating Wilderness," *Wild Earth*, Spring 2001, 28–32. Scott's article is essential reading to understand wilderness areas in the United States.
6. Public Law 88-577 (16 U.S.C. 1131-1136), 88th Cong., 2d Sess., September 3, 1964, in *The Wilderness Act Handbook*, 4th ed., rev., ed. Jay Watson and Ben Beach (The Wilderness Society, Washington, D.C., August 2000).
7. Michael Soulé, "A Vision for the Meantime," special issue, *Wild Earth* 1992, 7–8.
8. Scenic Quality Rating Criteria worksheets, U.S. Forest Service.
9. Assistant Secretary of Agriculture Rupert Cutler during the Carter administration reined in the Forest Service on purity. His directive to the Forest Service is well worth reading. Rupert Cutler, Memo: "Policy for Evaluating Wilderness Potential of National Forest Roadless and Undeveloped Areas," Assistant Secretary of Agriculture to Chief, Forest Service, November 2, 1977. During the Nixon administration, Assistant Secretary of the Interior Nat Reed similarly straightened out the National Park Service and the Fish and Wildlife Service on their outlandish purity standards.
10. Roadless inventory procedure, Southwestern Region, Forest Service, 1971.
11. *Report on the Proposed Gila Wilderness, Gila National Forest, New Mexico* (U.S. Department of Agriculture, Forest Service, Southwestern Region, Albuquerque, New Mexico, 1974), 37. Friends and I worked hard throughout the 1970s to get Aeroplane Mesa into the Gila Wilderness. The 1980 New Mexico Wilderness Act gave us a victory.

12. Ernie Dickerman and Doug Scott of The Wilderness Society worked closely with members of Congress to shoot down the Forest Service's purity arguments. See, for example, Ernest Dickerman, "Eastern Wilderness Areas," *Congressional Record Senate*, February 21, 1973, 44–54.
13. Frank Church, "The Wilderness Act Applies to the East," *Congressional Record Senate*, January 16, 1973.
14. Henry Jackson, "Eastern Wilderness Areas Act," *Congressional Record Senate*, January 11, 1973.
15. James Buckley, "Eastern Wilderness Areas Act," *Congressional Record Senate*, January 11, 1973.
16. John Saylor, "Legislation to Save Eastern Wilderness," *Congressional Record House of Representatives*, January 11, 1973.
17. Jim Eaton, personal communication.
18. Robert H. MacArthur and Edward O. Wilson, *The Theory of Island Biogeography* (Princeton University Press, Princeton, N.J., 1967).
19. Scialdone and Magee, *New Mexico Wilderness Alliance*.
20. Dave Foreman, Kathy Daly, Barbara Dugelby, Rosanne Hanson, Robert E. Howard, Jack Humphrey, Leanne Klyza Linck, Rurik List, and Kim Vacariu, *The Sky Islands Wildlands Network Conservation Plan* (The Wildlands Project, Tucson, Ariz., 2000), 49; Dave Foreman, Kathy Daly, Robert Howard, Reed Noss, Matt Clark, Kurt Menke, and David R. Parsons, *New Mexico Highlands Wildlands Network Vision* (The Wildlands Project, Richmond, Vt., 2003), 70.
21. S. K. Skagen, C. P. Melcher, W. H. Howe, and F. I. Knopf, "Comparative Use of Riparian Corridors and Oases by Migrating Birds in Southeast Arizona," *Conservation Biology* 12 (1998): 896–909.

14. Land Management Reforms for Implementing the North American Wildlands Network

1. Dave Foreman, Kathy Daly, Barbara Dugelby, Roseann Hanson, Robert E. Howard, Jack Humphrey, Leanne Klyza Linck, Rurik List, and Kim Vacariu, *Sky Islands Wildlands Network Conservation Plan* (The Wildlands Project, Tucson, Ariz., 2000), 173–183; Dave Foreman, Kathy Daly, Reed Noss, Matt Clark, Kurt Menke, David R. Parsons, and Robert E. Howard, *New Mexico Highlands Wildlands Network Vision* (The Wildlands Project, Richmond, Vt., 2003), 176–220; Brian Miller, Dave Foreman, Michelle Fink, Doug Shinneman, Jean Smith, Margaret DeMarco, Michael Soulé, and Robert Howard, *Southern Rockies Wildlands Network Vision: A Science-Based Approach to Rewilding the Southern Rockies* (Southern Rockies Ecosystem Project, Denver Zoological Foundation, the Wildlands Project, Boulder, Colo., 2004).
2. This has been the strategy of anticonservation think tanks like the Heritage Foundation, Cato Institute, and so on. During the Clinton administration, they developed detailed proposals to weaken public lands conser-

vation and to give extractive industries free rein. When Bush was elected president, they were able to hit the ground running.

3. Colorado Division of Wildlife, *DOW Insider*, June 2003.

4. Brian Miller, Katherine Ralls, Richard P. Reading, J. Michael Scott, and James Estes, "Biological and Technical Considerations of Carnivore Translocation: A Review," *Animal Conservation* 2 (1999): 59–68.

5. David S. Maehr, Reed F. Noss, and Jeffrey L. Larkin, eds., *Large Mammal Restoration: Ecological and Sociological Challenges in the 21st Century* (Island Press, Washington, D.C., 2001).

6. Wendy M. Brown and David R. Parsons, "Restoring the Mexican Gray Wolf to the Mountains of the Southwest," in Maehr et al., *Large Mammal Restoration*, 180.

7. David P. Onorato and Eric C. Hellgren, "Black Bear at the Border: Natural Recolonization of the Trans-Pecos," in Maehr et al., *Large Mammal Restoration*, 254–255.

8. Thomas McNamee, "Tinkering with Nature," *High Country News*, March 31, 2003.

9. Jim Yuskavitch, "Leave It to Beavers," *Forest Magazine*, Spring 2002, 20–24. This article is a good popular overview.

10. Michael E. Soulé, James A. Estes, Joel Berger, and Carlos Martinez del Rio, "Ecological Effectiveness: Conservation Goals for Interactive Species," *Conservation Biology* 17, no. 5 (October 2003): 1238–1250.

11. Committee for Biological Commentary on Utah Wilderness Issues, "Utah Biologists Speak Up for Biodiversity: Recommendations for Designating New Wilderness Areas," Southern Utah Wilderness Alliance Newsletter Insert, Summer 1995.

12. Michele R. Crist and Bo Wilmer, "Roadless Areas: The Missing Link in Conservation," The Wilderness Society, September 2002.

13. Reed Noss, "A Reserve Design for the Klamath-Siskiyou Ecoregion," *Wild Earth*, Winter 1999–2000, 72.

14. The Wilderness Society, "Wild Alert," e-mail June 11, 2003; Lisa Dix, e-mail alert, "Bush Administration Guts the Roadless Rule," American Lands, June 12, 2003.

15. Section 2(c), Public Law 88-577 (16 U.S. C. 1131–1136) 88th Cong., 2d Sess., September 3, 1964.

16. James R. Strittholt and Dominick A. DellaSala, "Importance of Roadless Areas in Biodiversity Conservation in Forested Ecosystems: Case Study of the Klamath-Siskiyou Ecoregion of the United States," *Conservation Biology* 15, no. 6 (December 2001): 1742–1754.

17. Dave Foreman and Howie Wolke, *The Big Outside: A Descriptive Inventory of the Big Wilderness Areas of the United States* (Harmony Books / Crown, New York, 1992).

18. The AUM, or animal unit month, is the standard unit of measurement of grazing for leasing. An AUM is one cow and her calf grazing for a month or five sheep grazing for a month.

19. Andy Kerr, "The Voluntary Retirement Option for Federal Public Land Grazing Permittees," *Wild Earth*, Fall 1998, 63–67.

20. Mark Blaine, "Reform on the Range," *Forest*, Fall 2003, 50.

21. These solutions are covered in more detail in Foreman et al., *New Mexico Highlands*, 181–184.

22. Thomas J. Valone, Marc Meyer, James H. Brown, and Robert M. Chew, "Timescale of Perennial Grass Recovery in Desertified Arid Grasslands Following Livestock Removal," *Conservation Biology* 16, no. 4 (August 2002): 995–1002.

23. David Krueper, Jonathan Bart, and Terrell D. Rich, "Response of Vegetation and Breeding Birds to the Removal of Cattle on the San Pedro River, Arizona (USA)," *Conservation Biology* 17, no. 2 (April 2003): 607–615.

24. Daniel Imhoff, *Farming with the Wild: Enhancing Biodiversity on Farms and Ranches* (Sierra Club Books, San Francisco, 2003), 20–42, 141–143, 149–150.

25. Imhoff, *Farming with the Wild*, 24–27.

26. *WILDALERT: Don't Pave the Parks*, The Wilderness Society, January 31, 2003.

27. Southern Utah Wilderness Alliance, "The War on Wilderness," *Redrock Wilderness*, Summer 2003, 6–7.

28. Maureen Hartmann, "An Evaluation of Wildlife Crossing Structures: Their Use and Effectiveness," *The Road-RIPorter* (Wildlands Center for Preventing Roads), January–February 2002.

29. John Davis, "Wildlands Philanthropy: Private Wealth Protecting Public Values," *Wild Earth*, Summer 1998, 19–22.

30. Brian Czech, "A Transdisciplinary Approach to Conservation Land Acquisition," *Conservation Biology* 16, no. 6 (December 2002): 1488–1497.

31. Andy Stahl, "Our 100 Years War," *Forest*, Fall 2003, 5.

32. Lisa M. Ellis, Manuel C. Molles Jr., and Clifford S. Crawford, *Seasonal Flooding and Riparian Forest Restoration in the Middle Rio Grande Valley*, Final Report to Jennifer Fowler-Propst, U.S. Fish and Wildlife Service, June 10, 1996, 37.

33. Anna A. Sher, Diane L. Marshall, and Steven A. Gilbert, "Competition between Native *Populus deltoides* and Invasive *Tamarix ramosissima* and the Implications for Reestablishing Flooding Disturbance," *Conservation Biology* 14, no. 6 (December 2000): 1744–1754.

34. Elizabeth G. Daerr, "On the Rebound," *National Parks*, January–February 2002, 49.

35. Federal Interagency Committee for Management of Noxious and Exotic Weeds, eds., "Pulling Together: A National Strategy for Management of Invasive Plants," 2nd ed., U.S. Government Printing Office, 1998.

36. "Exotic Plant Management Teams," leaflet, U.S. National Park Service, http://www.nature.nps.gov/biology/invasivespecies/emptbrochure.pdf.

37. James E. Byers, Sarah Reichard, John M. Randall, Ingrid M. Parker, Carey S. Smith, W. M. Lonsdale, I. A. E. Atkinson, T. R. Seastedt, Mark

Williamson, E. Chornesky, and D. Hayes, "Directing Research to Reduce the Impacts of Nonindigenous Species," *Conservation Biology* 16, no. 3 (June 2002): 630–640.

38. Foreman et al., *New Mexico Highlands*, 200–201.
39. L. Hannah, G. F. Midgley, T. Lovejoy, W. J. Bond, M. Bush, J. C. Lovett, D. Scott, and F. I. Woodward, "Conservation of Biodiversity in a Changing Climate," *Conservation Biology* 16, no. 1 (February 2002): 264–268.

15. Hope for the Future

1. Dave Foreman, Kathy Daly, Barbara Dugelby, Roseann Hanson, Robert E. Howard, Jack Humphrey, Leanne Klyza Linck, Rurik List, and Kim Vacariu, *Sky Islands Wildlands Network Conservation Plan* (The Wildlands Project, Tucson, Ariz., 2000). The Spring 2000 issue of *Wild Earth* is largely devoted to the Sky Islands Wildlands Network.
2. Aldo Leopold, "Conservationist in Mexico," *American Forests* 43, March 1937, 118–120. This important essay has been reprinted in David E. Brown and Neil B. Carmony, eds., *Aldo Leopold's Southwest* (University of New Mexico Press, Albuquerque, 1995), 201–208, and in *Wild Earth*, Spring 2000, 57–60.
3. Kim Vacariu of the Wildlands Project in Tucson deserves high praise for bringing together such a diverse constituency.
4. Alexandra Koelle, "Cougar Corridors: Restoring the Missing Link in California's Chino Hills," *The Road-RIPorter*, Wildlands Center for Preventing Roads, Spring Equinox 2003. See also Pat Brennan, "Erasing Development," *Orange County Register*, October 28, 2002. The South Coast Wildlands Project Web site is www.scwildlands.org.
5. Peter H. Singleton, William L. Gaines, and John F. Lehmkuhl, *Landscape Permeability for Large Carnivores in Washington: A Geographic Information System Weighted-Distance and Least-Cost Corridor Assessment* (United States Department of Agriculture, Forest Service, Pacific Northwest Research Station, Research Paper PNW-RP-549, December 2002).
6. See www.cascadespartners.org.
7. Michael Soulé and Reed Noss, "Rewilding and Biodiversity as Complementary Goals for Continental Conservation," *Wild Earth*, Fall 1998, 26.
8. Aldo Leopold, *A Sand County Almanac: And Sketches Here and There* (Oxford University Press, New York, 1989), 201–203. Rod Nash builds on Leopold's theme in Roderick Nash, *The Rights of Nature: A History of Environmental Ethics* (University of Wisconsin Press, Madison, 1989).
9. Leopold, *Sand County Almanac*, 203–204.
10. David Ehrenfeld, *The Arrogance of Humanism* (Oxford University Press, New York, 1981), 207–208.
11. Ian Tattersall, "A Hundred Years of Missing Links," *Natural History*, December 2000–January 2001, 65.

12. J. T. Heinen and R. S. Low, "Human Behavioural Ecology and Environmental Conservation," *Environmental Conservation* 19, no. 2 (1992): 110.

13. Rurik List, a leading Mexican conservation biologist and board member of the Wildlands Project, was a main organizer of this project.

14. Tom Butler, personal communication, September 14, 2000. He expands on these thoughts in Tom Butler, "Optimism and Hope," *Wild Earth*, Fall–Winter 2002, 8–9.

15. Reed F. Noss, "The Wildlands Project Land Conservation Strategy," special issue, *Wild Earth* 1992, 10.

Index

About the Author

For over thirty years, Dave Foreman has been one of North America's leading conservation activists, thinkers, and visionaries. He is currently the director of The Rewilding Institute. He lives in his hometown of Albuquerque, New Mexico, next to the Sandia Mountains, which first inspired him as a haunt of wildness.